The Roots of Witchcraft—Italy's Old Religion Lives On

The present trend of post-modern Witchcraft shows a strongly Celtic influence. But Italian Witchcraft, or Stregheria, pre-dates Celtic Witchcraft by centuries. When Celtic peoples were still living in primitive dwellings, Southern European civilizations were the glory of the earth. Italian Witchcraft is a proud legacy of the Etruscan civilization and the Roman Empire. It has been passed down through countless generations and it is alive and well both in Italy and wherever persons of Italian descent have settled.

Stregheria is a passionate Magick. In order to show that they came freely to practice the Craft, Aradia, the fourteenth-century Holy Strega, instructed Italian Witches to be naked during rituals and be sexual with each other. Today's Stregas may not choose to intermingle so freely, but an earthy passion still powers Stregherian rites. It was not and is not a religion for those who are embarrassed by or ashamed of their all-too-human nature. Stregheria welcomes and empowers the many sides of humanity—mind, body, and spirit.

Italian Witchcraft makes Stregheria accessible to everyone. Witches whose rituals are steeped in the Wiccan tradition can enhance their rites with the passionate spice of Stregheria. Novice Witches can create identity by self-training in a complete Magickal tradition. Italian Witchcraft is a gift to today's practitioners of the Craft.

ABOUT THE AUTHOR

Raven Grimassi was trained in the Family Tradition of Italian Witchcraft. He has also been an initiate of several other traditions including Brittic Wicca and the Pictish-Gaelic Tradition. Raven has been a teacher and practitioner of the Craft for over 25 years. His former students include authors Scott Cunningham and Donald Kraig. Raven is the author of several books on Wicca and Witchcraft including *The Wiccan Mysteries* which was awarded Book of the Year 1998 and First Place—Spirituality Book by the Coalition of Visionary Retailers. It is his life's work to ensure the survival of ancient Witch lore and legend along with traditional ancestral teachings on the Old Religion.

The author has been both a writer and editor for several magazines over the past decade, including *The Shadow's Edge* and *Raven's Call* magazine, a Journal of pre-Christian religion. Raven has appeared on both television and radio talk-shows in the San Diego area, in his efforts to educate the public about the positive practices and natures of Wicca and Witchcraft. He lectures on a variety of such topics as folk lore, magick, and ritual structure. Raven is active in lecturing, holding workshops, and teaching formal classes.

TO WRITE TO THE AUTHOR

If you wish to contact the author or would like more information about this book, please write to the author in care of Llewellyn Worldwide and we will forward your request. Both the author and publisher appreciate hearing from you and learning of your enjoyment of this book and how it has helped you. Llewellyn Worldwide cannot guarantee that every letter written to the author can be answered, but all will be forwarded. Please write to:

Raven Grimassi
℅ Llewellyn Worldwide
P.O. Box 64383, Dept. K259-3
St. Paul, MN 55164-0383, U.S.A.
Please enclose a self-addressed stamped envelope for reply,
or $1.00 to cover costs. If outside U.S.A., enclose
international postal reply coupon.

ITALIAN WITCHCRAFT

WITCHCRAFT

The Old Religion of Southern Europe

RAVEN GRIMASSI

2000
Llewellyn Publications
St. Paul, Minnesota, USA 55164-0383

SECOND EDITION
Second Printing, 2000
(Previously titled *Ways of the Strega*)

First edition, one printing, 1995

Cover design by Anne Marie Garrison
Cover photograph (landscape) by Bernard Boutrit, Woodfin Camp & Associates; cover inset photo by Photodisc. Interior art by Charles Godfrey Leland (pp. 2, 56, 86, 135, 140, 144, 148, 151, 154, 158, 162, 171, 176, 220, 232, 240); Gustave Doré (pp. 31, 74, 250); Shadowhawk (pp. 5, 24, 54, 65, 94, 207, 210, 248); Lady Morgan (p. 52); Wendy Froshay (pp. 69, 97, 112, 114, 116, 117, 118, 126-128, 132, 205); Tom Grewe, and clip art sources.
Interior design and editing by Matthew Segaard

Library of Congress Cataloging-in-Publication Data
Grimassi, Raven, 1951–
    Italian witchcraft: the old religion of southern Europe / Raven Grimassi
        p. cm.
    Rev. ed. of: Ways of the strega.
Includes bibliographical references and index.
ISBN 1-56718-259-3
 1. Witchcraft—Italy. 2. Magic—Italy. I. Grimassi, Raven, 1951- Ways of the strega. II. Title.
BF1584.I8 G75 2000
133.4'3'0945—dc21

Llewellyn Publications
A Division of Llewellyn Worldwide, Ltd.
P.O. Box 64383, Dept. K259-3
St. Paul, Minnesota 55164-0383, U.S.A.
www.llewellyn.com

Printed in the United States of America

DEDICATION

To Diane, who was there from the beginning; nothing is forgotten;
to my Mother, for her tales of Old Italy and for all that she taught me;
to my madrina Teresa who initiated my first rite of passage;
and to my Uncle Arturo and cousin Fulvio, who always fill in the missing pieces.

TABLE OF CONTENTS

Part 3: Aradia and the Teachings

Part 4: Appendices

Preface to the Second Edition

My purpose in writing this current edition is to clarify aspects of the earlier material and to correct some of the misunderstandings that critics appeared to have had of the first edition material. I have also introduced a new chapter on Tuscan Witchcraft along with several new appendices that should serve to enhance the overall material presented in this book. Some revisions have been made in many of the chapters as either corrections or additional information. I believe this current edition is a much-improved presentation of the Old Religion in Italy.

There are several elements appearing in this book that many people feel are drawn from modern Wiccan sources such as the Gardnerian Tradition. I have included an appendix that will demonstrate that the concepts I present here are much older than Gardnerian Wicca or any other twentieth-century Wiccan Tradition. One exceptionally verbal critic pointed to what he called "clear Gardnerian markers" in the older Italian concepts appearing in *Ways of the Strega*. In the appendix I have taken each so-called modern marker and presented pre-Gardnerian references that clearly indicate an earlier existence.

Many modern writers appear unfamiliar with the deeper levels of Aegean/Mediterranean paganism and classical Witchcraft as it appeared in ancient Roman times. The popular focus has been upon Celtic research, resulting in a bypass of southern Europe and its contributions to the practices and beliefs found in modern Wicca/Witchcraft. This has led to a misunderstanding of the parallels residing in modern Wiccan and Witchcraft Traditions.

When debating origins we can easily find ourselves in the old argument of which came first, the chicken or the egg. Because books on Gardnerian Wicca were primarily responsible for launching the Wiccan movement, the major attention has always been focused on the related writings by Doreen Valiente, Ray Buckland, and others. This in turn created an interest in Witchcraft as it appeared in the British Isles and northern Europe in general. Later, this interest would bring forth a harvest of Celtic Traditions. In time many people came to simply accept that all the tenets, rites, and practices originated with Gardnerian Wicca. However, just because Gardner, and those of his lineage, popularized such material does not mean that such things did not pre-exist elsewhere.

It is clear from the writings of Gerald Gardner and others that he incorporated material into his Wiccan Tradition from other cultures and other writers. Aleister Crowley and Doreen Valiente can be included among those who contributed various ritual poems, verses, and concepts. In his books *Witchcraft Today* and *The Meaning of Witchcraft*, Gardner writes of his visits to Italy and of his interest in Roman Paganism. He notes the similarities between Wiccan practices and the scenes depicted in the murals at Pompeii. He also mentions the similarities between ancient Roman Mystery Cults and modern Wiccan concepts. From his comments we can be sure that Gardner was studying Roman paganism during the time he was writing about Wicca.

Doreen Valiente indicated that the writings of Charles Leland on Italian Witchcraft first drew her to the Old Religion. The well-known version of the Charge of the Goddess written by Valiente contains verses almost identical to Leland's earlier Italian version. Aleister Crowley spent several years in Sicily studying and practicing Occultism. Everywhere one looks at Gardnerian Wicca, and the people who helped shape it in the early days, one can find a connection to Italy of some kind or another. Despite all of this, critics are still quick to declare that Stregheria is based upon Gardnerian Wicca.

As this book will demonstrate, many of the aspects, tools, symbols, and concepts commonly associated with modern Wicca also appear in ancient Greek, Etruscan, and Roman culture. In the vast majority of cases such things are traceable in the Aegean/Mediterranean to a time predating any contact with the Celts. The classic five-pointed star appears in archaeological sites near Cuma, Italy, dating from 700 B.C. Pentagram rings, dating from 525 B.C., have been found near the city of Crotona in southern Italy. The eight-spoked wheel design, representative in modern Wicca of the eight Sabbats, is a symbol found in Greek archaeological sites near Syracuse, dating from 600 B.C. The book *Decorative Symbols and Motifs for Artists and Craftspeople* (Dover Publications, New York, 1986) is an excellent research source of these and other ancient symbols.

Taken individually, any isolated aspect of ancient Aegean/Mediterranean concepts found also in modern Wicca might be a coincidence. However, as this book will demonstrate, the vast majority of them appear in modern Wiccan tenets and practices, and this is something that cannot reasonably be ignored. To this we must add the fact that the writings of Leland not only contain the same basic elements as Gardnerian Wicca, but also predate them by over half a century. Once the evidence in this book is considered as a whole, it will be clear that the chronology for origins lies with Leland's writings on Italian Witchcraft, and with Aegean/Mediterranean Paganism in general.

Preface to the First Edition

The purpose of this book is to provide not only a workbook on "how to do it," but also the reasons why Italian Witchcraft is being done and how it works. The book was also written to dispel the erroneous conclusion, prevalent today, that Witchcraft is a modern religion originating from Gerald Gardner and his work on Wicca. As the evidence in this book will demonstrate, the Old Religion clearly predated Gardnerian Wicca.

Over the years I have become concerned with the preservation of ancient traditions and ancient beliefs. While it is important to be open to new and unique ways, I feel it is equally important to bear in mind that the Old Ways are the foundation upon which the New Age rests. The New Age represents knowledge and the Old Ways represent wisdom; one might say that the Old Ways are the "DNA" within the body of the New Age.

Having been born a first generation Italian-American, I grew up on stories about the Old World and its customs. My mother used to tell me these wonderful tales of Italian spirits and the beautiful witches of Benevento, Italy. Not surprisingly, other first generation Italian-Americans with whom I have spoken also knew the same stories. Many of them knew the same spells and folk traditions. Italian culture, by its very nature of family focus and respect for tradition, has preserved the Old Ways from generation to generation.

As former editor for *Raven's Call* magazine (a journal of pre-Christian European religion), I have corresponded with many individuals of southern European heritage. A common theme appears in the majority of their letters, one of "disconnection" from the Wiccan Community as a whole. Since the rise of modern Wicca, stemming from the works of Gerald Gardner, the main focus of study and research has been upon northern Europe (specifically upon the British Isles).

People of southern European heritage find it difficult, if not impossible, to locate material providing a connection to their own Pagan roots. Many search in vain among the bountiful texts on Celtic and other northern European works relating to Wicca and Paganism. Others have had to make do with whatever survived within their family traditions.

In response to this situation, I bring twenty-five years of research into the history of Witchcraft in Italy. This lonely quest led me to the study of trial transcripts from the Italian Inquisition, through endless research notes by Italian scholars, to antique bookstores, and through a fascinating maze of fact and fantasy. In the end I was convinced not only of the authenticity of the material that I (and others) had previously possessed, but also of the reality that much of the Old Religion has survived relatively intact throughout Italy.

When most people think of Witchcraft/Wicca they generally associate it with Celtic religion, having its roots in northern and western Europe. While this may be true when strictly employing the English word "Wicca," it is not true of Witchcraft in general. Actually the practice of the Old Religion (called in modern times Wicca and Witchcraft) was well established in Italy long before it was recognizable in any Celtic lands, as I will clearly demonstrate in this book.

Professor Marija Gimbutas, in her excellent books, *The Goddesses and Gods of Old Europe*, and *The Language of the Goddess*, states that the Goddess Cult (with a horned male consort) first appeared in Old Europe (circa 7000 B.C.–3500 B.C.). She describes this region as encompassing Italy and Greece, and also extending into Czechoslovakia, southern Poland, and the western Ukraine. According to Gimbutas, the religion of Old Europe survived the patriarchal invasion of the Indo-Europeans longest in the Mediterranean region, up to a period of around 1500 B.C. She also states that remnants of it appear in both Etruscan and Roman religion.

Italy is a land steeped in antiquity and tradition. Great civilizations such as the Etruscan and Roman Empires once flourished amid her beautiful hills and valleys. When other European people were still living in primitive dwellings, great cities and temples adorned the Italian landscape. In Italy, shamanism had already evolved into religion, which, in turn, evolved into various Mystery Traditions, at a time when northern and western Europeans were still considered barbarians.

The Old Religion of Italy first began to form around the beliefs of early, pre-Etruscan Italians. The mystery teachings and the magickal practices were further developed and refined by the Etruscans, who appeared in Italy around 1000 B.C., establishing the great Etruscan Empire. The Etruscans were known historically for their great magickal and mystical knowledge. With the rise of the Roman Empire, other factors began to influence Italian religion.

The soldiers comprising the Roman armies carried the Pagan religion of Italy into all parts of the known world, and returned with aspects of all the religions they encountered.

They also planted the seeds of Italian Paganism in every land that they conquered, which accounts for many of the similarities between southern and northern European practices.

Roman religion went on to eventually become the greatest eclectic tradition in all of history. The Roman Senate libraries contained the great mystery texts of Etrusca, along with the teachings of other lands conquered by Rome. This placed Italy in a unique situation for, in effect, she preserved the world's religious concepts and wove them into a living mosaic. Here they have remained a silent testimony to the ways of our European ancestors.

In the far-off villages of the Roman Empire lived the rustics who had little contact with the ways of the Roman cities. They were not concerned with the great gods usually associated with Roman mythology, such as Jupiter and Vulcan. Their gods were deities of the fields and forest upon whom the rustics still depended for their livelihood.

Over the course of time, Rome outlawed magickal practices and Dianic cults such as that of the King of the Woods at Nemi. The priestesses of Diana took refuge in the isolated villages near Lake Nemi, and the temple of Diana fell into ruins. Cultured and educated Romans looked down upon the country dwellers, whom they viewed as uncouth simpletons. Yet it was here in these rural villages that the Old Religion of Italy was maintained, separate and independent of Roman religion.

The purpose of this book is to give the reader a clear picture of the history, practices, and beliefs of Witchcraft as both a religion and a magickal system. If what I have written here can provide those who feel disconnected with a sense of belonging, then my labor will have been well worth the effort.

ACKNOWLEDGMENTS

I wish to thank Llewellyn Publications for seeing the value in reintroducing this book. My thanks to all my students, and the initiates of Clan Umbrea, for understanding my absence while I worked on this manuscript. And last, but certainly not least, a special thanks to all the critics and supporters of my work. It is your input that keeps me motivated and determined to improve my writings on the Old Religion.

Copyright Permission Acknowledgements

The author wishes to express his gratitude to the following publishers for permission to reprint the many quotations employed in this book..

The Citadel Press: from *Witches* by T. C. Lethbridge. Copyright 1962. From *Witchcraft Today* by Gerald Gardner. Copyright 1973. Fourth paperbound printing.

Johns Hopkins University Press: from *The Night Battles: Witchcraft & Agrarian Cults in the Sixteenth & Seventeenth Centuries* by Carlo Ginzburg. Copyright 1983.

University of California Press: from *Goddesses and Gods of Old Europe* by Marija Gimbutas. Copyright 1982.

The University of Chicago Press: from *The World of Witches* by Julio Caro Baroja. English Translation. Copyright 1964. Also from *Occultism, Witchcraft, and Cultural Fashions*. Copyright 1978. Paperback edition.

University of Texas Press: from *Folklore by the Fireside: Text and Context of the Tuscan Veglia* by Alessandro Falassi. Copyright 1980. By permission of the author and the University of Texas Press.

Introduction

Today we hear the terms Wicca, the Craft, the Old Religion, and Witchcraft. Also popular is the term Neo-Pagan. Generally, these terms are used in reference to the Nature Religions which embrace a Masculine/Feminine concept of Deity. Practitioners of the Old Religion are referred to as Wiccans, Crafters, Witches, and Neo-Pagans.

In Italian, there are two words used for the word "witch." The first is *Strega* (pronounced stray-gah) and the second is *Stregone* (pronounced stray-go-nay). Literally, Strega means a "female witch" and Stregone means a "male witch." The old Italian word for Witchcraft is Stregheria (pronounced stray-gah-ree-ah). In modern Italian, the word Stregoneria (from the root word strego, "to enchant") is used for witchcraft, but this word actually means sorcery and it is not appropriate to apply it to the religion of Witches. The Italian word for coven is Boschetto (pronounced boss-ket-oh), which means "a grove." Traditionally, Witches met within the forest to practice the Old Ways and from this practice originated the term "a grove of witches."

The persecution of Witches in Italy did not become violent until the late fourteenth century, and even then the Church struck out mainly against organized groups. The solitary village Witch was generally tolerated, being also the village healer and counselor; thus, Italian Witchcraft remained relatively intact throughout the Middle Ages. In northern Europe, the violent persecution of Witches began almost 100 years earlier, and it included solitaries as well as covens.

In central Italy, Witches of old worshiped the goddess Diana and her consort, the god Dianus. Outside Rome, in the Alban Hills region, they gathered in the ruins of the sanctuary of Diana at Lake Nemi. During the Middle Ages, Witches celebrated in the city of Benevento, at the site of a sacred walnut tree. What these Witches came to worship were the forces of Nature, personified as gods and goddesses.

In fourteenth-century Italy, a Wise Woman who called herself Aradia brought about a revival of the Old Religion, La Vecchia Religione. From her efforts there arose three separate Traditions, which were originally one. Today these Traditions are known as the Fanarra, Janarra, and Tanarra. Collectively they are referred to as the Triad Traditions.

The Fanarra are centered in northern Italy, and are known as the Keepers of the Earth Mysteries. The Janarra and Tanarra occupy central Italy. The Janarra are the Keepers of the Lunar Mysteries, and the Tanarra are the Keepers of the Stellar Mysteries.

The "leader" of each Tradition is called a *Grimas* (pronounced gree-mahs), and each Grimas has a working knowledge of the other two Mystery Traditions. It is the duty of a Grimas to maintain the integrity of the Tradition and to ensure its survival. Initiates are trained in the Ways of each Tradition (respectively), and if they choose to become Priests and Priestesses, they can begin training in the mystery teachings of the other two Traditions.

The Aridian Tradition, originally established in North America as a branch of the Tanarra, is based upon a blending of the Triad Traditions in an attempt to restore the original Tradition which Aradia had returned to the people. It is however a modern Tradition and as such does contain some modern elements. The Aridian name is derived from an old Italian village called Arida. Several of the first followers of Aradia were said to come from this village, and therefore the name was chosen as a connection with the Old Country. Unlike the Triad Witches in Italy, Aridians have adopted a few Wiccan elements into their ways, having been more exposed here in the United States. Still, Aridians consider themselves to be the spiritual descendants of those who formed the first of Aradia's groves in Italy. This is also true of the Triad Witches. Please note that rituals in this book are modern Aridian rites and not Old World rites.

Being of a Nature religion, Aridians acknowledge the polarity of gender within the Natural Order, and personify this as the God and Goddess. The year is divided up into the god-months (from October through February) and the goddess-months (from March through September). Balance is essential within a Nature religion, and therefore the Goddess and the God are viewed as equal but different manifestations of Divine Consciousness. During the god-months, celebrations are performed with ritual robes, and in the goddess-months everyone worships without clothing. The rites themselves are, in part, drama plays symbolizing the interplay between the forces of Nature.

At first, the rituals of the Strega may seem anachronistic, inasmuch as they focus on fertility and agricultural themes. In truth, these aspects easily translate into our modern lives; fertility becomes our personal growth and well-being, and the agricultural themes become our own prosperity and career involvements. If we are fertile in our minds and our hearts, then our relationships increase and prosper. If we celebrate the cycles of growth and prosperity, then we draw this positive energy into our work and our careers.

The Fanarric Teachings are concerned with the mysteries of what are commonly referred to as ley lines. They also contain the secrets of the Earth's Power, and the use of various places (and objects) for directing energy. Janarric Teachings preserve the mysteries of Lunar Energy, and their use in magick and Nature. Tanarric Teachings reveal the secrets of ancient stellar cults, Star Lore, and the nature of Stellar Forces.

Common to all three systems are the arts of herbalism, divination, magick, ritual, and other aspects associated with the Old Religion. Each Tradition enhances these arts, with their own individual mystery teachings. During the latter part of the fourteenth century, the original Tradition divided into three separate Traditions, in order to safeguard the Mystery Teachings during the era of persecution by the Christian Church.

Today, these Old Traditions are fading away within modern European communities. Centuries of Christian propaganda and contemporary life have rendered the Old Religion an unattractive anachronism. Yet, isolated groves still hold to the Old Ways in many remote mountain villages throughout Italy. Seaports such as Naples still contain small Janarric groves, and Benevento, once the capital of La Vecchia Religione, continues to provide sanctuary for a handful of hereditary groups.

In the grove structure of the Aridian Tradition there are several offices or positions of authority. Each group is led by a *Sacerdotessa* (High Priestess) who rules with a *Sacerdote* (High Priest). Second to these offices is the *Dama D'onore* and *La Guardia*, known in English as the Lady's attendant (the Maiden) and the Guardian. These are quite similar to the Gardnerian ranks, which Gerald Gardner borrowed from Italian Witchcraft (see chapter 9 for details). Usually these positions lead to the higher ranks, as they are generally considered to be training periods for the High Priest(ess)hood.

The Guardian is responsible for the conduct of new initiates within the ritual circle and, traditionally, for the safety of the Sacerdotessa. This was an essential duty during the time of the Persecution, and remains in place now largely out of respect for tradition. The Maiden is responsible for maintaining the altar and assisting the Sacerdotessa during the rites.

Three stages of advancement exist within the Old Religion. These are marked by initiation ceremonies through which power and knowledge is passed to the initiate. Prior to the Persecution, this structure was quite different. Originally a person was simply a worshipper within the Cult, and he or she could go on to become a Priest or a Priestess of the Old Ways, if desired. All were considered to be Witches within this Community, regardless of their position.

The Priest(ess)hood oversaw and directed the rites, while the populace provided the energy to empower them. As a Priestess or a Priest displayed special skills and talents, they were elevated to the rank of High Priestess or High Priest. In this office they represented the presence of Goddess and God within the ritual drama.

During the Middle Ages, Italian Witchcraft was influenced by Hebrew mystics (who were also being persecuted) and, beginning with the eighteenth century, by Masonic groups as well. During the late 1800s and early 1900s, many Witches in Italy were also Masons. It is not difficult to see the minor Masonic influence in some Strega symbols and rituals.

When Aleister Crowley lived in Italy, from 1920 to 1923, he studied with Italian Occultists and Witches. He established the Abbey of Thelema in Sicily, and had the walls of the villa painted with murals depicting sexual encounters between the Horned God and the Great Goddess. In 1923, Italian authorities told Crowley to leave Italy, and had the murals covered over with whitewash. He then returned to England with what he had learned of Italian Occultism/Paganism. In 1947, he died at a boarding house in Hastings.

Gerald Gardner met Crowley sometime after 1937, and became an initiate member of the Order of the Temple of the Orient. It may have been from Crowley that Gerald Gardner first learned of Italian Witchcraft, or possibly from the writings of Charles Leland which were quite popular during this era. We do know that Gardner later spent some time himself in Italy investigating the Roman Mystery Cult at Pompeii. Much of what Gardner borrowed from the Strega Tradition is now erroneously attributed to his original writings and those of Doreen Valiente (see chapter 9).

I hope that the reader will enjoy both the similarities and differences between Wicca and the Strega Tradition, as portrayed in this book. In the end it is really not important who wrote what, or when it was written. It is only important that it survives, and this is why I have written this book. I hope that you find it a worthy addition to your library.

Part 1
An Overview

A Lasa

2

1

Beliefs of the Strega

Among the cliffs and scrubby moors of northern Italy there dwell today descendants of an ancient people whose stubborn and exotic mystery has provoked historians to conflict, linguists to despair, archeologists to poetry, and poets to philosophy. For almost two thousand years the astounding secret of their existence was kept without living whisper save in the anachronistic echoes, recorded for the first time in this book, of Tuscan Catholic peasant voices calling through unbroken generations upon the pagan deities of their remarkable ancestors.

Margery Silvers
Foreword to Charles Leland's *Etruscan Magic & Occult Remedies*
(1963 reprint of 1892 text)

It is midnight and in the woods, beneath the Full Moon, kneels a lovely young woman. In her hands she holds a small red flannel bag filled with salt and containing a special amulet. She carries wine and water, and with them she blesses herself, tracing a pentagram upon her body. Looking up toward the Moon, she calls out and identifies herself as a daughter of Aradia.[1] A gentle breeze lifts her hair softly away from her shoulders, and as moonlight filters down through the leaves of the forest, she is tenderly embraced by a goddess. The religion that she practices, and the magick that she possesses, is ancient and powerful. She is one who is called a Strega, and her arts have been passed to her through timeless generations.[2]

The Strega are the Witches of Italy, and there is much that is still secretive about them. The openness of the New Age is not yet a part of their culture, and they continue to practice the Old Ways of pre-Christian European religion. In a formal sense, theirs is the Old Religion, known in Italy as La Vecchia Religione. The art of Witchcraft itself, in Italian, is called Stregheria. Among themselves, the Strega simply refer to their religion as "La Vecchia" or sometimes as "The Ways."

Italian is a Latin language, and employs the use of gender in its word and sentence structure. A female Witch is called a Strega, a male is called a Stregone, and the plural for Witches is Streghe. In modern times some Witches prefer the use of the words *Maga* for female and *Mago* for male, although this applies more to users of magick than to Witches in general. For the purposes of simplification, in this book I have elected to use the word Strega to encompass all of these. In other words, no gender is meant to be represented by the word Strega, and it will apply to practitioners of "the Old Religion" in general, both in the singular and plural.

In Italy, and in American cities with large Italian populations, Witches of the "old school" can still be found. In almost every city or village, someone can point you to a Strega who can cast or cure the Malocchio (the "evil eye"), or use olive oil and herbs to heal or to divine the future. In the heart of the Strega, the "spirits of old" live on, for theirs is an ancient belief. Sit quietly and they will tell you tales of the Elven Race, and of the *Lasa* who are known as The Old Ones. You will learn of the sacredness of fire, and of the forces behind Nature. The voice of the wind shall whisper to you as the Strega speak, and you shall know and understand.

The old beliefs of pre-Christian Europe live on among these people. Theirs is still a world in which charms and amulets can attract or banish. Secret hand gestures can invoke protection or draw power. Incantations are taught as an art, with emphasis upon meter and tonal quality. Signs and omens are read in the clouds and in the flight of birds. The future is revealed in drops of olive oil upon the surface of consecrated water, or in visions appearing within crystals. The crescent-crowned Goddess and the stag-horned God of the early Clans are still worshipped by the Strega. They are known by many names among the Witch Clans: Fana and Faunus, Jana and Janus, Tana and Tanus. The most common names for the God and Goddess of Italian Witchcraft are Diana and Dianus. The most ancient names are *Uni* and *Tagni*.

Nature is viewed as the manifestation of spiritual forces or laws. Magick is the art of understanding the interplay between these forces, and the ways in which they can be influenced. This hidden "mechanism" behind the Physical World (dimension) is animated, and kept in order, by a host of spirits and deities. Ancient techniques have been preserved through which the "favor" of these beings can be acquired, and personal desires can be granted. This usually involves various offerings and rites designed to connect with the entity that has influence over the things that you desire.

In northern Italy lies the region of Toscana, or Tuscany. In this area dwell the descendants of an ancient people related to the Etruscans. It is here that the Old Religion of Italy has been preserved by Witches, who have passed down their Craft through unbroken lines for countless generations. The Craft Tradition in Tuscany is quite unique, even by Italian standards. In it we

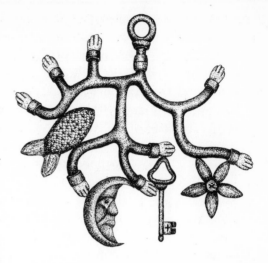

Figure 1
The Cimaruta

can see the remnants of early Etruscan religious belief. The myths of Tuscan Witchcraft are largely those of spirits who were once Etruscan Gods. The magick of Tuscany is one of Pagan simplicity, and bears little resemblance to modern ceremonial practices.

Tuscan Witches believe that their Craft is a legacy that must be passed on to at least one other person before they die. If they do not accomplish this, it is said to interfere with the proper advancement of future lives. In the Tuscan structure, a Witch is reborn in human form many times, becoming more and more powerful. Eventually the individual may become a powerful spirit or possibly even a demi-god.

The magickal focus is largely upon spells, omens, and natural objects. These are employed in amulets, talismans, charm bags, and divination (see Figure 1). Natural actions such as a "falling star" or fruit dropping from a branch may be employed in spells. Here an incantation might be recited, linking the falling action to a wish that someone may fall in love, or perhaps that an enemy might "fall."

Ritual circles are seldom used for spell casting or other works of magick. A large flat rock within a field would serve adequately for any Tuscan Witch. Symbols might be laid out in patterns around power objects placed upon the flat rock, and the Witch's wand (the primary tool of Tuscan Witches) would be passed over them, forming ritual gestures. Metered tonal chants are always employed in every act of magick, which is one of the most cherished arts of Tuscan Witchcraft.

The religious focus of this tradition is upon the God Tagni and the Goddess Uni. The universe that they rule is comprised of sixteen "houses," four in each of the four quarters. The gods of destiny dwell in the north. In the east are the major gods, in the south dwell the astral entities, and in the West dwell the beings of the Underworld. Tagni and Uni also rule over a hierarchy of powerful spirits that exert power and influence over the Earth.

The list that follows will show most of these "spirits" and the "gods" with whom they actually correspond.

Tuscan	Greek/Roman	Tuscan	Greek/Roman
Teramo	Mercury	Tesana	Aurora
Nortia	Fortuna	Spulviero	Aeolus
Aplu	Apollo	Fanio	Faunus
Losna	Diana/Luna	Alpena	Flora
Turanna	Venus	Tituno	Vulcan
Pano	Pan	Verbio	Verbius
Maso	Mars	Dusio	Eros
Silviano	Silvanus	Jano	Janus
Esta	Vesta	Meana	Fate
Faflon	Bacchus		

These spirits/deities are evoked for many purposes and are more a part of everyday life in Tuscany than would most likely be true of other Craft regions. The lore of Tuscany is so pervasive that even the average Christian is knowledgeable in it.

Teramo is a messenger spirit who is evoked to carry requests to the gods and to aid in the sending of spells. Losna is the spirit of the Moon, and is evoked to aid in all works of magick. Turanna has influence over matters of love. In the Old Religion of Tuscany everything is the result of either a spirit's or a god's action, or that of a Witch. That is one reason why everyday life is so closely tied to the Old Ways.

As in most Craft Traditions, the basic elemental forces are revered, and living entities are associated with the seemingly magickal properties of the elements. Likewise, Nature is seen to be filled with spirits that inhabit objects and places. The Fauni and Silvani are spirits of the woods. Monachetto are Gnome-like spirits, and the Linchetto are elven spirits.

In Tuscan Witchcraft, the north quarter is a place of great power. The Elemental Beings of the North are called *Pala*. In the South are the *Settiano*, who are spirits of Elemental Fire. In the West are the *Manii*, who are spirits of Elemental Water, and in the East are the *Bellarie* who are spirits of Elemental Air. In the early lore, the Lasa were also spirits associated with the Underworld. Through the interaction of these beings, vegetation flourishes, rains fall, and life cycles continue. These spirits are the inner forces of Nature.

Closely linked to the belief in these spirits is a large tradition of magickal cures, incantations, spells, and rites for attracting love, banishing evil, and assuring physical comforts. All of these have been passed down through old family lines, where the belief that Witches are born again to their descendants is quite strong. Even though much of this lore is known to non-Witches, the secrets of the practical art are closely guarded by hereditary family Traditions.

The Strega believe in Clan spirits known as the *Lare*, who protect the homes and families of the Strega. They also preserve the family bloodlines and traditions. The Lare assist the Strega to be reborn again among those whom they have known and loved in the previous life. Small Lare shrines are set in the west or the east part of the home, and offerings are made there on important family occasions, such as births, deaths, marriages, and so on.

Traditionally candles are lighted and offerings of wine, milk, and honey are placed in a single bowl before the Lare shrine. In earlier times, these spirits were known as the *Lasa*, and were considered to be the first spirits known upon the earth.

There are many different types of spirits in Italian folklore. Some of the most common and widely known are the *Folletto*. All Folletto travel in the wind, and can be seen at play, causing swirls in the dust (or "knots of winds" in Italian). They are said to be somewhat like butterflies, and are almost always moving about. Traditionally, the Folletto are known to be friendly toward humans, but can be mischievous and annoying at times. It is not uncommon for the Folletto to lift up a woman's dress in the wind, or knock over objects with a sudden gust. They are magickal beings, and have a particular attraction to sexual situations. In northern Italy, certain Folletto are called the *Basadone* (woman-kisser[s]) and are known to steal kisses from women with a passing breeze. The female spirit is known as a *Folletti*, which is also the term for the group as a whole.

Another type of Folletto is a spirit called the *Linchetto*. Actually they belong to the Elven Race, and are specifically night elves. Linchetto are native to the Tuscan region of Italy, which was once the old Etruscan Kingdom. These elves are said to cause "nightmares" and odd noises in the night. Linchetto hate disorder and will not dwell in any such element. One old technique to drive away the Linchetto was to spill seeds upon the floor surrounding the bed. The night elf would come and try to pick up the seeds, usually leaving in frustration. Another technique was to place a lock of curly hair over the bed. The Linchetto would try all night to straighten it, then flee in despair.

The Italian *Fata* are spirits of the woods and water. They are beautiful, gentle, and kind. The Fata are excellent shape-shifters, and often appear in human or animal form. There are many legends in which someone has stopped to help an animal or an old person, only to discover a Fata. Those who helped a Fata in disguise were always richly rewarded, but anyone who was cruel to them was in grave danger. The *Lauru* is a Folletto spirit with black twinkling eyes, long curly hair, and clothes of the finest velvet. They are said to be mischievous, but when treated with respect may reveal hidden treasure or winning lottery numbers.

Italian folklore also extends to inanimate objects, which are believed to contain power. Among the most common are keys made of gold or silver, scissors, horseshoes, pearls, and coral (especially red coral). Other objects such as a clove of garlic, a red ribbon, a pair of crossed straight pins, and a pinch of salt can all be employed to provide protection. In the chapters that follow, all of these aspects of Stregheria are expanded upon in greater detail, along with many other unique traditions left to us through the rich legacy of Italian Witchcraft.

ENDNOTES

1. Aradia was a Strega who lived and taught in Italy during the fourteenth century. She was largely responsible for the revival of Witchcraft in Italy during the Middle Ages. See chapter 20, "The Strega's Story" for further information.

2. See chapter 2, "Italian Witchcraft" for historical evidence of the antiquity and survival of Italian Witchcraft.

2

Italian Witchcraft

I forsee that a day will come, and that perhaps not so very far distant, that the world of scholars will be amazed to consider to what a late period an immense body of antique tradition survived in Northern Italy, and how indifferent the learned were regarding it; there having been in truth only one man, and he a foreigner, who earnestly occupied himself with collecting and preserving it.

Charles Leland
Aradia; Gospel of the Witches, 1899

It has become currently popular in the Neo-Wiccan community to dismiss "The Old Religion" as a reconstructed system, a contemporary creation based upon ancient concepts. Some modern writers insist that there is no evidence of a Wiccan tie to any ancient and authentic way of worship. Others say that Witches have always been portrayed as evil in ancient times and that there can be no similarity between ancient references to Witches and the image of Witches portrayed by Wicca today.

In this chapter we will look at all of these issues and present some compelling evidence that Witchcraft was indeed an ancient religion, and that Witches were not inherently evil, but simply maligned by a "solar" patriarchal society which was opposed to the "lunar" matriarchal society. We

shall see that the Christian image of Witchcraft is one that grew out of fear and ignorance, giving way to prejudice and discrimination.

I have made liberal use of various quotations within this chapter, and I ask the reader
to please indulge me. It is important here to introduce the conclusions of others who
came before me, in order to present a convincing argument for my case. Time-proven
techniques of magick and esoteric religious belief are integral parts of the Old Religion in
Italy. They have carried and maintained the Old Ways for centuries, allowing them to
survive the persecution during the Middle Ages. A little patience with this chapter will be
well worth your time.

HISTORICAL SUPPORT FOR ANTIQUITY AND SURVIVAL

In the book *Etruscan Magic & Occult Remedies*[1] (published in 1892), author and folklorist
Charles Leland writes of his investigation into Italian Witchcraft:

> But I was much more astonished to find that in Tuscany, the most enlightened por-
> tion of Italy under all Roman rule, an old pagan faith, or something like it, has
> existed to a most extraordinary degree. For it is really not a mere chance survival of
> superstitions here and there, as in England or France, but a complete system, as this
> work will abundantly prove.[2]

Leland later implies that he was taken into the Witches' community in his book *Legend
of Florence* (1895), in which he states:

> The witches of Italy form a class who are the repositories of all the folklore; what is
> not at all generally known, they also keep as strict secrets an immense number of
> legends of their own, which have nothing in common with the nursery or popular
> tales, such as are commonly collected and published . . . Lady Vere de Vere, who has
> investigated witchcraft as it exists in the Italian Tyrol, in an admirable article in La
> Rivista of Rome (June 1894) tells us that "the Community of Italian Witches is
> regulated by laws, traditions, and customs of the most secret kind, possessing special
> recipes for sorcery" which is perfectly true. Having been free of the community for
> years, I can speak from experience. The more occult and singular of their secrets are
> naturally not of a nature to be published. . . .[3]

What should be of particular interest here to modern Wiccans is Leland's (and Lady
Vere de Vere's) use of the present tense when speaking of Witchcraft in their time. For
those who believe that the Craft was invented by Gerald Gardner, bear in mind that this
was written over half a century before any of Gardner's books. Indeed, many aspects of
the Old Religion found in Gardnerian Wicca can also be seen in the earlier writings of

Charles Leland and James Frazer. Despite this fact, many people insist on attributing such origins to Gardnerian Wicca.

After consulting with Lady Vere de Vere (Italian Folklorist) and Professor Milani (Director of the Archaeological Museum in Florence), Leland wrote of Italian Witchlore in *Legends of Florence*:

> *That this is of great antiquity is clear, for out of this enchanted forest of Italian Witchcraft and mystical sorcery, there never came anything great or small which was not at least of the Bronze Age, if not the Neolithic Age.*[4]

In *Aradia; Gospel of the Witches* (1899) Leland writes of the popular Christian image of the Witch, but goes on to say:

> *But the Italian Strega or sorceress is in certain respects a different character from these. In most cases she comes of a family in which her calling or art has been practiced for many generations. . . .*[5]

Again we find Leland's use of the present tense when describing Witches in Italy, circa 1880.

Worthy of mention also, in Leland's book, is the story about the walnut Witches. Manuscripts from old witch trials in Italy speak of this walnut tree, which (it is said) had always been there and was in leaf all year long. For centuries, legends were told of the great Witch gatherings in the town of Benevento, at the site of an ancient walnut tree. In the year A.D. 662, Saint Barbato converted the Duke of Benevento (a pagan) to Christianity and had the tree cut down. The Witches replanted the walnut tree from seed, and legend says it still stands in Benevento. Bottles of Strega Liquore, manufactured in Benevento today, bear labels upon which appears the old walnut tree with a group of Witches and satyrs dancing around it.

There are several chapters in *Etruscan Magic & Occult Remedies* that contain some very interesting statements supporting the existence of the Witch Cult in Italy during the nineteenth century, and implications of its existence dating back to the days of antiquity. In chapter 10, we find a section titled "Witches and Witchcraft," with these words:

> *. . . and it is interesting to know that in the city of Florence in the month of January, 1891, there were people who believe in a prehistoric Shamanism which is stronger and mightier than that of the Church. Ages have lapped over ages, the Etruscans and Sabine-Latin and Roman and Christian cults have succeeded one to the other, but through it all the witch and wizard, humble and unnoted, have held their own.*[6]

In chapter 8 we find a section titled "Diana and Herodias" which contains the following words:

It is remarkable that while witchcraft was regarded in later times among Northern races as a creation of Satan, it never lost in Italy a classic character. In this country the witch is only a sorceress, and she is often a beneficent fairy. Her ruler is not the devil, but Diana . . . it is true enough that the monks imported and forced into popular Italian superstition strong infusions of the devil. Yet with all this, in the main, the real Italian witch has nothing to do with Satan or a Christian hell, and remains as of yore a daughter of Diana. There is something almost reviving or refreshing in the thought that there is one place in the world—and that in papal Italy itself— where the poison of diabolism did not utterly prevail.[7]

So what was the basis of the evil Witch image? There are several ways to understand this distorted image, and we turn to the writings of the Roman poet Horace to begin our quest. In the *Epodes of Horace*, written around 30 B.C., he tells the tale of an Italian Witch named Canidia. Horace describes her as an old toothless hag with wild unkempt hair, who casts evil spells upon those who offend her.

Horace goes on to say that Proserpine and Diana grant power to Witches who worship them, and that Witches gather in secret to perform the mysteries associated with their worship. He speaks of the Witches' book of incantations (*Libros Carminum*) through which the Moon may be "called down" from the sky. Other ancient Roman writers such as Lucan and Ovid produced works that clearly support the same theme. This would seem to indicate that during this era such beliefs about Witches and Witchcraft were somewhat common knowledge. In Epode 5 we read:

. . . Night and Diana, who command silence when secret mysteries are performed, now aid me; now turn your vengeance and influence against my enemies' house . . .

In Epode 17 we find these words (addressed to Canidia):

Now already I yield to your mighty art, and suppliant beseech you by the realms of Proserpine, and by the powers of Diana, not to be provoked, and by your books of enchantments that are able to call down the fixed stars from heaven, Canidia, at length spare your magic words, and turn backward your swift wheel . . . (Canidia replies) . . . must I, who can move waxen images and draw down the moon from the sky by my spells, who can raise the vaporous dead, and mix a draught of love lament the effect of my art, availing nothing upon you?[8]

We know from the writings of Roman times that Proserpine and Diana were worshipped at night in secret ceremonies. Their worshippers gathered at night beneath the Full Moon and shunned the cities where the solar gods ruled. It is only logical that the city dwellers would fear them because they met in secret when "decent" people were asleep in bed. Out of their fear came the imaginings common to ignorance and prejudice. All unexplained ailments and disasters were in turn believed to come from these Witches who met in secret (for surely they were plotting against the "good folk"). From generation to generation, prejudicial beliefs were passed on, in time becoming common knowledge. In this same way prejudicial beliefs about various minorities are kept alive today. One generation teaches another through comments and attitudes, and soon distortion becomes "fact."

It is not surprising that the unsophisticated, country-dwelling Pagan bore the image of the toothless evil hag, cursing the cattle and fields of her "good" neighbors. Since Witchcraft was predominantly matriarchal, the men who ruled the cities (and wrote the history) looked down upon Witches as rebellious and dangerous to the established order. In a patriarchal society, a woman who uses magick and worships in secret, having no need of patriarchal society or religion, can only be seen as an evil, crazed woman. In the traditional Halloween witch image, perhaps we

Roman Sword and Fasces

are seeing the worst fears of a patriarchal society: a woman turned loose without the constraints of patriarchal rules or religious dogma. Add to this, in later times, the arrival of Christianity and its passion to convert pagans, and its need to discredit Pagan ways in order to firmly establish Church doctrine, and what other image of a Witch could there be but an evil one?

The fact that some Witches went "renegade" in order to fight the Church, employing Satan, who the Church itself viewed as a powerful enemy, in the end served only to verify the evil nature that Christianity attributed to Witches. The majority of Witches chose not to denigrate the Old Ways in such a manner, and went "underground," almost completely disappearing from history.

It is interesting to note, however, that in Italy there were both "good" and "evil" Witches. In chapter 10 of *Etruscan Magic & Occult Remedies*, Leland writes :

> *True, there are witches good and bad, but all whom I ever met belonged entirely to the buone (good). It was their rivals and enemies who were* maladette streghe *(evil witches), et cetera, but the latter I never met. We were all good.*[9]

This "witch war" theme between good and bad Witches is similar to that of the Benandanti and the Malandanti,[10] of whom I have written in other chapters.

Despite the fact that the Church taught that all Witches were evil, their ancient cult still maintained a following and continued on through the centuries. Mircea Eliade wrote in his book *Occultism, Witchcraft, and Cultural Fashions*, concerning the existence and modern study of Witchcraft:

> *It suffices to say that, as work progressed, the phenomenon of witchcraft appeared more complex and consequently more difficult to explain by a single factor. Gradually it became evident that witchcraft cannot be satisfactorily understood without the help of other disciplines, such as folklore, ethnology, sociology, psychology, and history of religions . . . for instance, even a rapid perusal of the Indian and Tibetan documents will convince an unprejudiced reader that European witchcraft cannot be the creation of religious or political persecution or be a demonic sect devoted to Satan and the promotion of evil. As a matter of fact, all the features associated with European witches are—with the exception of Satan and the Sabbath—claimed also by Indo-Tibetan yogis and magicians.*[11]

Clearly there is a common thread running through many ancient practices and beliefs. It is through our look back into time that we find the roots of Witchcraft. In his book *The World of Witches*, Julio Baroja writes of southern Europe:

> *There seems to have been a flourishing cult of Diana among European country people in the 5th and 6th Centuries A.D., and she was generally looked upon as a Goddess of the woods and fields, except by those trying to root out the cult, who thought she was a devil.*[12]

In the author's notes for chapter 4, Baroja adds that the cult also worshipped a male deity called Dianum. This may be of interest to modern writers on Wicca who claim that witches never worshipped Diana, or a God and Goddess consort, in ancient times.

In A.D. 906, Regino of Prum wrote in his instructions to the bishops of the Kingdoms concerning Witches:

> *They ride at night on certain beasts with Diana, goddess of the pagans, and a great multitude of women, that they cover great distances in the silence of the deepest night, that they obey the orders of the goddess . . . by speaking of their visions (they) gain new followers for the Society of Diana. . . .*[13]

It is interesting to note that the label "Society of Diana" mentioned by Regino continues to be associated with Witches throughout the centuries in Italy, as recorded in witch trials by the Italian Inquisition. It appears with greater frequency in trial transcripts during the later part of the fourteenth century and into the late fifteenth century. A brief chronology[14] follows to summarize this unbroken chain of European Witchcraft through the centuries:

700 B.C.: Hesiod, in his Theogony, speaks of the Witch, Circe.

30 B.C.: Roman poet Horace in his Epodes of Horace associated Witches with the goddess Diana in a mystery cult.

A.D. 314: Council of Ancyra labeled as heretics witches who believed that they belonged to a "Society of Diana." Council concluded that they were deceived by Satan.

A.D. 662: Saint Barbato converted Romuald (Duke of Benevento) to Christianity. On Saint Barbato's bidding, Romuald had the "witches' walnut tree" cut down. This walnut tree was the gathering place of Witches who worshipped Diana, well known in the region. In A.D. 680, Saint Barbato attended the Council of Constantinople, where he spoke out against the "witches of Benevento."

A.D. 906: Regino of Prum, in his instructions to the bishops, claimed that pagans worshiped Diana in a cult called the Society of Diana.

A.D. 1006: 19th book of the *Decretum* (entitled *Corrector*) associated the worship of Diana with the common Pagan folk.

A.D. 1280: Diocesan Council of Conserans associates the "Witch Cult" with the worship of a Pagan Goddess.

A.D. 1310: Council of Trier associated Witches with the Goddess Diana (and Herodias).

A.D. 1313: Giovanni de Matociis wrote in his *Historiae Imperiales* that many lay people believed in a nocturnal society headed by a queen they call Diana.

A.D. 1390: A woman tried by the Milanese Inquisition for belonging to the "Society of Diana" confessed to worshipping the "Goddess of Night" and stated that "Diana" bestowed blessings upon her.

A.D. 1457: Three women tried in Bressanone confessed that they belonged to the "Society of Diana" (as recorded by Nicholas of Cusa).

A.D. 1508: Italian Inquisitor Bernardo Rategno wrote in his *Tracatus de Stigibus* that a rapid expansion of the Witch Cult had begun 150 years earlier. He concluded this from his study of trial transcripts from the Archives of the Inquisition at Como, Italy.

A.D. 1519: Girolamo Folengo (Italian poet) associated a "Mistress" known as Gulfora with Witches who gathered to worship at her court, in his *Maccaronea*.

A.D. 1526: Judge Paulus Grillandus wrote of Witches in the town of Benevento who worshiped a goddess at the site of an old walnut tree.

A.D. 1576: Bartolo Spina wrote in his *Quaestrico de Strigibus*, listing information gathered from confessions, that "witches" gathered at night to worship "Diana," and had dealings with night spirits.

A.D. 1647: Peter Pipernus wrote, in his *De Nuce Maga Beneventana* and *De Effectibus Magicis*, of a woman named Violanta, who confessed to worshipping Diana at the site of an old walnut tree in the town of Benevento.

A.D. 1749: Girlamo Tartarotti associated the Witch Cult with the ancient cult of Diana, in his book *Del Congresso Nottorno Delle Lammie*. In his *A Study of the Midnight Sabbats of Witches* he wrote: "The identity of the Dianic Cult with modern witchcraft is demonstrated and proven."

A.D. 1890: Author Charles Leland associated the Witch Cult with the goddess Diana, as a survival of the ancient ways, in his books: *Etruscan Magic & Occult Remedies*, *Legends of Florence*, and *Aradia; Gospel of the Witches*.

Professor Carlo Ginzburg, author of *Night Battles: Witchcraft & Agrarian Cults in the 16th & 17th Centuries*, and *Ecstasies: Deciphering the Witches' Sabbath*, presents compelling evidence of Witchcraft as the survival of a hidden shamanistic culture that flourished across the European continent (and in England) for thousands of years. Ginzburg was formerly a history professor in the Instituto di Storia Medioevale e Moderna at the University of Bologna. He is currently professor of Italian Renaissance studies at the University of California at Los Angeles. In *Ecstasies*, Ginzburg presents important information supporting the antiquity of the Witch Cult. Although burdened with the Christian image of evil Witches, but armed with the knowledge of pre-Christian European religion, Ginzburg links those accused of practicing Witchcraft to an ancient fertility cult which he believes was once widespread throughout central Europe.

Ginzburg has an interesting approach to the study of Witchcraft. Most scholars who study Witchcraft look at the trial transcripts, dismiss the statements as "too fantastic," and therefore conclude that such a cult never existed, but was due to some kind of hysteria. Ginzburg looks at the material as though the statements indicate what the people themselves actually believed, and then goes on to try to understand why they would have believed themselves to have participated in such fantastic events. A great deal of

Witchlore can be discerned by such an approach, and allows us to view the material contained in various transcripts as a peek into the folklore of the Middle Ages.

Through this line of investigation emerges an ancient shamanistic practice involving organic hallucinogens, employed to send the practitioners off into other realms of consciousness. This, of course, resulted in fantastic stories of flight, mythical creatures, orgies, and wild Sabbats (not to mention whatever may have been contributed to the trial transcripts for its own agenda by the Inquisition).

THE CULTURAL ASPECTS BEHIND SURVIVAL

The roots of Witchcraft clearly do go back to the shaman priests and priestesses of our forefathers. From their attempts to understand the world around them arose the beliefs and practices of what came to be Witchcraft. Women were viewed as magickal because of their ability to reproduce, and because they could bleed for days and not grow weak or perish. Men were in awe of women, and supported them in a matriarchal society. In time, as men began to go off hunting and warring, masculine images took on more importance. An inner patriarchal cult arose and demanded a place in the clan. Sadly, the matriarchal and patriarchal systems would not share equally in the clan life, and the former power began to collapse.

The concept of Deity in the Old Religion has its origin in the early stages of human development. When humankind began to wonder about the forces around them, personifying for simplification, the "gods" arose. This stage in human development was the origin of what eventually became the Nature religion of Witchcraft.

Our ancestors perceived a "consciousness" or "spirit" within all things. This, they called the *Numen*. It was the Numen that gave power to the forms in Nature. Power objects, stones, and charms were all valued for the power of their Numen. These indwelling spirits could be minor entities, or very powerful ones, depending upon the object possessed. Rare objects were believed to contain powerful Numen, while the more common objects contained the lesser ones. One major exception was the tree. Trees were always considered to contain very potent Numen.

In addition to the Numen, our ancestors perceived the Nature spirits, or Elementals. These are spirits who channel the life force into Nature. In the occult tradition they are called Gnomes, Sylphs, Salamanders, and Undines. Gnomes are linked to the Earth energies, Sylphs to Air, Salamanders to Fire, and Undines to Water. These are the physical and nonphysical elements that constitute created materials.

The rituals of Witchcraft indicate a concern for growth and sustenance, and clearly mark the peak of the cult at a time of agricultural development. The rites were designed to increase fertility of both plant and animal. Traces of the well-known "Slain God" mythos are still evident. In the modern rites of Aridian Witchcraft, layer upon layer of these ancient beliefs can be found, having been built upon each prior foundation (much as ancient ruins lay deeper beneath cities of antiquity). With the growing power of the new religion of Christianity, the Witch Cult began to retreat. Where once entire villages had gathered in celebration, now only handfuls of people came to worship. By A.D. 314 it had become a crime of heresy to believe in anything that was contrary to Christianity.

Trial transcripts and various treatise from the fourth century A.D. through the eighteenth century clearly document a continuing Witch Cult in Christian Europe. Some contemporary authors would have us believe that none of this was really going on during this era. I can only assume that they perceive these peasants to have been simply bored, and that the peasants therefore decided to commit suicide by fabricating involvement in a nonexistent cult.

However, consistent documented statements recorded by Italian Inquisitors clearly demonstrate that these peasants were worshipping Diana, in a cult whose practices can be traced back historically to at least the time of Horace. It is interesting to note that peasants on trial in the fifteenth and sixteenth century A.D. were being accused of the very same magickal practices that Horace, in the first century B.C., ascribes to Canidia, the Witch.

The Italian Inquisitor Bernardo Rategno wrote, in his *Tractatus de Strigibus*, of a rapid expansion of the "witches' sect" around 1375. He had studied trial transcripts of the past, and concluded that what he was dealing with in 1508 had begun to spawn sometime around 1375. Something had taken place in fourteenth century Italy from which arose an increase in the practice of Witchcraft.

In the book *Folklore by the Fireside; Text and Context of the Tuscan Veglia*, author Alessandro Falassi (professor of anthropology and director of the University of Colorado in Siena) relates the Italian custom known as the *veglia* (pronounced vay-yah). The word "veglia" is roughly translatable as "wake" and is similar to the Latin word vigilia, meaning to stay awake during the usual hours of sleep (a vigil). The veglia has always been a social occasion in which social rules and values have been discussed and transmitted in rural Tuscany; folklore has provided for centuries the means and messages of such crucial communicative events.

Falassi describes the scene in which Italian peasants once returned from the fields at sunset and gathered before the fireplace. Here, they would first tell fairy tales to the youngest children that contained various messages and morals intended to merge the child into the Tuscan community as he or she grew up. Next, the older children were told stories of their family members and ancestors, in order to establish a sense of who they were and who they had been. Lastly, they spoke of their religious beliefs and customs in order to preserve their traditions. It is because of traditions like the veglia that so much of hereditary Italian Witchcraft has survived and been passed on. Falassi writes of the veglia:

> *La veglia; the word and the custom that surrounds it have an old-fashioned ring to Tuscans today. Yet these fireside evenings and their homespun performances are not so far removed from contemporary people's experience, for it is only in the last decade or so that the occasion has lost its vitality . . . The veglia has lasted over 500 years without losing its function or meaning.*[15]

Traditionally, to attend a veglia one had to be a member of the family; "of the blood" as they would say. Other participants in the veglia could be relatives "of the same blood," or those acquired through marriage.

Throughout the Middle Ages, the veglia was held during the period of the year between the fall and winter sowing of the crops and Lent, even though the common rituals extended to cover the complete cycle of the year and all four seasons.

The fireside hearth was the center of the Italian Pagan's home, a place it has maintained for centuries. The family and the fireplace belonged to the mother of the home and it was she who tended the fire. In the center of the fireplace sat the "fire stone," a fireproof slab over which the fire burned. The umbilical cords of children born into the family were placed beneath the stone, a custom based on the folklore belief that this would keep the family together. This is an indication that the fire stone was an important element in the veglia family gatherings.

The main substance of the fire at the veglia was the *ceppo* (log) which was burned. This log always came from the part of the tree closest to the roots, connecting the log symbolically to the family roots. Ceppo is the Italian word for log, but can also mean "a group of houses" or "a family." A pregnant woman is sometimes called *ceppa inceppita*, which means a log ready to sprout a branch. The log was the symbol of marriage in Roman times, and the woman symbolized the tree of life, so it is easy to see that the symbolism of the veglia is quite ancient.

The fireplace was the center of the house, providing heat and light and the means by which food was prepared. It was the point at which Nature merged with human culture. Here also hung the items common to domestic family life, which were also symbols of the generative act of life and of the family. The female symbols were the kettle, the chimney, and the chain, symbolizing the womb, the vaginal passage, and the unifying principle of family. The male symbols were the fire poker and tongs (phallic representations), and the fire itself.

It was here in this setting that the family gathered to hear the old stories told and re-told. The fire which back-lighted the narrator was the explanatory principle and signifier of both magickal transformation and the metaphysics of the family. It only made sense that this would be the place where family values and world views would be shared among those of the same blood. It was here that hereditary witches were kept bound together from one generation to the next through the family tales of bloodlines and religious beliefs, mixed together with folklore and legend.

The earliest references to the veglia in literature date from the fifteenth century, although certainly this was a much older practice. In the Strega Tradition, gatherings at the time of the Full Moon are referred to as the *Veglione* (pronounced vay-yoe-nay), although the slang term *Tregua* (tray-gwah), meaning "respite," is more commonly used. The root word of Veglione is clearly Veglia. Veglione means "to dance all night"; today that word is the name of a traditional Italian dance.

The ritual gathering at the time of a Full Moon was a respite from the burdens of daily work and drudgery for the Pagan peasants of old Italy, hence the slang word Tregua. This was also true of the yearly celebrations of the great festivals, many of which were adopted and altered by the Church, making it easier for the Pagans to celebrate in the open under the guise of Christian worship. Open worship of the saints became a useful cover for the worship of the old gods, as witches adapted to the ruling class of the period.

Many modern witches see Catholics simply as Pagans who accept Jesus as divine, and certainly many aspects of Italian Paganism have survived in Roman Catholicism. Clearly Mary is the goddess image, the "mother of god," and Jesus is the slain god born at the Winter Solstice, linked to themes of resurrection maintaining the ancient cycle of the Green Man.

The fire of the veglia is still kindled today by Italian Witches in the form of the "Spirit Flame," which burns upon the altar. Placed directly in the center of the altar is a bowl that holds the blue flame symbolizing the presence of the ancient spirit of the Old Ways. In a real sense, however, this is more than a symbol, as the Strega invoke the ancient ones directly within the flame and draw their power from divine fire. Fire is one of the most ancient forms of divinity and appears to have been a common focus in most ancient cultures.

In the book *The Golden Bough*, by James Frazer, there is a chapter dealing with the sanctuary of the Goddess Diana at Lake Nemi in Italy. In this chapter Frazer makes reference to the divine fire:

> *For the perpetual holy fires of the Aryans in Europe appear to have been commonly kindled and fed with oak-wood, and in Rome itself, not many miles from Nemi, the fuel of the vestal fire consisted of oaken sticks or logs as has been proven by a microscopic analysis of the charred embers of the Vestal fire . . . if Diana was a queen of the woods in general, she was at Nemi a goddess of the oak in particular. In the first place, she bore the title of Vesta, and as such presided over a perpetual fire, which we*

have seen reason to believe was fed with oak-wood. But a goddess of fire is not far removed from a goddess of the fuel which burns in the fire; primitive thought perhaps drew no sharp line of distinction between the blaze and the wood that blazes.[16]

Here again we see the ancient connection between the log, fire, and the female spirit (which is the setting for the veglia). Literally it was "folklore by the fireplace" which preserved so much of the Strega's ways.

Fortunately, the persecution of Witches in Italy began almost 100 years later than it did in northern Europe, and even then the local village witch was generally tolerated as the Church searched mainly for organized groups. The persecution of Witches was not as fierce in Italy, although indeed many Witches (and non-Witches) were burned by the Inquisition in its war against religious freedom. However, more often than not, the majority of Witches in Italy were either flogged or imprisoned for short term. This more tolerant attitude, along with the tradition of the veglia, helped many family traditions survive the centuries of persecution that destroyed or severely fragmented so many of the Witch traditions of northern Europe.

RUSTIC BELIEFS BEHIND SURVIVAL

As previously mentioned, in the Old Religion of Italy there are certain spirits called the Lare, who are both protectors and preservers. In Roman mythology, the Lare were ancestral spirits and guarded the family. A small Lare "house" was placed upon the hearth. Each Lare house had a receptacle for offerings that consisted of wine, honey, milk, and flowers.

The focal point of a family is their home, and in ancient times the focal point of a house was the hearth (the Latin word *focus* means hearth); the hearth held the fire, which provided heat and upon which the meals were prepared. A prayer was said to the Lare every morning, and special offerings were made at family festivals. These spirits were originally gods of the cultivated fields, worshipped by each household at the crossroads where its allotment joined those of others. Later Lare were worshipped in houses, and the household Lar (singular of Lare) was conceived of as the center of the family, and of the family cult. The image of the Lar was usually a youthful figure dressed in a short tunic, holding in one hand a drinking horn and in the other a cup.

In early Etruscan times, these spirits were called the Lasa. In Tuscany, the name Lasa still applies to various spirits. Aradia, who lived in Tuscany during the fourteenth century, taught mortals about the Lasa and about fire. The flame became a symbol of the Spirit of the Old Religion. Aradia associated the light of fire with personal enlightenment. She taught that we all bear a spark or flame of Divine Consciousness within us. This was our Spirit or Soul. Fire is an ancient symbol of Deity and of worship (Moses and the burning bush, etc.). To early humankind it provided warmth and protection, as well as a method of food preparation. The possession of fire was essential to long-term survival. Today it appears on the Aridian altar as the Spirit Flame, which represents the presence of Deity.

In La Vecchia, the Lare represent not only ancient family ties, but also the spirits who protect and preserve the Old Religion (and its followers). It is also largely because of the Lare belief that the Old Religion was never totally destroyed during the violent Witch persecutions of the Middle Ages. The Lare Cult maintains a strong family connection, and it is for this reason that the hereditary Witches of Italy retained a cohesive Family Tradition down through the centuries.

Generation after generation has remembered and honored their predecessors, passing on the ancient traditions of the Old Religion. Even today among the mainstream populace many elements of the ancient cult still exist. The tradition of the Good Witch Befana filling stockings hung on the hearth is a living remnant of the Old Religion. It is interesting to note that children write their wishes upon bits of paper that they place in the hearth to be carried up the chimney (connecting fire, Lare, and Befana). For more information on Befana, see the appendix.

ENDNOTES

1. Originally titled *Etruscan Roman Remains*, when first published in 1892. Renamed in 1963 reprint by University books.

2. Charles Leland was an American folklorist who spent his final years in Italy researching Italian Witchcraft and Tuscan folklore. Author of many books and articles on this subject, Leland's works were clearly the foundation for much of Gerald Gardner's reconstructive material on Wicca.

3. Introduction, page 9. Reprint by University Books, 1963.

4. Preface, pages 8–9.

5. Page 252, *Legends of Florence*, Macmillan & Co., 1895.

6. Preface, page 5, *Aradia; Gospel of the Witches*. Reprint Phoenix Publishing, Inc., 1990.

7. *Etruscan Magic & Occult Remedies*, page 196. Reprint University Books, 1963.

8. *Etruscan Magic & Occult Remedies*, pages 150 and 152.

9. *The Works of Horace*, pages 177–178. Reprint, David McKay Publisher, 1884.

10. *Etruscan Magic & Occult Remedies*, page 197.

11. The Benandanti and Malandanti were two different factions of witches who fought against each other in ritual combat.

12. *The World of Witches*, page 65. English translation, University of Chicago Press, 1964.

13. *The World of Witches*, page 60.

14. Compiled from the collective works of Carlo Ginzburg, Julio Baroja, Alfredo Cattabiani, and Charles Leland. Although some of the references address events outside of Italy, it must be remembered that the Church directed them from Rome, and that the Councils and individuals mentioned here were accountable to the Pope in Italy (and also for a time at Avignon).

15. *Folklore by the Fireside*, page 2, University of Texas Press, Austin, 1980.

16. *The Golden Bough*, page 190. Reprint 1 volume abridged edition, Macmillan Co., 1972.

17. See chapter 21, "Teachings of the Holy Strega," for additional information.

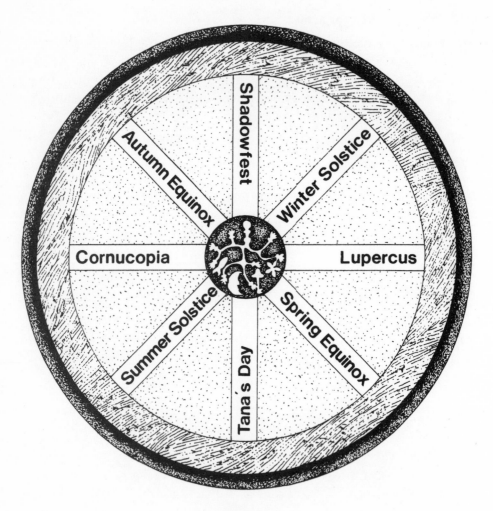

Figure 2
Wheel of the Year

3

Festivals of the Seasons

Aradia taught that participation in the Trequenda Festivals brought Witches into harmony with Nature. It aligned them with the energy patterns which flowed across the earth. Aradia promised that the traditional powers of Witchcraft would be bestowed through continuous participation in the Wheel of the Year.

from the text

In Italy, Witches do not use the word Sabbat for their seasonal rites. The Italian word is *Treguenda* (Tray-gwen-dah), and is similar in meaning to that of Sabbat. Webster's Dictionary lists Sabbat as Old French for Sabbath (old English as well). The word "Sabbatical" (French: Sabbatique) is defined in the dictionary as "of or suited to the Sabbath" and "a period of rest that occurs in regular cycles." The word "Treguenda" has as its root the word *Tregua* which means "a respite, or a truce." It is interesting to note that a "Tregua" (Tray-gwah) is also slang for the Full Moon ceremony. Respite translates as "an interval of temporary relief or rest (as from work, etc.). In modern Italian the word Triguenda means "quarterly, every three months." It is easy to see the relationship between Sabbat and Treguenda as periods of rest.

In early times, the followers of the Old Religion were farmers and craftsmen. Their lives were largely spent in toil. Their religion provided times in which they could set aside their work and enjoy a social and spiritual celebration. These festivals were indeed "respites," or "periods of rest occurring in regular cycles."

THE EIGHT TREGUENDAS

In the modern Aridian Tradition there are eight Treguendas: four major and four minor. The major rites occur in October, February, May, and August. These are the Spiritual Festivals and are considered of greater importance. The minor festivals occur on the Spring and Autumn Equinox, and on the Summer and Winter Solstice. These are the Earth Festivals, and are seasonal/agricultural in nature. While many people believe that the ritual observance of these times is of Celtic origin, the fact remains that these seasonal rites were observed in ancient Roman times in southern Europe, as we shall discover in this chapter.

The agricultural year was vital to ancient Romans and to later Italian farmers. Ancient Romans held various festivals every month; thus, it is easy to find similar celebrations occurring near the same dates as modern Wiccan festivals. Roman farmers were aware of the Equinoxes and Solstices and their place in the Wheel of the Year; this was also noted in the Greek and Roman Eleusinian Mystery Cult. The rites of the Lesser Eleusinian Mysteries were celebrated at the Spring Equinox; the Greater Mysteries at the Autumn Equinox. Such rites focused upon the descent of the Goddess into the Underworld and her ascent in the Spring.

Just as we have no historical records to indicate that any specific sect of Celts celebrated the eight Sabbats within any specific cult, so too it is with Italian traditions. We know that the basic themes of each Sabbat are native to Aegean/Mediterranean festivals occurring at the same time of year as northern European festivals. A simple study of Greek and Roman festivals will clearly demonstrate this (see the appendix for more parallels). To obtain a good overview of ancient Italian festivals originating from Etruscan and Roman influences in Italy, let us look at the Wiccan festivals of the year and note the Italic counterparts.

Samhain (October 31/November 1):

According to Italian tradition the dead return to the human world beginning on the night of November eve and continue until the second night (3 nights in all). In the fifteenth century, the Roman Catholic Church (in an attempt to disband Pagan practices) officially claimed the day of celebration calling it *Ognissanti* or All Souls. As early as the tenth century this old Italian pagan celebration had already concerned the Christian monks who encountered it among the people. The Church allowed this practice to continue because of the conversion opportunities it presented; the monks began cooking large vats of fava beans for the poor which they placed on street corners in honor of the departed souls of the faithful. A free sermon accompanied each serving of free food.

Winter Solstice (December 21):

December was marked by Roman festivals to the sun god Sol and to the agricultural god Saturn. The intimate connection between the sun and the growing of crops called for an invocation of both aspects of deity.

Imbolg (Candlemas):

In Gardnerian Wicca it is a time of purification. The month of February was sacred to the Roman god Februus who was a god of purification and death. The purification rites of the Lupercalia were also celebrated in February. This ritual occasion was later transformed into a festival honoring St. Simon. In the seventh century, the Roman Church renamed it "The Presentation to the Lord." The date was changed to the 2nd of February in hopes of putting an end to the rival Pagan celebrations. By providing a conflicting time of worship, the Church ensured the presence of common folk who would not want to be counted absent from the Christian celebration, nor discovered as preferring the Pagan celebration, for fear of the resulting retribution by the Church. The Church festivals then coincided with the month dedicated to purification in Roman Paganism: to Iunio Februata and the ritual of the Lupercalia. By removing all these pagan presences, and above all, Juno, the 2nd of February became the Purification of the Blessed Virgin. This time was then known as Candelora or Candlemas because people were blessed by candles distributed to the faithful by the Church. These candles were believed to possess protective virtues against calamities, storms, and the agony of death. The same practices and beliefs were earlier observed by Pagan farmers who once lit torches for Juno's protection.

Spring Equinox (March 21):

March was marked by the festival of Liberia, who was also known by the name Proserpine (Persephone). Proserpina was (among other things) a goddess of Spring whose ascent from the Underworld was marked by rituals performed in the Eleusinian Mysteries at the Spring Equinox.

Bealtaine/May Day (April 30/May 1):

May was marked by the Spring festivals of the Floralia. Flora was the Roman goddess of gardens and flowers. Her week-long Spring celebrations culminated on May 1st with a grand festival.

Summer Solstice (June 22):

The Roman festival of Vesta occurred in June. Vesta was the goddess of the hearth and of sacred fire itself. The Lare (ancestral spirits) were under her domain. These Lare were originally spirits of cultivated fields. They are derived from the Etruscan Lasa who were spirits of fields and meadows. The Lasa are identical to the old concepts of fairies throughout Europe. The Mid-Summer festival is connected to fairies and magickal times. In the Roman festival of Vesta, with her Lare, we see the theme of the Queen of the Fairies on Mid-Summer's Eve.

Lughnasadh/Lammas (July 31/August 1):

The festival of Ops occurred in August. Ops was the goddess of the fertility, creative forces, and earthly energies. She was the wife of Saturn, who was the Roman god of agriculture, and thus we have the harvest association. In Roman Mythology she was identified with the goddess Fauna/Fatua.

Autumn Equinox (September 21):

In the Eleusinian rites of the Roman and Greek cults this was the time of the descent of the Goddess into the Underworld. This ancient Aegean/Meditteranean theme is the classic Wiccan mythos as viewed by most Traditions.

The modern Aridian rites of the festival year are based upon the myths of the Old Religion, which are collectively referred to as "the Mythos." These myths employ the names of various deities to personify the ways of nature, and to portray the life of humankind, as well as the process of death and rebirth. In essence, the myths are a drama play, Earth is the stage, and we are the players. Within the heroes and villains of the play, we find our own inner selves struggling with the forces of light and darkness. The seasonal year represents the journey of the Soul as it moves through the cycles of the natural world and the supernatural world.

The religious Aridian year begins at the end of October and is marked by the celebration known as Shadowfest, or in Italian, as La Festa dell' Ombra. The following is a summary of each Treguenda:

> **Shadow Fest** *(La Festa dell' Ombra) - October 31: Celebration of the Pro-Creation. In the Mythos, the union of the God and Goddess.*

> **Winter Solstice** *(La Festa dell' Inverno) - December 21/22: The birth of the Sun God, from the Union in Shadow Fest. Celebration of light, hope, and promise.*

> **Lupercus** *(Festa di Lupercus) - February 2: Celebration of purification, and the beginning of fertility. In the Mythos, the puberty of the Sun God.*

> **Spring Equinox** *(Equinozio della Primavera) - March 21/22: Celebration of the ascent of the Goddess from the Underworld Realm of Shadows. Celebration of awakening fertility.*

Tana's Day *(La Giornata di Tana) - May 1: In the Mythos, the Courtship of the God and Goddess. Celebration of the return of the Goddess to the World. Celebration of life, and of the fullness of fertility.*

Summer Solstice *(La Festa dell' Estate) - June 21/22: In the Mythos, the marriage of the God and Goddess. Celebration of life, and growth.*

Cornucopia *(La Festa di Cornucopia) - August Eve: Celebration of Plenty, and of a ripe harvest. In the Mythos, the God is preparing to sacrifice Himself for the world to continue.*

Autumn Equinox *(Equinozio di Autunno) - September 21/22: Celebration of the Harvest. In the Mythos, the God dies and departs to the Underworld. The Goddess then descends to seek her lost lover.*

A common modern term for the eight rites is the "Wheel of the Year." It is thought o as a spinning wheel, turning and weaving the patterns of life. On the physical level, it i symbolic of the changing seasons. On the spiritual level, it is symbolic of the "seasons o the soul." The Mythos, which is an integral part of each rite, symbolizes the journey o the soul through a variety of existences. In the Mystery Teachings of the Wheel, we dis cover that we are the characters in the Mythos. Everything is symbolic within each Mythos and represents various aspects of the encounters facing a Soul as it passes from life to life. Through a study of the Mythos, and routine participation in each Treguenda one can gain spiritual enlightenment.

The Mythos of the Full Moon ceremony weaves its way through each Treguenda and completes the Spiritual Vision. Understanding the Full Moon ceremony is essential to unlocking the Mysteries. It is interesting to note that the ancient teachings connect the light of the Moon to the passages of the soul.

In the old Mythos, the God would rise up each day and travel across the sky from eas to west. As he did so, he collected the souls who had left the body during his absence Then he would descend into the Underworld and deliver them to the Goddess. She would then take them to the Realm of Luna (which was the Moon). As more and more souls were gathered, the light of the Moon increased until it was full. As these souls were reborn back into the World, the light of the Moon would decrease.

Aradia taught that participation in the Treguenda Festivals brought Witches into har mony with Nature. It aligned them with the energy patterns that flowed across the earth Aradia promised that the traditional powers of Witchcraft would be bestowed through continuous participation in the Wheel of the Year.

In ancient Rome, a festival known as the Saturnalia was held in December. This par ticular mythic rite was to have more impact upon later European customs influencing the

Old Religion than perhaps any other. In the pre-Republican calendar, the festival started on December 17, and usually ran for several days, ending on the Winter Solstice. Bonfires blazed during this time, and the celebration was marked by orgies, carnivals, transvestism, and gift giving.

Masters and slaves changed places and the world was turned upside down for a short period. All of this was overseen by a temporary king called "The Lord of Misrule." These Saturnalian revels and orgies were not tamed until the fourteenth century, when the Catholic Church had enough power to finally exert its "authority" over both the government and the people.

The person chosen to play the Lord of Misrule had to be a young, attractive man, strong and virile. For thirty days prior to the festival he was allowed to indulge himself in any and all pleasures as he pleased. He was dressed in royal robes and was treated like a king. In point of fact, this young man represented the god Saturn, in whose honor the festival originated.

The Romans considered Saturn to be a god of cultivated fields and sprouting seed; according to legend he was the first king of Latium and first introduced agriculture. At the end of the festival he was slain upon the altar of Saturn by having his throat cut. His blood was then given to the fields so that his vitality passed into the soil, revitalizing the life within the Earth and ensuring a bountiful harvest for the next year. In the classical period of Horace and Tacitus, this king was a buffoon figure, but in earlier times he was the sacrificial king.

In the book *The Golden Bough*, by James Frazer, we read these words:

> *We can hardly doubt that in the King of the Saturnalia at Rome, as he is depicted by classical writers, we can see only a feeble emasculated copy of that original, whose strong features have been fortunately preserved for us by the obscure author of the Martyrdom of St. Dasius. In other words, the martyrologist's account of the Saturnalia agrees so closely with the accounts of similar rites elsewhere which could not possibly have been known to him, that the substantial accuracy of his description may be regarded as established; and further, since the custom of putting a mock king to death as a representative of a god cannot have grown out of a practice of appointing him to preside over a holiday revel. . . .*[1]

In Italy today, the winter festival of *Carnevale* (the Carnival) closely resembles the revels of the Saturnalia, with the exception of the literal slaying of the king, of course. Frazer writes of this in *The Golden Bough*:

> *The resemblance between the Saturnalia of ancient and the Carnival of modern Italy has often been remarked, but in the light of all the facts that have come before us, we may well ask whether the resemblance does not amount to identity. We have seen that in Italy, Spain and France, that is, in the countries where the influence of Rome has*

*been the deepest and most lasting, a conspicuous feature of the Carnival is a burlesque
figure personifying the festive season, which after a short career of glory and dissipation
is publicly shot, burnt, or otherwise destroyed, to the feigned grief or genuine delight of
the populace. If the view here suggested of the Carnival is correct, this grotesque personage is no other than a direct successor of the old king of the Saturnalia. . . .*[2]

In ancient Rome, a pig was sacrificed at the Saturnalia. In later times, this was substituted with a trickster character, and in more recent times by a great buffoon who ruled as
the King of the Carnival. This character was carried about upon a throne as he reclined,
wearing the costume of a pig.

Traditionally, a fava bean was baked into a focaccia cake, and the young man
among the contestants who found the bean became the Lord of Misrule. The custom
of placing a fava bean in a focaccia cake still takes place at Carnival in Italy, along
with many tamed versions of the original revels of the Roman Saturnalia. In *The
Aquarian Dictionary of Festivals* by J. C. Cooper, the author comments on the ancient
and modern associations of the Saturnalia:

> *The characteristics of this time passed from Rome into Europe, persisting into
> medieval times, having also a Lord of Misrule.*[3]

Ritual Dancers

Frazer's book deals with the Slain God Mythos which is an integral part of the Old Religion. In *The Golden Bough*, we find these words from Frazer:

> *We may conclude with a fair degree of probability that if the King of the Wood at Aricia lived and died as an incarnation of a sylvan deity, he had of old a parallel at Rome in the men who, year by year, were slain in the character of King Saturn, the god of the sown and sprouting seed.*[4]

Clearly we can see, in all presented here, the Slain God Mythos of the Western Mystery Tradition; the Lord of the Vegetation (formerly the Lord of the Woods) sacrificed in the harvest. It is interesting to note that yet another northern European Craft Mythos originated in Italy. There are still those, however, who claim that Stregheria is not native to the Meditteranean/Aegean region but is a system created from modern Gardnerian Wicca. The fact that almost every tenet of Gardnerian Wicca also appears in ancient Greek and Roman beliefs and practices seems to escape the logic of these critics. In reality, it is only natural that the witches of Italy would absorb various cultural, religious, philosophical, and theological aspects found in southern Europe. See the appendix for a further outlining of these parallels, which I have presented for those who wish to approach this subject with an open mind.

ENDNOTES

1. *The Golden Bough* by James Frazer, page 678. MacMillan Company, 1 volume abridged, 12th printing, 1972.

2. *The Golden Bough*, page 678.

3. *The Aquarian Dictionary of Festivals*, page 192. The Aquarian Press, 1990.

4. *The Golden Bough*, page 679.

OTHER SOURCES

Bunson, Matthew. *A Dictionary of the Roman Empire*. Oxford University Press, 1991.

Cardini, Franco. *Il giorno del sacro, il Libra delle feste* (Sacred Days, the book of Festivals). Milano: Rusconi Libri, 1989.

Catabiani, Alfredo. *Calendario; Le feste i mitti le leggende e i ritti dell'anno* (The Calendar; festivals, myths, legends and rituals of the year). Milano: Rusconi Libri, 1988.

Field, Carol. *Celebrating Italy*. New York: William Morrow & Co, 1990.

Kravitz, David. *Who's Who in Greek and Roman Mythology*. Clarkson N. Potter, Inc., 1975.

4

Tuscan Witchcraft

But there is, withal, as I have remarked, a great deal of mystery and secrecy observed in all this cult. It has its professors: men, but mostly women, who collect charms and spells, and teach them to one another, and hold meetings; that is, there is a kind of college of witches and wizards, which, for many good reasons, eludes observation.

Charles Leland
Etruscan Roman Remains, 1892

Witchcraft in Tuscany is unique among other types of Witchcraft in Italy. In Tuscany the roots of the Old Religion stretch back into Etruscan times, and contain less Roman influence than many other forms of Italian Witchcraft. In the Neolithic period of Italy there once existed the culture now referred to as the Cult of the Great Goddess. Archaeological discoveries dating from this period include an abundance of icons portraying a mother goddess and a male consort. Some archaeologists, such as Marija Gimbutas, believe that the Etruscans were the inheritors of surviving beliefs and practices from this ancient cult, and another known as the Cult of the Dead, both of which once thrived on the Italian peninsula. This area was part of what is now called Old Europe, a region inclusive of Italy, Greece, Czechoslovakia, southern Poland, and the western Ukraine.

Extremely archaic concepts flourished in the region of Old Europe long after the rise of Christianity. This was particularly true throughout the Italian peninsula. Hellenistic and Roman writers were often astonished to discover traces of primitive conceptions and practices within the old Etruscan lands that were quite unlike those commonly acknowledged in Greece and Rome. Among the most noteworthy were the suggestions of an animistic conception of the supernatural and the omnipresent importance of omens, signs, and the divinatory arts.

The ancient Etruscans embraced the high social and religious status of women, a remnant of the matrifocal religion that once flourished in Old Europe. Also worthy of mention is the belief in the material survival of the dead in their burial places. The Etruscans placed personal items, games, tools, and furnishings in their tombs. In archaic Roman religion we also find similar practices associated with burial sites. Archaeological evidence of such practices in the Neolithic burial mounds left by the indigenous Cult of the Dead is abundant. So great was the antiquity of Etruscan beliefs and practices that the ancient Romans themselves referred to Etruscan religion as "The Old Religion."

The Etruscan civilization rose to power in Italy sometime around 1000 B.C. Some scholars have theorized that the Etruscans were not indigenous to Italy, but were an Indo-European people. However, a linguistics study of the 10,000 inscriptions left by the Etruscans has convinced the majority of linguists that the Etruscans were a non-Indo-European people native to Italy who adopted many customs, crafts, and styles of eastern Mediterranean culture by way of trade.

The Etruscans believed in the ultimate power of supernatural forces. All acts of Nature were seen as initiated by a god or a spirit. Various signs and omens preceded the appearance or action of any supernatural being. This was the catalyst to the presentation of sacred offerings, an attempt to establish a beneficial relationship between spirits, deities, and humankind. Connected to the Etruscan belief in the power of omens and signs is the ancient myth of the animal guide or ancestor. This prehistoric concept was widespread throughout Italy and remained linked to pastoralism and transhumance as evidenced in the archeological studies of the Apennine Bronze Age.

Early nomadic tribes in Italy believed in an animal spirit that guided and protected them. The Piceni tribe, for example, believed their guide was a woodpecker, the Sabellians a bull, the Lucani a wolf, and the Ursenti a bear. The people of this era practiced a custom known as *Ver Sacrum*, the sacred springtime. This required a selected portion of each tribe to leave and settle in another area each spring season. Therefore, the animal guide was extremely important to beliefs and practices of such a pastoral-nomadic people.

As humans evolved into an agrarian society, the spirits of meadows and forests were transformed into spirits of the plowed and seeded fields. These were the Lasa spirits,

Etruscan Protective Spirit

beings sharing an intimate ancestral relationship. Under Roman rule these spirits were called Lare, and were transformed into spirits of home and family. Making the Lare protectors of the family preserved the memory of their former ancestral nature.

The Etruscans further developed and refined many early Pagan beliefs, creating a mystical and magical tradition famous throughout the classical world. Centuries before the Romans came to power, the Etruscans worshipped the Great Mother Goddess Uni and her consort Tinia. These deities oversaw a host of spirits and demi-gods and displayed power over the forces of Nature and human destiny. The pantheon of the Etruscans was not unlike the Olympic gods of Greece, although they worshipped another set of gods who were above them. These deities were called the Involuti or *gods of the mists.*

The Witches of Tuscany are the descendants of the Etruscan race. For centuries they have kept their existence secret, whispering on moonlit nights to the ancient deities of their ancestors. Unbroken generations have passed on the Old Ways through family bloodlines, preserving the ritual and magical knowledge of ancient Italian Witchcraft. In the early seventeenth century, Francesco Guazzo (an Ambrosian monk) wrote of hereditary Italian witches in his book *Compendium Maleficarum.*

In chapter six Guazzo writes of the "inherited taint" of Witchcraft found in children born to Witches. Several chapters deal with ceremonies in which children are dedicated to the Witch Sect, and other ceremonies, including Witch weddings. Guazzo states that all of these are designed to "propagate the race of witches."

In the nineteenth century, Charles Leland encountered Maddalena, an Italian Witch from Tuscany. Leland wrote in his *Memoirs* concerning Maddalena:

> *A young woman who would have been taken for a Gypsy in England, but in whose face, in Italy, I soon learned to know the antique Etruscan, with its strange mysteries, to which was added the indefinable glance of the Witch. She was from the Romagna Toscana, born in the heart of its unsurpassingly wild and romantic scenery, amid cliffs, headlong torrents, forests, and old legendary castles. I did not gather all the facts for a long time, but gradually found that she was of a Witch family, or one whose members had, from time to immemorial, told fortunes, repeated ancient legends, gathered incantations, and learned how to intone them, prepared enchanted medicines, philtres, or spells. As a girl, her Witch grandmother, aunt, and especially her stepmother brought her up to believe in her destiny as a sorceress, and taught her in the forests, afar from human ear, to chant in strange prescribed tones, incantations or evocations to the ancient gods of Italy, under names but little changed, who are now known as folletti, spiriti, fate, or lari—the Lares or household goblins of the ancient Etruscans.*

Maddalena supplied Leland with a great deal of Witchlore, much of which he later published in his books *Legends of Florence* and *Legends of Virgil*. Leland's book *Etruscan Roman Remains* was inspired by his contact with Maddalena, and is Leland's most complete work on Italian Witchcraft. Near the end of his life, Leland obtained some material from Maddalena that he published as *Aradia; Gospel of the Witches*. This text was quite different from anything Maddalena had taught Leland about Italian Witchcraft. When comparing this material with the bulk of what Maddalena earlier supplied to Leland, it becomes apparent that the Aradia material did not represent the type of Witchcraft actually practiced by Maddalena.

Leland's *Legends of Florence* and *Legends of Virgil* both present a fascinating glimpse into the Old Religion of Italy. Much of the material focuses on tales of an obscure matrifocal religion wherein goddesses have been reduced to Nature spirits over the course of time. These legends reflect themes of conflict between female and male entities, all resolving in victory for the former. The goddess Diana still retains her divine status in these old tales, and appears as the patroness and protector of all witches.

Agricultural themes are prominently featured in Maddalena's material. A spirit known as Bughin forms seeds. Another spirit named Palo presides over planting and Segetia guards the seed within the earth. Segesta protects the new plant sprout, Patana tends the plant as it grows, and Patelena opens the ear of grain. Patella prepares the grain for its first touch by sunlight and moonlight. Once the grain is exposed, spirits of the night come in the form of fireflies and impart their mystical powers to the grain. A spirit known as Talena (the spirit of the night) oversees this process.

Robigo is the spirit of the harvest and Remle is the spirit of mills. When the grain is harvested, Witches make ritual cakes from it to be used in a sacred meal beneath the Full Moon. In the mythos provided by Maddalena, the seeds (that later became the plants) extracted the secrets of the Underworld as they lie within the dark warm soil. When the ears opened to reveal the new grain, spirits came to learn new secrets and to impart old ones. In this manner, the Witches receive all of these mystical secrets when they eat the ritual cakes. Leland speaks of this connection with the underground in *Etruscan Roman Remains*:

> *For there are in the earth deep mysteries; the earth-worm and mole are full of them because the foot of the sorcerer passes over them, and gives power, the salagrana or stalagmite, and different metallic ores are really holy, from being subterranean, and yet sparkling with hidden occult light when broken they meet the sun; and plants which send their roots deep down into the earth draw from it mystic forces which take varied magic forms according to their nature when brought up into light and air. Owing to the inability of my informant to express herself clearly, I had difficulty for a long time in understanding this properly chthonic theory; when I did master it, I was struck by its Paracelsian character—this belief in a "geomantic force" which Chinese recognise as Fengshui.*

Plants, and particularly herbs, have been associated with Witches since classical times. In the writings of Homer, Witches dwell in forest glades. Ovid places Witches living among "herb-clad hills." By the Hellenistic period we find references to Witches dwelling in cities and procuring their herbs from urban settings and graveyards. Accounts from this era say that Witches performed their rituals at night upon rooftops.

It is interesting to note that the ancient Greek word for witch is *pharmakis* (herbalist) and it is from this word that the Modern English word pharmacy is derived. The Romans replaced the Greek with the Latin word *venenum*, a word referring specifically to poisonous herbs. From this was derived the word *veneficium*, the Latin word for Witchcraft. At this stage the Latin word for witch became *venefica*, where earlier it had been saga meaning "a wise woman" or "sorceress." It is clear from ancient accounts that Aegean/Mediterranean Witches knew how to heal and how to harm with herbs. In the Witchlore of this region each plant contained a spirit called a Numen, and it was this indwelling spirit that gave the plant its potency. The principle of the Numen later evolved into the concept of the fairy or Nature spirit.

In Tuscan Witchcraft there is a very intimate relationship between fairies and Witches. Both share in a stewardship of Nature and possess an understanding of the secret inner knowledge of magick. In Tuscany the Queen of the Fairies is known as Alba or Turanna, the latter being the oldest name and one of Etruscan origin. Aldeganno is a fairy spirit of ivy, and Turabug is the spirit of rue and the guardian of reeds or canes. Rue and ivy are among the most magickal of plants employed in Tuscan Witchcraft. In Tuscan Witchcraft, rue, ivy, salt, and wine are used to evoke the Goddess and to call upon spirits and fairies. In *Etruscan Roman Remains*, Leland writes of Etruscan beliefs still found among the Tuscan peasants:

> There are also a few records of certain plants, showing how the belief that many herbs and flowers have an indwelling fairy, and are in fact fairies themselves, still survives, with a degree of personification which has long since disappeared in most other European countries.

Connected to the Tuscan belief in fairies are the three spirits of Fate known as Maratega, Rododesa, and Befana. They spin the lives of all humans, weaving the patterns of each individual's existence, and then cutting the thread of life when the design is completed. Divination is an important aspect of Tuscan Witchcraft, and is used to catch a glimpse of the pattern being woven by the Fates. Befana is also an ancestral spirit whose sacred symbol is the woven stocking, a symbol of spinning and weaving. Stockings are traditionally hung by the fireplace on the night of January 6th in anticipation of a visit from Befana. The fireplace is a symbol of family life and unity, as from ancient times it has been a place of gathering for food, warmth, and companionship. On her special night Befana fills the children's stockings with gifts, connecting her with the new generation each year.

Attilio is a spirit of the fireplace and is associated with Lare, the ancestral spirits dwelling in or near the hearth. Setlano is a spirit of fire evoked for divination. Traditionally, while a fire burns in the hearth, the pattern of the flames and the appearance of any sparks all combine into a divinatory observance. Elemental beings of fire known as Salamanders may appear in the dance of the flames as omens. Mena, a spirit of love and marriage, is said to manifest in the form of a serpent. Young men and women ask questions to the fire and observe any changes. Those hoping for love may call upon the spirit known as Marta. She is also known to ignite passion as suggested by her association with fire divination.

Primitive practices are a keystone of Tuscan Witchcraft and a sign of the great antiquity of this tradition. Many aspects of this old form of Witchcraft have been preserved in the records of the Inquisition in Italy. One case concerning a woman named Elena Draga is worthy of particular consideration. In 1571 she was brought before the Inquisition for using Witchcraft to heal people. One of her spells called for a piece of raw meat to be rubbed on a wart. Then the meat was to be buried in the soil so that as it rotted the wart would also waste away.

In another spell Elana washed a sick person with water, waited for the ebbing tide to occur in the third or fourth phase of the moon, and then poured the soiled water into the ocean tide. As the tide carried away the soiled water, so too was the disease believed to disappear. This observance of the phases of moon and the ocean tide was a common feature of healing practices in the coastal regions of Italy. Author Dino de' Antoni came across it in his research into Chioggian witchcraft and magick, and noted it as one of the few entirely non-Christian aspects of healing to survive into sixteenth century Italy. By this period it was common in popular folk magick to find spells that required gesturing the sign of the cross, sprinkling holy water, or saying the Lord's Prayer. However, in the case of Elena Draga we find that Tuscan Witches are still using the older pre-Christian forms of magick.

The preservation of traditions of any kind is central to the Italian way of thinking. Charles Leland noted this in his field research into Italian Witchcraft in the late nineteenth century. In his book *Etruscan Roman Remains* we read:

> *There is in Northern Italy a mountain district known as La Romagna Toscana, the inhabitants of which speak a rude form of the Bolognese dialect. These Romagnoli are manifestly a very ancient race, and appear to have preserved traditions and observances little changed from an incredibly early time. It has been a question of late years whether the Bolognese are of Etrurian origin, and it seems to have been generally decided that they are not. With this I have nothing whatever to do. They were probably there before the Etruscans. But the latter at one time held all Italy, and it is very likely that they left in remote districts those traces of their culture to which this book refers. The name Romagna is applied to their district because it once formed part of the Papal or Roman dominion, and it is not to be confounded with La Romagna proper. Roughly speaking, the region to which I refer may be described as lying between Forli and Ravenna. Among these people, stregeria, or witchcraft—or, as I have heard it called, "la vecchia religione" (or "the old religion")—exists to a degree which would even astonish many Italians. This stregeria, or old religion, is something more than a sorcery, and something less than a faith. It consists in remains of a mythology of spirits, the principal of whom preserve the names and attributes of the old Etruscan gods, such as Tinia, or Jupiter, Faflon, or Bacchus, and Teramo (in Etruscan Turms), or Mercury. With these there still exist, in a few memories, the most ancient Roman rural deities, such as Silvanus, Palus, Pan, and the Fauns. To all of these invocations or prayers in rude metrical form are still addressed, or are at least preserved, and there are many stories current regarding them.*

Despite this nature to preserve traditions, Tuscan Witches are very protective of their ways, and rarely discuss anything with people who are not initiates or blood relatives. In *Etruscan Roman Remains* Leland writes of this:

But there is, withal, as I have remarked, a great deal of mystery and secrecy observed in all this cult. It has its professors: men, but mostly women, who collect charms and spells, and teach them to one another, and hold meetings; that is, there is a kind of college of witches and wizards, which, for many good reasons, eludes observation. It was my chance to become acquainted in Florence with the fortune-teller referred to, who was initiated in these secrets, and whose memory was stocked to an extraordinary and exceptional degree with not only magical formulas but songs and tales. Such familiarity with folk-lore and sorcery as I possess, resulted in confidence—the end being that I succeeded in penetrating this obscure and strange forest inhabited by witches and shadows, faded gods and forgotten goblins of the olden time, where folk-lore of every kind abounded to such excess that, as this book shows, I in time had more thereof than I could publish. To do this I went to strange places and made strange acquaintance, so that if the reader will kindly imagine something much out of common life, and often wild and really weird—i.e., prophetic—when fortune-telling was on the cards, as the dramatic accompaniment of every charm and legend in this book, he will but do it justice. To collect volumes of folk-lore among very reticent Red Indians, and reserved Romanys is not unknown to me, but the extracting witchcraft from Italian strege far surpasses it. I too was among the shadows.

The extraordinary tenacity with which the peasants of Tuscany have clung to their old faith is an inherited character passed on from their Etruscan ancestors. The ancient Roman historian Livy said of the Etruscans that they were *"a race which excelled all in devotion to religious rites and in the art of cultivating them."* Throughout all the wars and transformations that reshaped Italy, the peasants of Tuscany have remained essentially the same race. Again in *Etruscan Roman Remains*, Leland writes:

Englishmen and Frenchmen are the result of modern mixtures of peoples, but the Italians are absolutely ancient, if not prehistoric. There are families in Italy who find their family names in Etrurian monuments on their estates. And Cicero, Tacitus, Livy, Virgil, and many more testify that all their divination and religious observances were drawn from and based on Etruscan authority. "This," says Muller, "was shared by the common people. There were in Italy schools, like those of the Jewish prophets and Gallic Druids, in which the system was thoroughly taught." And there is the last relic of these still existing among the Tuscan witches.

ETRUSCAN ROOTS OF TUSCAN WITCHCRAFT

One of the reasons why so much of the Old Ways has survived in Tuscan Witchcraft lies within the people themselves. All of their patterns of thought and tradition are derived from thousands of years in which religious art and passionate faith influenced almost every facet of life. These patterns have imprinted what might be called a *predisposition* within the genetic memory of the Tuscan witches, a factor transmitted through heredity. The passion that once inspired religious and theological expression on Etruscan vases, mirror art, and in jewelry was the very same spirit that created the Etruscan concepts of deities, goblins, spirits, and elves, along with their myths and legends. From this spirit is derived the mentality that created all the mystical and magickal concepts that have evolved into Tuscan Witchcraft.

Even today we still find remnants of Etruscan religious beliefs in many cultures, and oddly enough the modern clown figure is one example, as we shall soon see. Many of these elements are rooted in the Neolithic Cult of the Dead. In this primitive sect it was believed that the souls of the dead lingered, awaiting a chance to be reborn into the physical world. These spirits had to be appeased, and therefore offerings were placed and various ceremonies were performed.

Crude mounds were constructed for the dead and in these primitive tombs were placed the personal items formerly the property of the buried person. A small passageway was left in the mound so that the spirit could come and go as it pleased.

The Cult of the Dead also produced spiral designs that marked its tombs. Spiral symbols are often employed in owl motifs because of the circular patterns of their feathers, especially around the eyes. The spiral itself symbolizes many things other than owls, including serpents, renewal, and mystical forces in general. But the owl is of particular interest to us in this chapter, and many of its connections to Witchcraft will be explored later as the chapter continues.

The simple clown figure, typically present at carnivals, dates back to Etruscan times. In Etruscan tomb art, we find depictions of entities wearing checked as well as dotted clothing, sporting large beak-like noses, and carrying something resembling a slapstick. In some images the clothing bears black and white checks and in other images their clothing is multicolored. These colors were also connected in Etruscan religion with ancestral spirits. Even today, the mythical figure known as Befana (in part an ancestral spirit) traditionally wears an apron of multicolor. See the appendix for more information related to Befana.

In Etruscan tomb art, the beings wearing this type of clothing represented spirits of the dead and death itself. Their appearance at carnivals and festivals once symbolized the brevity of life and served to remind people to enjoy it to the fullest. They also symbolized the attendance of one's ancestors at the festival, a mystical family reunion. In Tuscan Witchcraft, as in most forms of Italian Witchcraft, we find an emphasis upon family lineage and the honoring of one's ancestors. The belief that a person's soul can become a powerful spirit in the Afterlife is an old Etruscan concept, and is reflected in the Etruscan beliefs surrounding the Lasa spirits (the fairy folk of Old Italy). So to honor one's ancestors was to assure oneself of good rapport with the Lasa.

The beak-like noses appearing on the Etruscan characters, mentioned earlier, are remnants of Neolithic worship in ancient Italy. The earliest deity icons found in the Italian peninsula depict deities that are part bird and part human. Typically the birds are waterfowl, and symbols etched into the icons indicate a connection to the Moon and to rain and fertility. Over the following centuries, as this theme evolved in ancient Italy, we find the bird transformed into both a scavenger and a bird of prey. For example, Tulchulcha (an Etruscan deity of the dead) has the beak of a vulture, and instead of a slapstick he later carries a large hammer. By classical times the bird itself is no longer the deity at all, and simply accompanies one as its sacred animal. An example of this is Athena and the owl.

In Tuscan Witchcraft there are several obscure elements that suggest a connection between Athena and the Witch sect of Old Italy. First we find an Amazon cult in Athens that worshipped a statue of Artemis bearing a shield, spear, and helmet. These are the classic items associated with Athena. The Amazon's statue in Athens appears to be a composite image of Athena and Artemis, as opposed to the classical Greek image of Artemis as a maiden wearing a hunter's tunic and sandals. In ancient Rome Witches were identified with owls, also the sacred bird of Athena.

Charles Leland gives us an interesting related tale in *Legends of Florence* that he obtained from Maddalena. In this tale we find a Tuscan story about the rivalry between a god associated with water and a goddess. In Greek mythology there are tales of the rivalry between Athena and Poseidon. As we will discover there are several other elements found in both stories that may indicate a connection of great antiquity.

The olive tree was associated with Athena in Greek mythology, and she was said to have created it on the Acropolis during a competition with the sea god Poseidon for the mastery of Attica. Poseidon created the horse as his challenge to Athena. The gods of Olympus favored the olive tree and thereby Poseidon lost the contest. In Maddalena's tale, the god Biacone kills a magickal serpent sent by the goddess, as a demonstration of his claim to possess greater power. The goddess then resurrects the serpent by touching it with an olive twig, a sign of her claim to greater power. In the context of a competition it is interesting to see the olive twig appear in our tale of rivalry, yet another indication of the antiquity of Maddalena's themes. The horse also appears in Maddalena's legend, as Biacone rides in a chariot drawn by horses.

It is interesting to note that horses were forbidden in the sanctuary of the goddess Diana, patroness of Italian Witches. Here may lie another obscure connection between witches and Athena, perhaps an archaic memory of Poseidon as an adversary.

Also worthy of consideration are the Greek myths relating tales of animosity between the Centaurs and the Amazons who worshipped Artemis in Athens (as already noted). Perhaps the Centaurs are symbols of Poseidon, reminders of the conflict between Poseidon and Athena. Another cult creature shared by Athena and Artemis is the owl, one of the symbols of Italian Witchcraft in Tuscany.

The owl and its connection to Tuscan Witchcraft are shrouded in the distant past. Any unquestionable link between Athena and Witches, through the owl, is most likely lost now in time. Although if it, in fact, ever existed, I think it is not too great a leap in logic to associate the inner secrets of Witchcraft with the owl as a symbol of wisdom. We do know that the ancient Romans believed that Witches could transform into owls, and some scholars believe that the word Strega is derived from the Latin word *strix*, meaning owl. The word strix refers specifically to a screech owl, which was also the type of owl sacred to Athena.

The owl is, among other things, a symbol of death and darkness. In Etruscan religion the owl was an attribute of the deity of darkness and night. Archaeological excavations at Pyrgi and Santa Marinella have revealed altar carvings depicting Minerva (Athena) as a deity in Etruscan chthonic cults. This connects Minerva/Athena with themes related to classical Roman Witches who worshipped goddesses of the night and darkness such as Diana, Hecate, and Proserpina (Persephone).

Ancient Roman writers such as Horace, Lucan, and Ovid all portray Witches as members of a chthonic sect involved in the worship of Diana, Hecate, and Proserpina. In these ancient tales we find the moon as central to the magickal workings of Italian Witches. Even the modern Witches' theme of "drawing down the moon" appears in Horace's writings circa 30 B.C. Before Horace the concept was known in ancient Greece as *kathairesis*.

The earliest mention of a witch in Aegean/Mediterranean culture can be found in the tale of Circe, written by Homer circa 800 B.C. Some may argue, however, that Circe was a sorceress and not a Witch. In connection with Circe, Homer also lists three features commonly associated with Witchcraft. These features are streams, hills, and dog-like beasts. More important is the fact that these features consistently appear in the literature of Witchcraft spanning nine hundred years from the time of Homer to Lucan.

Also worthy of note is that the roots of Witchcraft lie in the shamanic practices that eventually evolved into magickal systems. Circe was depicted as one of the great magick users of ancient Greece. Magick is deeply connected to Witchcraft, and the merging of magick with shamanic practices and pre-Christian religion had certainly taken place by 800 B.C., as indicated in the ancient Mystery Cults of Greece and Egypt.

Proserpina

In ancient myths Proserpina is linked to the Underworld goddess Hecate Triformis, of whom Porphyry wrote: *The moon is Hekate . . . her power appears in three forms: Selene in heaven, Artemis on earth, Hekate in the Underworld.* Hesiod wrote in the Theogony (circa 700 B.C.) that Hecate ruled over the three great mysteries: birth, death, and life. Diana also shared a three-fold nature as indicated by the writings of Horace (*Songs,* 3:22):

O maiden goddess, guardian of hill and grove, thou that, thrice invoked, givest ear to young mothers when in travail and rescuest them from death, goddess of the triple form, thine be the pine that overhangs my dwelling . . .

In the first century B.C., Catullus says of Diana in his Hymn to Diana:

. . . Diana whose name is Trivia—the crossroads her sacred places—nightgoddess, queen of underworld. Threefold Diana . . .

And Ovid writes (*Met.* 7:94-95):

He swore he would be true by the sacred rites of the threefold goddess . . .

The connection of Diana to Witches and Italian Witchcraft is a long-standing Mediterranean tradition. Beginning with Horace in the first century B.C., we find historical references to Diana as the Witches' goddess, references that continue even after the rise of Christianity. A sect known as the "Society of Diana" is mentioned in the records of the Inquisition as late as the eighteenth century A.D. Among the ancient Romans, Diana was connected to childbirth, and offerings were placed at her shrine near Lake Nemi to ensure an easy labor. In Roman mythology Diana was also the chaste maiden, and in the writings of Horace we see her as a hag goddess associated with Hecate. In these themes we find the traditional triformis aspect of the goddess: maiden, mother, and crone.

Some of the material recorded by the Inquisition, related to the Society of Diana, may contain remnants of the beliefs rooted in the Neolithic Cult of the Great Goddess. As noted earlier, humanoid bird deities were among the first icons produced during Neolithic times in what is now Italy. This leads us again to the owl, which in turn leads us to Italian Witches, the theme of flying, and festivals of the dead (related to the Cult of the Dead mentioned earlier).

44

The ancient Roman Witches, known as *striges*, were believed to possess the ability to appear as either an owl or a human. The tenth-century writings of Regino of Prum speak of processions of spirits of the dead accompanied by Witches. Regino calls this group the "Society of Diana" and says it is led by the goddess Diana. Here we see the Neolithic elements of primitive religion evolved into a structured sect.

In Witchcraft during the Middle Ages we see strong elements of the ancient chthonic religion of Old Europe. Many of the aspects of the ancient Mystery Cults of the Aegean/Mediterranean region are present in Witchcraft at this time and later. The gatherings for festivals, sacred meals, libations of wine, fertility rites, and the worship of a horned god and goddess consort are all features of the Greek and Roman cults. We see associations of this nature not only in the rites of Bacchus/Dionysus but also in the rites of Eleusis. In the latter we also find the theme of the Descent of the Goddess and the Lord of the Underworld, a common mythos in modern Wicca/Witchcraft.

By the time of the Middle Ages folklore and folk magick were well rooted in the worship or veneration of various Saints. The Church allowed this transfer of ancient pagan spirit worship to saint worship because it kept the peasants from reverting back to the Old Ways of their ancestors. Thus the needs of the peasants were fulfilled and the Church was satisfied to keep its flock by whatever means. Unfortunately this also included violence and death, as seen in the torture and execution of people accused of practicing Witchcraft.

By the fifth century Christianity had assimilated Mediterranean Paganism and as the power of the Church moved into northern Europe it readily absorbed the Celtic and Teutonic elements that closely resembled Mediterranean paganism. These new elements merged with the original aspects of classical Witchcraft and were mixed together into the earlier structure of ancient Greek and Roman Witchcraft.

Today Witchcraft is more often expressed in northern European rather than Mediterranean terms. This is due to the fact that most modern writers on Witchcraft are neither well versed in classical Witchcraft literature, nor fluent enough in Latin or Italian to study the southern European material. Most modern studies in Witchcraft/Wicca are written in English, and the majority of writers on the subject have nationality roots connected to the British Isles. This, together with the fact that most writers are primarily interested in their own cultural roots, has created a tendency to both perceive and present Witchcraft as being primarily Celtic in nature.

During the Renaissance period we find many of the Aegean/Mediterranean elements of classical Witchcraft appearing in the trial records of the Inquisition. In Guazzo's *Compendium Maleficarum* we discover many interesting aspects of the Witches' sect. According to Guazzo, a large black goat sits upon a throne during these rites. Ritual circles are traced upon the ground with beech twigs, and spirits of earth, air, fire, and water are called to the rituals. Present at the rites is a man in the vestments of a priest who reads from a black book. Guazzo notes that Witches hold religious ceremonies, and that some of their rites are expiatory in nature. He also focuses on hereditary Witches and their children who attend these ritual celebrations.

One of the primary aspects of Tuscan Witchcraft is the hereditary element. Charles Leland noted this in his nineteenth-century field studies into Italian Witchcraft. The portrayal of Tuscan Witches depicted by Leland confirms not only the antiquity of their beliefs and practices but also the tenacity for survival inherent in this ancient sect. Fortunately, Leland is not the only source of information we can turn to regarding the Witch sect in Italy circa 1896. In volume three of *Folk-Lore; Transactions of the Folk-Lore Society* (published March 1897) we find an interesting account of Neapolitan Witchcraft. The author, J. B. Andrews, tells us:

> *The Neapolitans have an occult religion and government in witchcraft, and the Camorra; some apply to them to obtain what official organizations cannot or will not do. As occasionally happens in similar cases, the Camorra fears and yields to the witches, the temporal to the spiritual.*

Andrews goes on to say that the Witches of Naples are divided into "special departments of the art" and he lists two as "adepts" in the art of earth and sea magick. Andrews also implies that a third specialty may exist as adepts of star magick. Andrews tells us that Italian Witches perform knot magick, create medicinal herbal potions, construct protective amulets, and engage in the arts of healing.

Andrews concludes his article with information he collected while interviewing Italian Witches. During these interviews Andrews asked from what books these Witches gathered their information. They replied that their knowledge was entirely traditional, and is "given by the mother to the daughter." The Witches also informed Andrews that blood is exchanged from a vein in the arm, and the new member is given a mark under the left thigh. Although the Moon is not specifically mentioned, the Witches do report to Andrews that such ceremonies are performed at midnight.

Perhaps the most telling sign of the antiquity and survival of Tuscan Witchcraft lies in the fact that these Witches still wear a charm called the *Cimaruta*. Author Fredrick Elworthy, in his book *The Evil Eye* (John Murray, London, 1895), describes the Cimaruta and provides a drawing of it along with another depicting an ancient Etruscan charm of striking similarity. This Etruscan charm is now housed in the Bologna Museum. The word Cimaruta means "the top sprig of rue." The Etruscans incorporated the rue into the background designs engraved on the backs of polished mirrors. It more often than not accompanies mythical and magickal themes portrayed in Etruscan mirror art.

The symbols attached to the rue charm are all aspects of the Old Religion. Although the individual items vary from region to region in Italy, there are common ones appearing on most Cimaruta pieces: fish, Moon, key, blossom. The fish is a symbol of fertility and abundance, a remnant of the fertility rites of Old Europe. The Moon symbolizes the night and occult powers as well as allegiance to the Goddess and her consort.

The blossom (typically a vervain flower) is a sign of protection. The vervain is also sacred to the fairies, and in Italian folklore the goddess Diana is called the Queen of the Fairies. Therefore, this symbol displays a kindred nature between Witches and fairies.

In Tuscany, family Witches still gather beneath the Full Moon to honor the ancient ways. The solitary Witch, whether living in a town, village, or city still remains to read fortunes, dispense charms, or to brew the healing potions. This has been the way of Witches for countless centuries. It is comforting to know that the Old Guard is still there, and that the Old Ways have been preserved among the peasant Witches of Tuscany.

Ceres, with Horn of Plenty

5

The Moon and Witchcraft

The children gather wood, and the fathers kindle the fire, and the women knead their dough, to make cakes to the Queen of Heaven . . .

The Old Testament: Jeremiah 7, 18

In "The Teachings of the Holy Strega"[1] we find evidence that Aradia once taught her disciples that the souls of the "dead" dwelled upon the Moon. Although modern followers of her teachings now agree that Aradia used the Moon as a symbol for Astral Realms, this former concept was not unknown in many ancient cultures.

That the Moon is an abode of the "departed" has been believed for ages. In the *Egyptian Book of Respiration* (manuscript translated from the original in the Louvre, Paris), Isis breathes the wish for her brother Osiris "that His soul may rise to heaven in the disk of the Moon." Plutarch once wrote:

> *. . . of these soules the Moon is the element, because soules doe resolve into her, like as bodies of the dead into the earth.*

Initiates of the Aridian System believe that Aradia used the Moon as a representation of the Astral Plane, and of its Lunar Realm in particular.

The cycles of the Moon mark the Astral tides and cycles, and serve to indicate points in time through which the Astral spheres of influence may be tapped.

The phenomenon of the Moon that attracted early humankind was the sequence of its phases, waxing and waning. Many ancient cultures linked these phases to periods of loss and gain, to fertility, and to aging and dying. The origin of Moon worship is no doubt connected to the changing of its form each month, and to its lighting of the night sky. The Moon itself became the focal point of early lunar cults and was viewed as the Goddess Herself.

In the sanctuary of Diana, at Lake Nemi, the Moon was viewed as the dwelling place of the Goddess Diana and her company, as well as the resting place of those Witches who passed from the physical life on Earth. According to early lore of the Strega, the "shadow" areas of the Moon were believed to be the sacred groves of the Goddess Diana, where she hunted with her sacred hounds, and the bright areas were thought to be the plains.

The Janarra Witches, who are the descendants of those Witches who worshipped at Nemi, practice a form of lunar ritual that dates back to ancient times. The ancient theme of "becoming like the Moon" can be seen in the Janarric Rites of Initiation. Initiates who choose to become priests or priestesses are taken nude beneath the Moon and then "painted" white. This is usually done with a white powder (or ointment) which is applied over the entire body, including the hair.

The Rites of Initiation are linked to the phases of the Moon. The first

The Enchanting Moon

degree is the New Moon, the second degree is the Half Moon, the third degree is the Full Moon, and physical death is the Waning Quarter, and is considered to be a ritual of Initiation into the Great Mystery. Thus there are four degrees of Initiation, in accordance with the lunar phases.

Ritual worship and religious consideration of the Moon varies in many parts of the world, depending upon the cultures that embrace Moon worship in a given place. Between the Tropic of Capricorn and the Tropic of Cancer, the Moon is considered to be feminine in nature. Remainders of ancient people such as the African Bushmen, Australian Aborigines, Congo Pygmies, Chaco Indians, and some Brazilian tribes view the Moon as male. Nearly all Moon-oriented cultures connected the phases of the Moon with the rhythm of Nature, the human cycles of fertility, and life and death.

As a heavenly being, the Moon was believed to encounter various situations with other celestial beings. Many cultures believed that the three dark days of the Moon were due to certain evil creatures who devoured, and later regurgitated, the Moon. The eclipse of the Moon was seen in many different ways. These run from the Moon Goddess periodically descending to earth, to the lore of Italian Witches who once believed that the Sun and Moon mated from time to time, in order to give birth to new stars in the heavens (to replace those which have fallen). It is apparent that even the ancient Hebrews once worshipped the Goddess of the Moon, as recorded in such Biblical scriptures as Jeremiah 7, 18:

> *The children gather wood, and the fathers kindle the fire, and the women knead their dough, to make cakes to the Queen of Heaven . . .*

Even Mount Sinai was linked to the worship of the Assyrian Moon God called Sin. The word Sinai meant "of Sin" or "place of Sin." The ancient Hebrews were known to have called Egypt Sinim (which means Moonland), and it was through their stay in Egypt that the Hebrews became knowledgeable in the ways of Moon worship.

Throughout the history of humankind, the Moon has played an important part in measuring time, and in signaling the planting and harvesting of various plants of both mundane and magickal nature. The beginnings and endings of various concerns became linked to the waxing and waning stages of the Moon. In Witches' herbal lore, the phases of the Moon are significant in the planting and picking of herbs. Magical herbs are often planted at the New Moon to ensure the waxing of their powers; then they are harvested at the Full Moon when they are most potent. Today we know that the Moon does indeed influence the growth of plants, and the phases of the Moon affect the pharmaceutical nature of plants. It is interesting to note that one of the definitions of the word "pharmaceutical"[2] is to practice Witchcraft.

Italian and Greek witches were said to have the power to draw the Moon down from the sky. Old tales abound of people trying to pay them to do so, in order to disrupt the month. The origin of this belief is unknown, but today it is said that these Witches drew down the etheric power of the Moon for magickal purposes.

During the time of Christian persecution of Witches, a superstition arose which said that having the light of the Full Moon fall upon you could lead to insanity. This was no doubt devised to keep people from joining in Pagan lunar rites at night. It is recorded in the Bible that to kiss your hand to the Moon is a sin against God. This act was originally a ritual salute to the Moon (the throwing of a kiss). The ancient Hebrew leaders apparently had a difficult time keeping their people from worshipping the Moon.

Weather lore is, of course, associated with the Moon in such ancient beliefs as a ring around the Moon meaning rain was imminent. Storms and winds were once linked to lunar phases, and Janarric Witches linked astrological associations to the phase of the Moon at a person's birth, along with the season in which it occurred, as well as the time of day or night. This is a complete system based entirely upon the Moon, and is similar to today's astrology, with its own signs and so on.

The earliest symbolic representation of the Moon deity is a stone, which appears in ancient art to be either a crude pillar or perhaps a cone of some sort. Early legends tell of this stone having fallen from the sky as though it had come from the gods themselves. It is interesting to find that both the symbol and the legend appear in early Greek, Assyrian, and Etruscan/Roman legends. In Chaldea, the Moon goddess known as Magna Dea was worshipped in the form of a black stone obelisk, as was the Arabian goddess, Al-Uzza. Goblet d'Alviella, in his book *Migration of Symbols*, shows a series of drawings in which the Moon stone is carved (maintaining the general form) into the goddess image of Diana of Ephesus.

It is interesting to note that the ancient Ephesians claimed that the statue of Diana had fallen from the sky. It is likely that this story has preserved the ancient legend of the

Figure 3
Ancient Italian Moon Tree

Moon stone itself. It appears that the original stone was carved over a period of time into a human image. An ancient Italian carving discovered at the site of the Barberini Palace in Rome (see Figure 3) pictures the Moon hidden in a secret place within an altar; the pillar of stone along with a Moon tree are included in the image.

The ancient glyph known as the Moon Tree appears in the Old Religion. Variations of this symbol can be found in ancient Etruscan, Assyrian, Greek, and Roman art. Trees have long been viewed as symbolic bridges to other worlds. In European folklore, doorways to the fairy kingdoms sometimes appear at the base of certain trees in various folk tales. In some mythologies, a tree becomes the vehicle for enlightenment, as in the case of the god Woden who hung on a tree for several days. This theme is recalled in the tarot card of The Hanged Man. Sometimes trees bear a forbidden fruit or in some way contain the key to a higher consciousness (as in the Judaic/Christian myth of the Garden of Eden). The association with the Moon in tree lore is quite ancient and is connected to the Moon deity itself, as well as to the themes of forbidden fruit and enlightenment.

A tree or wooden pillar frequently appears in ancient art as a symbol of the Moon. The Moon Tree symbol pictured in Figure 4, below, typical of Assyrian art design, is quite ancient and appears over and over again in religious art. At times the Moon Tree is

Figure 4
Ancient Assyrian Moon Tree

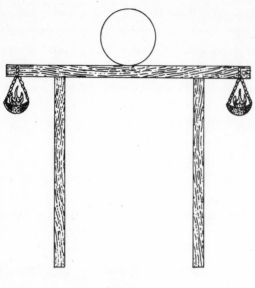

Figure 5
Moon Portal

depicted as an actual tree and other times it may appear as a truncated pole or a stylized pillar. In some ancient myths the Moon Tree was cut down and carved into a boat for a slain god or a coffin, as in the myth of Osiris.

In art forms, the Moon Tree is often shown bearing thirteen blossoms or thirteen torches (there are always thirteen Moons in a year, being either Full Moons or New Moons). In Assyrian art, the Moon Tree sometimes appears bearing ribbons similar to the European Maypole. Images have been found which depict the Moon Tree enclosed in a shrine or trellis work, recalling the fact that the Moon goddess was first worshipped in a grotto or a grove of trees (which was the case in ancient Italy).

When Witches gathered at the site of the temple of Diana, at the sanctuary of Lake Nemi, two upright pillars of wood were erected which supported a cross beam of wood (forming a "doorway") on the northeast shore of the lake. The Witches would kneel and wait for the Full Moon to rise until it appeared (from their angle) to "sit" upon the crossbeam. At this point they would rise and pass through the doorway structure in a symbolic act of passing into the lunar realm. This structure was often referred to as the Moon Tree, or Moon Portal.

Lanterns or oil lamps were hung from the ends of the crossbeam and when the Moon "sat" upon the center of the beam a triangle of light could be seen (see Figure 5). This was the mystical sign of access to the Astral or Lunar Dimension, sometimes referred to as the magickal sign of the enterer. To this day Italian Witches enter and exit the ritual circle at the northeast point, and still employ a version of this ancient Moon portal.

The inner teachings of the Old Religion deal with the esoteric meaning of the Moon Tree. In this aspect it is seen to represent the Mysteries themselves, and in a practical sense the structure of the Old Ways. The Moon Tree bears a single white fruit which is the sacred food of enlightenment. In the Mythos, the tree is located in the center of the sacred grove of Diana at Nemi, guarded by the Hooded One. The Hooded One is a powerful warrior who is not easily vanquished. Symbolically, the Moon Tree represents our system of beliefs, and the fruit of the tree is the enlightenment that arises from its teachings.

The Guardian of the Grove represents our conscious mind, which keeps us from embracing the mystical vision by always questioning and discounting our "supernatural" experiences (or those of others). It is through the practice of magick, and through the experience of mystical encounter, that we form the mentality necessary to defeat the Guardian. Once the Guardian can be defeated, then the fruit of the Moon Tree is within reach. To taste of its essence is to receive initiation from the gods themselves.

ENDNOTES

1. See chapter 21 of this book, "The Teachings of the Holy Strega" for further information.

2. *Webster's Dictionary*, 1970.

Dusio—The Trickster

6

Catholicism and the Craft

It is the most natural thing in the world that there should be certain blendings, compromises, and points of affinity between the Stregheria—witchcraft, or "old religion," founded on the Etruscan or Roman mythology and rites—and the Roman Catholic: both were based on magic, both used fetishes, amulets, incantations, and had recourse to spirits. In some cases these Christian spirits or saints corresponded with, and were actually derived from, the same source as the heathen. The sorcerers among the Tuscan peasantry were not slow to perceive this.

Charles Leland
Etruscan Roman Remains, 1892

In Italy today, many Catholic traditions have preserved the old Pagan ways. The two most obvious examples are the reverence for Mary (as the "Mother of God"), and the belief in the intercession of saints (a remnant of Pagan worship related to specific spirits who have power over various aspects of life). The Fanarric Witches of northern Italy maintain the belief that the Goddess was the first of all that came to be, and that she created the God. In this sense she can be thought of as the Mother of God. They also believe in a host of various spirits who can be persuaded to assist them in life through the use of offerings, prayers, and spells.

Many modern Strega simply consider Catholics to be Pagans who have accepted the divinity of Jesus. There are some interesting concepts in both the Old and New Testaments that resemble Strega beliefs and may well be the foundation of such an idea. According to the New Testament, the Magi were the first to seek out Jesus after "seeing" his star. Legend claims that the Magi were astrologers and sorcerers, and associates them with the lands of Chaldea, Egypt, and Persia. These are all places that have an occult history dating far back into antiquity. The tale of the Magi recorded in the Book of Matthew seems to indicate that these mystic Pagans were among the first to pay homage to Jesus.

In the Book of Proverbs (chapter 8, verse 2), we find a personage called "Wisdom" conceived of in the form of a female divinity who "stands at the crossroads," a phrase used in ancient times concerning the Witches' goddess. Wisdom speaks of being present both prior to and during the process of Creation. In verse 30 (The Jerusalem Bible) she claims to have been God's assistant during the process of Creation:

> *I was by his side, a master Craftsman, delighting him day after day, ever at play in his presence, at play everywhere in his world, delighting to be with the sons of men.*

In the Book of Wisdom (found only in the Catholic version), Wisdom is praised with these words (chapter 7: 22-27):

> *For within her is a spirit intelligent, holy . . . penetrating all intelligent, pure and most subtle spirits; for Wisdom is quicker to move than any motion; she is so pure, she pervades and permeates all things . . . She is a reflection of the eternal light, untarnished mirror of God's active power . . . although alone, she can do all; herself unchanging, she makes all things new . . .*

Connected to this concept of the feminine aspect of Divinity is the word *Ruach*. In Hebrew, this word is of feminine gender and would properly be defined in the sense of feminine divinity. When we read in the account of Creation (Book of Genesis) that the "spirit of God moved upon the face of the waters," the Hebrew word used here for spirit was Ruach. In the New Testament this has been translated into "Holy Spirit," as in the Trinity concept of "Father, Son, and Holy Spirit." Hebrew mystics of the Kabbalah[1] considered Ruach to be associated with the element of air, and thus with spirit as well. Among early Kabbalists, the sound of a word denoted its elemental association; soft sounds were associated with air, hard sounds with earth, hissing sounds with fire, and muted sounds with water.

It is not necessary, however, to look to Catholicism in order to find remnants of earlier Pagan worship. Aspects of Stregheria still survive today in both Italy and America, even among those who would not readily identify themselves as being members of La Vecchia Religione. They employ various prayers to a host of saints, lighting candles, and placing assorted objects as required by tradition. Saints such as St. Anthony, St. Jude, St. Anna, and St. Simon have replaced the old Pagan gods, to whom similar prayers and offerings were once made.

Charles Leland, in his book *Etruscan Magic & Occult Remedies*, records the old connection between Witches and Catholicism, of which he writes:

> *As for families in which stregheria, or a knowledge of charms, old traditions and songs is preserved, they do not among themselves pretend to be even Christian. That is to say, they maintain outward observances, and bring the children up as Catholics, and "keep in" with the priest, but as the children grow older, if any aptitude is observed in them for sorcery, some old grandmother or aunt takes them in hand, and initiates them into the ancient faith.*[2]

Much of their magick is mixed with Catholic rites and saints, the origins of which date back to ancient times. Certain saints, such as Anthony, Simon, and Elisha, are viewed as demi-gods, and their magickal rites of evocation are performed in cellars.

BEFANA AND BEFANO

Perhaps one of the most unlikely remnants of Witchcraft in Catholic Italy is the annual tradition of Befana, the "Good" Witch. On January 6th, children set out stockings to be filled with presents by Befana, a curious tradition to have survived in a Catholic Christian nation. Curious, unless you realize that the Old Religion never totally disappeared in Italy.

The antiquity of the Befana tradition will become clear, and we discover that she may well be a surviving memory of Fauna, a goddess of the Old Religion. In order to fully understand this we will first look at the "modern" Befana. Although rapidly disappearing, the tradition of the Befana and Befano procession is still observed in some Italian cities. Early in the evening people gather together dressed in the scruffiest and oldest clothing possible. Their faces are blackened with charcoal, and pieces of frayed rope serve as imitation hair. La Befana and her husband Befano are dressed in peasant costumes of the Middle Ages; both have humped backs and carry long staffs. Befano does not seem to serve any particular role in the procession, other than as a consort to Befana.

In their homes, meanwhile, children are busy writing their wishes on pieces of paper, which are then placed in the hearth and allowed to float up the chimney. As they do this they chant the following rhyme:

> *Befana, Befana*
> *you are my lady*
> *you are my wife*
> *Throw something down to me*

> *A small orange or a pefaninos*
> *or a piece of pecorino.*

Pefanino is a small biscuit made in the shape of Befana, and *pecorino* is a special type of cheese made from goat milk.

La Befana moves through the streets with her husband Befano and her entourage. She is accompanied by a makeshift band of three or four musicians and a live horse. The procession tours the neighborhood, calling out to the children at each house. Here they sing the Befana song, and the Befana dances with Befano:

> *Upon the mountain the snow is falling*
> *And is blown on the wind before*
> *And with a light step she descends to us*
> *A spirit that is dear to us all*
> *A spirit that many here love*
> *Who comes every year to find you*
> *She has arrived with us "la Befana"*
> *Every heart is full of joy*
> *From among the valleys, villages and countryside*
> *Our Befana has arrived here*
> *She has brought a large sackful of presents*
> *That she wants to give to you dear children*
> *who promise to be good for their mothers and fathers.*

The tempo changes at this point and the following verse is repeated twice:

> *And now you friends that are here*
> *We want to sing and dance*
> *And a veglione we want to do*
> *With the Befana and Befano*
> *And we want to salute you all*
> *Friends we shall always remain*
> *And the Befana before she goes*
> *Wishes you all happiness and prosperity.*

Having done this, the Befana and the people in her procession are given a glass of wine, some treats, or even a little money from the householder, and then they move on to the next house.

In her book *Celebrating Italy*, Carol Field tells of Befana and her ancient association to Hecate. Here she writes:

The good and bad sides of the Befana are like the good mother/bad witch of fairy tales, two aspects of a single person. The Befana may bring wonderful presents, but she can also be a grotesque woman with a sinister black face, associated in some accounts with Hecate, Queen of the Night.[3]

On page 301 of Field's book, there is a reprint of an etching of Befana done by Bartolomeo Pinelli in 1825. In this drawing Befana is seated, surrounded by an abundance of fruits, grains, and other harvest items. In her hand she holds a stalk of fennel, upon which a stocking is suspended. Here she represents the Great Mother amid the fruits of the Earth.

Field recounts a recent experience she had, in which she observed the burning of an effigy of Befana during a New Year's celebration. A procession began at sunset, wandering through the village and up to a site upon a hill, where a pyramid-style stack of corn sheaves, brushwood, and pine branches had been erected. An effigy of Befana was placed on the top of the stack, which was then set on fire by the men of the village. The torching of the stack, and the parade preceding it, is always led by the oldest man of the community. Chestnuts, symbols of fertility, are roasted on the fire. It is said that if the smoke blows to the east, it is an omen of a year of abundance. If it blows to the west, then the crops will be poor. Once the fire has died, people remove the embers and scatter them over the fields that will later be planted. This is very much like the Sacrificial King Mythos (the Slain God).

It is likely that originally Befano was the sacrificed deity, and that in time this was altered to appease the onlooking Christian officials (burning the female Witch was something that the Church would gladly sanction). It is quite interesting to see that these things have been preserved down through the ages, and are still practiced today. The fact that Befana has a male consort, is associated with the Goddess Hecate, with Witches, and with the Harvest Mother confirms the antiquity of contemporary Craft theology. Hecate was the goddess of night, and of magick. Crossroads were sacred to her, and it is interesting to note that spirits called Lare were protectors of the crossroads. Befana brings gifts to the hearths within a family's home. Lare dwelled in or near the family hearth, and it is partly because of the Lare cult within the Old Religion that the Old Ways have been preserved through family lines. The Lare were originally gods of the cultivated field and Befana is shown surrounded by the harvest, another connection of considerable antiquity.

There are two books written in Italian that present the associations of Befana with certain seasonal rites, and reveal her connection to the Goddess in ancient times. The first, *The Sacred Day, a Book of Festivals* (Il giorno del Sacro, il libro delle feste) is written by Franco Cardini (professor of history at the University of Florence). This book focuses on festivals and their connections with myth, rituals, and magickal rites. The other book, by Alberto Cattabiani, is titled *The Calendar: Festivals, Myths, Legends, and Rites of the Year* (Le feste; miti, leggende e i ritti dell 'anno). The author of *Celebrating Italy* draws upon these research texts throughout her book. A wealth of information can be found in these books supporting the survival of pre-Christian cults into modern times.

The worship by Witches of a masculine deity is easily documented. Unfortunately, the Horned God of the Old Religion, as he oversaw the Sabbath rituals, was portrayed as the Devil by the Church. Many engravings and woodcut prints from the Middle Ages portray this Christianized distortion of the seasonal rites. Fortunately, Italian Witches have managed to maintain the presence of the Goddess Diana in the Witch Cult throughout the ages.

It is interesting to note that Jan Ziarnko, in 1612, produced an engraving for the work *Tableau de l' inconstance*. In this engraving (see Figure 6) he displays a horned entity sitting upon a throne. To its right sits a woman who is labeled in the text as the Queen of the Sabbath. Kneeling before them are worshippers who are presenting a small child. All about, people are involved in dancing and feasting. The fact that people kneel to the throned individuals addresses the issue of worship. The importance of this image is that it shows a male and a female entity overseeing the Sabbath. In the picture, we note that they do not participate as would a High Priest or High Priestess. The Sabbath is being performed *for* them. This addresses the issue of Deity. Are we seeing Befana and Befano before they were dethroned by the Christian Church?

THE CYCLE OF THE YEAR

The ancient seasonal festivals of the old gods still remain in Italy, disguised as days of feast in honor of various Catholic saints. These feast days occur throughout the year, marking the ancient Pagan cycles of growth, decline, and renewal. The cycle of Winter first appears in November and weaves its spell through January as the Earth seems to wane, and seeds lay beneath the ground where they await their rebirth in the Spring. In Italy it is a time when the wheat has been sown and the fruits have been gathered. The harvesting of olives for olive oil is the seasonal labor of November and December. The veil between the world of spirits and humankind grows thin, and tradition says that those who dwell in the Spirit World feel an attraction to the living and return for visitations.

According to Italian tradition, the dead return to the world of the living on the night of November eve, and continue until the second night (three nights in all). In Sicily it is the custom to set an extra place at the table for the return of departed relatives. Sicilian families are also known to set a banquet out before the family tomb as they gather on November 2 to honor the dead.

During the Roman Empire, early Italians associated the fava plant with the dead, due to the single black stain on an otherwise perfect white petal. The Romans served fava

Figure 6
Lord and Lady of the Sabbat

beans at funeral banquets, honoring the connection of the dead with the fava plant. This association has remained constant in Italian Witchcraft, and fava bean soup is still a traditional meal served on November eve. A bowl of fava bean soup is placed outdoors as an offering to the spirits at midnight and then buried after sunrise on November 1.

In the tenth century, Christian monks encountered this celebration and were concerned with the problem of what to do with this Pagan tradition. They decided to cook up large batches of fava soup and offer them up for the souls of the dead. Hungry peasants took great delight in the vats of fava bean soup that the monks set out on street corners. The Church allowed this practice to continue because of the conversion opportunities it presented, but it wasn't until the fifteenth century that the Church officially claimed the day of celebration, calling it Ognissanti, or All Souls' Day.

In modern Italy, celebrants still eat festival treats called *ossi da morto* (bones of the dead) and *fave dei morte* (fava of the dead), which are sweets similar to cookies, but fashioned in the shape of skeletons and fava beans. In Sicily, special ritual breads are made in the form of a corpse laid to rest, along with figures made of sugar in the shape of traditional heroes and characters from Italy's past.

As winter approaches in December, the old gods make their appearance in the form of various saints now associated with the holiday season in Italy. December 13 is the festival of Santa Lucia and is marked by Pagan customs that include the observation of omens predicting the weather for the outcome of the next year's crops. Santa Lucia, or Saint Lucy, was born in Sicily in the second century A.D. and was a Christian martyr, according to inscriptions found in Syracuse (Sicily) dating from the third/fourth century A.D. In northern Europe, the Italian figure of Lucia is pictured with blond hair and wears a crown of candles upon her head—interesting how images are altered by culture. In Italy, Santa Lucia is actually a Christianized goddess dating back to early Roman times, when she was called Lucina, the Goddess of Light.

December ends with the theme of birth, whether in the image of the Son of God or the Sun God. January begins the closing of the Winter cycle and introduces the curious figure of Befana, the Good Witch. On the night of January 5, Italian children hang stockings to be filled by Befana, in much the same manner as is associated with the Santa Claus custom. Games such as tombola are still played during the holidays—this is a game that dates back to the ancient Roman festival of Saturnalia. Neapolitans wrap dried figs in laurel leaves and exchange them at New Year's, a custom going back to Roman times, when friends gave jars of dates and figs filled with honey and a bay leaf, meant to assure good fortune for the coming season. These are just a few of the many surviving Pagan traditions that are still alive in Italy today.

In her book *Celebrating Italy*, author Carol Field writes of January:

> *Later on January 17, for the feast of Sant'Antonio Abate, when a pig is slaughtered, people eat dried chestnuts, invoking fertility at the precise time the greatest source of plenty has been slaughtered. Whoever finds the black bean cooked into a sweet focaccia becomes King of Epiphany and although he is destined to be dethroned, he no longer meets the fate of the King of the Wood, who was sacrificed in the forest.*

In early Roman times, whoever received a fava bean inside one of the ritual cakes was made master of the Saturnalia revels. As late as the fourteenth century, the custom (although altered by Christianity) was still practiced at this seasonal festival, which by then

Catholic Monks with the Scrolls of Aradia

had been changed to the festival of Epiphany. Curiously, however, the name of the festival was *Festa del Re* (the Festival of the King), which retained the earlier Pagan meaning.

Another custom of this festival still observed in Italy today is when lots are drawn for pieces of the festival cake. Whoever finds a black bean in his slice is proclaimed king of the banquet and must choose a queen to rule with him over the festivities. Families still purchase a focaccia cake to be left near the fireplace for Befana at the time of Epiphany (Befana will be burned in effigy at the end of the season). Unfortunately, these old customs are beginning to disappear as the upcoming generation seems to not share a love of the Old World Traditions.

The last festival of January is the festival of Saint Anthony, the patron saint of animals. In the old days he was the god of the forest. His festival day falls on January 17, which in Italy is "the brief moment between the end of the old year and the sowing of seeds for the new." In the timing of his festival, we see that he is associated with a time when hunting was more important than agriculture, when the stag god was the King of the Woods, before he became the Harvest Lord. On this feast day, people take their animals to church to be blessed. The festival of Saint Anthony is followed by the last rite of winter, known popularly as Candelora (February 2), and known by Italian Witches as Lupercus. So ends the cycle of Winter, as it passes on its way toward the Spring.

Wrapped safely in the Roman Catholic celebrations of modern Italy lay the Pagan traditions that have connected humankind with the cycles of Nature since the time of our beginning. In most cases, only the names of the old gods have been changed to those of saints. Yet among the small isolated covens of hereditary Witch families, and the solitary Witches of remote Italian villages, the Old Religion remains unbroken, still clinging fragilely to the present. Perhaps in the Spring someone will plant a few more seeds and the Old Religion will continue to bear fruit into the future.

ENDNOTES

1. An ancient mystical Hebrew system that was designed to explore and explain the nature of divinity and the occult universe.

2. *Etruscan Magic & Occult Remedies*, page 237.

3. *Celebrating Italy*, page 299. William Morrow & Co., 1990.

7

The Watchers

The Watchers are called, or evoked, to guard the circle and to witness the ritual.
The guarding of a ceremonial circle is self-explanatory, but why are the rites to be
witnessed?

from the text

Found in Stregheria, and common to most Wiccan traditions, is the concept of the *Watchers*, who are viewed differently by the various systems. In this chapter we will look at the oldest concept of the Watchers, dating back to the early Stellar Cults. Among the Strega these beings are called the *Grigori*, and particularly so by the Tannarric Witches who are known as the "Star Witches." The Tannara have preserved the ancient Stellar Mysteries, and it is through their teachings that we can better understand who the Watchers/Grigori really are.

In the early Stellar Cults of Persia there were four "royal" stars (known as Lords) that were called the Watchers. Each one of these stars "ruled" over one of the four cardinal points common to astrology. This particular system would date from approximately 3000 B.C. The ancient ritual god-forms of the Watchers, pictured in this chapter, are performed at the associated cardinal points, while evoking them during the casting of a ritual circle (see Figures 7–10). There is a definite link between the "powers" of a Witch and the rapport with the Watchers. To assume the posture of one of these Watcher positions is to invoke the nature of that Watcher within your own psyche.

The Star Aldebaran, when it marked the Vernal Equinox, held the position of Watcher of the East. Regulus, marking the Summer Solstice, was Watcher of the South. Antares, marking the Autumn Equinox, was Watcher of the West. Fomalhaut, marking the Winter Solstice, was Watcher of the North.

Towers were constructed bearing the symbols of the Watchers as a form of worship, and their symbols were set upon the Towers for the purpose of evocation. During the "Rites of Calling," these symbols were traced in the air, using torches or ritual wands, and the secret names of the Watchers were called out.

In the Stellar Mythos, the Grigori themselves were gods who guarded the heavens and the Earth. Their nature, as well as their "rank," was altered by the successive lunar and solar cults which replaced the stellar cults. Eventually the Greeks reduced them to the Gods of the Four Winds, and the Christians to principalities of the air. Their connection with the stars is vaguely recalled in the Christian concept of heavenly angels.

Cabalists organized them into Archangels, which I assume they derived from the early Hebrew concept of a similar order of angels known as the Watchers. According to this belief, the Watchers were ruled over by four great Watchers known as Michael, Gabriel, Raphael, and Auriel. The Hebrews, no doubt, borrowed this whole concept from the surrounding cultures that were stellar and lunar in nature. The Hebrew religion was highly eclectic in ancient times.

In Italian Witchcraft, these ancient beings are the Guardians of the Dimensional Planes, protectors of the ritual circle, and witnesses to the rites that have been kept down through the ages. Each of the ruling Grigori oversees a "Watchtower," which is now a portal marking one of the four quarters of the ritual circle. In ancient times, a "Tower" was a term for a military fighting unit, and a "Watchtower" was a defending home unit, similar to a National Guard. In Italian Witchlore, the stars were once thought of as the campfires of the Grigori legions.

Originally, the Grigori were "lesser gods" who watched over the Earth and the Heavens. In the Aridian Mythos, they are the Guardians of the Four Entrances to the Realm of Aster, which is the home of the gods in Strega mythology. Outside of the Wiccan structure, the Watchers are most easily linked to the Judaic/Christian concept of "guardian angels." In the Old Testament (Daniel 4:13–17), reference is made to the Irin, or Watchers, who appear to be an order of angels (in early Hebrew lore, the Irin were a high order of angels who sat on the Supreme Judgment Council of the Heavenly Court). In the Apocryphal Books of Enoch and Jubilees, the Watchers are mentioned as "fallen angels" who originally were sent to Earth to teach men law and justice. In the *Secret Book of Enoch*,

Figure 7
Watcher Posture of the North

Figure 8
Watcher Posture of the East

Figure 9
Watcher Posture of the South

Figure 10
Watcher Posture of the West

the Watchers (called therein Grigori) are listed as rebellious angels who followed Sataniel in a heavenly war.

Gustav Davidson, in his *Dictionary of Angels*, portrays the Watchers as a high order of angels, known also as the Grigori. In Rabbinic and Cabalistic lore, the "good" Watchers dwell in the Fifth Heaven, and "evil" Watchers dwell in the Third Heaven. The Watchers of the Fifth Heaven are ruled over by the archangels Uriel, Raphael, Michael, and Gabriel. In the *Apocryphon of Genesis*, it is said that Noah is the offspring of a Watcher who slept with Bat-Enosh, his mother.

In the *Dictionary of Angels*, the Watchers are listed as the Fallen Angels who instructed humankind in the ancient arts. The most common associations found in various texts on medieval magick regarding the Watchers are as follows:

Araqiel: taught the signs of the earth

Armaros: taught the resolving of enchantments

Azazel: taught the art of cosmetics

Barqel: taught astrology

Ezequeel: taught the knowledge of the clouds

Gadreel: taught the making of weapons of war

Kokabeel: taught the mystery of the stars

Penemue: taught writing

Sariel: taught the knowledge of the Moon

Semjaza: taught herbal enchantments

Shamshiel: taught the signs of the Sun

It is these same angels who are referred to as the "Sons of God" in the Book of Genesis 6:4. According to Christian mythology, their "sins" filled the Earth with violence and the world was destroyed as a result of their intervention. This, of course, is the Biblical account and has little to do with Strega beliefs.

Richard Cavendish, in his book *The Powers of Evil*, makes references to the possibility of the giants mentioned in Genesis 6:4 being the giants or Titans of Greek mythology. He also lists the Watchers as the "Fallen Angels" which magicians call forth in ceremonial magick. (Read Genesis 6:1–7 for the background in Biblical reference.) Despite the debatable accuracy of information in books by Cavendish, he does draw some interesting parallels and even mentions that the Watchers were so named because they were stars, the "eyes of night."

St. Paul, in the New Testament, calls the Fallen Angels "principalities": *for we are not contending against flesh and blood, but against the principalities, against the powers ... against the spiritual hosts of wickedness in High Places.* It was also St. Paul who called Satan *the prince of power of the air,* and thus made the connection of Satan (himself connected to "a star," Isaiah 14:12–14) and etheric beings, for they were later known as demons and as principalities of the air.

This theme was developed further by Sinistrari, a French theologian of the sixteenth century, who spoke of an order of beings existing between humans and angels. He called them demons and associated them with the elemental natures of earth, air, fire, and water. This, however, was not a new concept, but was taught by certain Gnostic sects in the early days of Christianity.

Clement of Alexandria, influenced by Hellenistic cosmology, attributed the movement of the stars and the control of the four Elements to Angelic Beings. Sinistrari attributed bodies of fire, air, earth, and water to these Beings, and concluded that the Watchers were made of fire and air.

Cardinal Newman, writing in the mid-1800s, proposed that certain angels existed who were neither totally good nor evil, and had only "partially fallen" from the Heavens. This would seem to support Davidson's text, which places the Watchers in two different "heavens."

My purpose in presenting these associations is to show some examples of how a central theme can be divided and transformed. Today, even among Craft Traditions, there exists a great deal of confusion concerning the Watchers. Some systems view them as elemental rulers, demi-gods, guardians, spiritual teachers, or planetary intelligences. All of these concepts are indeed aspects of the Watchers. Do the Watchers have any association with the Judaic/Christian angels? Yes, but those associations are so distorted and biased that they serve only to cloud the issue.

To really understand the Grigori, we need only look to their role in Witchcraft as a Religion. Our first encounter with these entities usually occurs when casting a ritual circle in which to practice the rites. The Watchers are called, or evoked, to guard the circle and to witness the ritual (see Figures 7–10). The guarding of a ceremonial circle is self-explanatory, but why are the rites to be witnessed?

In answering this question, let us consider the relationship that exists between a Witch and the Watchers. When someone is first initiated, he or she is brought before the quarters where the Watchers have been evoked. The initiate is then presented before the Watcher and the initiate's Craft name is revealed. This is the first step in the bonding which must take place. From that moment on, the Initiate is "watched" and aided. This bond also serves as a safeguard, for every act of magick that a Witch performs is observed and noted by the Grigori.

The Watchers guard the portals to the Astral Realms, and can allow a magickal act to establish itself in the Astral substance, or can dispel the charge. This is why certain gestures and signs of evocation such as the pentagram were designed, so as to "announce" the presence of a trained practitioner to the presence of the Watchers (that is, one who had sworn not to misuse the arts). Once such signs and symbols are acknowledged by the Watchers, then the portals to other realities open more readily.

In the lore of Witchcraft, it is the Watchers who assist in the spiritual growth of a Witch and who "escort" the Witch to the next realm after physical death. Nothing is ever hidden from the Watchers, and in the end a Witch may come to know them as either the "Dread Lords of the outer spaces," or as the "Mighty Ones, the Guardians." This is not to be viewed as a situation in which these entities will "get you" if you're not "good," but rather as an assurance that karma will be delivered promptly.

As we saw in the first part of this chapter, the Watchers were linked to certain stars that marked the Solstices and Equinoxes, being the cornerstones of the year, if you will. On a greater scale, the Watchers oversaw the "seasons" of the Heavens as well. It is important to remember that the Watchers are stellar beings, not lunar. Their association with a lunar cult, rather than a solar, is obvious on a mundane scale. Stars are associated with the night, as is the Moon, for they share the heavens together. The Sun is seemingly alone (at least most of the time). The stellar and lunar cults are older than the solar cults, which later adopted (and adapted) the inner teachings of the previous ones.

Ancient lore reveals that the Watchers once had bodies of physical matter, but they evolved beyond the need for physical expression long before the rise of humankind. They became "Beings of Light," and this was most likely one of the first parallels between Watchers and angels. Yet, these Beings of Light were linked to the stars even before their evolution, for the old legends state that the Watchers came from the stars. In the early stellar cults, this association was so strong that the Watchers were considered to be stars who had descended to Earth.

From their original worship as demi-gods, the Watchers have come to be honored as a spiritual race that oversees the Worlds. In between, we have seen what became of them. Today, we acknowledge them as Guardians of the entrances and exits to and from the Worlds that connect to the Physical Plane. We also know them as the "Keepers of the Ancient Wisdom" and "Guardians of the Art."

8

The Powers of Light and Darkness

In the fighting that we do, one time we fight over the wheat and all the other grains, another time over the livestock, and at other times over the vineyards. And so, on four occasions we fight over all the fruits of the earth and for those things won by the Benandanti that year there is abundance.

Carlo Ginzburg
The Night Battles

In the Old Religion, each Tradition has as its foundation a mythos concerning the seasons. In most Traditions of northern Europe the foundation is the Oak King and the Holly King, but there is another mythos in southern Europe which reflects the roles of Divinity within the dance of Winter and Summer. In the Aridian Tradition, the aspects of the waxing year and the waning year are symbolized by the Stag God and the Wolf God, respectively. The Wolf God is called Lupercus and the Stag God is called Kern. Unlike the mythos of the Oak King and the Holly King, the Stag and Wolf gods do not slay each other "at the appointed time," but instead are slain by another.

In the Old Religion of Italy there are three aspects to the God. In these aspects we find the connections of Deity within the Physical World.

The three titles by which the God is known are The Hooded One, The Horned One, and The Old One. The Hooded One is commonly referred to, in many Traditions, as the Green Man or Jack-in-the-Green. He is covered with vegetation, or hooded in the green. The Horned One is a Stag-horned Deity and is the God of the Forests, or of the Wild. The Old One is the Sage, or Elder.

It is interesting to note that the earliest known representation of the Stag-horned God appears on a rock carving in Val Camonica (Italy) dating back to the fourth century B.C. (according to Miranda Green, Tutor in Celtic studies at the University of Wales College of Cardiff, and Honorary Research Fellow at the center of advanced Welsh and Celtic studies at Aberystwyth). In this carving the Stag-horned God is shown wearing a long robe; he is standing with his arms uplifted and a pair of antlers appears upon his head, which is human in appearance.

In Miranda Green's book *Symbol and Image in Celtic Religious Art*, a picture of the rock carving is reproduced (on her page 87). Engravings from the prehistoric period at Trois-Freres depict humans dressed in animal skins (including a stag disguise), engaged in hunting and ceremonial acts. Joseph Campbell, in his book *Primitive Mythology*, describes them as shaman dancers in animal disguise, involved in a hunting ritual. While these prehistoric carvings picture a human disguised as a stag, the carving in Italy portrays the stag itself as a deity.

The Powers of Light and Darkness

The three aspects of the God evolved out of the merging of the Hunter/Gatherer society into the agricultural community. The Hooded One was connected with the crops, and came after the time of the Stag God. He was the son of the Stag God. The Hunter/Gatherer came long before the agricultural community, and therefore the Animal Spirit was valued before the Plant Spirit. As humankind grew in spiritual maturity, the concept of the Old One was born. This was the human representation of Deity: the God man.

Other aspects of the God are simply variations of these three basic concepts. The Trickster aspect, for example, is associated with the Hooded One. We see this in the Celtic Legend of the Green Knight who tricked Gawaine, and again in the Roman Lord of Misrule who was sacrificed during the Saturnalia. In the Italian Tradition, the Raven (a renowned trickster) is associated with the Hooded One in his role as the Guardian of the Grove.

The common image of the Goat-foot God, or Pan-like God, is merely a domesticated version of the Stag God of the Forest. As humankind began farming, domesticated animals became more important than once-hunted animals, and thus the symbolism began to change. Pan, or Faunus, is simply the Stag God of the Forest as seen by an agricultural community which valued domesticated animals more than the wild animals of the forest.

The Winter months brought on the wolves that preyed upon both domesticated and wild animals. Wolves easily became symbols of the power of Winter, aiding in the decline of the other creatures during the harsh Winter months. Their connection with the Stag of the Forest (the Hunted and the Hunter) lies deep in the memories of early humankind. Thus the Stag God came to symbolize the waxing year, and the Wolf God came to represent the waning year.

THE STAG AND THE WOLF

The Stag and the Wolf God go back to the days of antiquity in the Witch Cult. An early Etruscan image, found on a vase from the sixth century B.C., shows the Goddess holding up a wolf and a stag. This is no surprise, for Italian Witchcraft originates from Tuscany, which is where the Etruscan civilization once flourished. The wolf, the "Howler of the Night," was the Goddess' principal cult animal. Its importance in the religion of Old Europe can be found in the numerous figurines and vessels that depict the Goddess with the wolf and stag.

Wolves were sacred to the Moon Goddess. Their lunar nature is indicated by the crescents that appear along with their images on ancient artifacts. More common today is the portrayal of the Goddess Diana with her hunting dogs (domesticated wolves), but the earliest statues of Diana show her with a stag. It is in Diana that we discover the seasons of the stag, and of the wolf.

The season of the waxing year is symbolized by the phenomenon of the cycle of regeneration and growth of the stag's antlers. Marija Gimbutas, Professor of European Archaeology at the University of California, Los Angeles, in her book *The Goddesses and Gods of Old Europe*, states:

> *The role of a deer in Old European Myth was not a creation of Neolithic agriculturists. The importance of a pregnant doe must have been inherited from a pre-agricultural era. [In this book she also states]: In some portrayals deer antlers and crescent moons merge together as they spin around a cross with knobbed extremities showing the four cardinal points of the world. Two pairs of opposed crescents and the goddess' dog can also be seen.*[1]

Again we see lunar connections, the Goddess, and also her dog (which is a wolf).

In the Strasbourg Museum of Archaeology there is an icon of a god which illustrates the ancient connection of the Old Religion with the stag and the wolf (a picture of this statue appears in the book *Symbol and Image in Celtic Religious Art* by Miranda Green, on page 102). It was discovered at the site of the mountain sanctuary of Le Donon (near a Celtic shrine to Mercury). The icon depicts a woodland god carrying the first fruits of the forest—a pine cone, acorns, and nuts—in an open bag underneath his left arm. He is shown wearing a wolf-skin, and a long hunting knife hangs on his left side. His boots are decorated with a small animal head at the top of each boot.

The god's ambiguity as a hunter/protector is shown, on the one hand, by the wolf-skin cloak and weapons he bears, and on the other hand by his close relationship with a stag who stands next to him as he gently rests his hand upon its antlers. It is in this icon that we see the connection of the God of the Old Religion with images of the stag and the wolf. He is shown as both the hunter and protector of all forest animals, the Guardian of the Grove, the Lord of the Trees, the Old One.

The image of the stag and the wolf also appears in icons of the Celtic god known as Cernunnos. The famous Gundestrup bowl contains a panel showing Cernunnos with a wolf standing to his left and a stag to his right. This seems to be a common theme in many different parts of Europe, and it seems likely that they all come from a common source.

In an early Roman mosaic, an interesting image actually captures the history of the transition from hunter/gatherer to agricultural community. In the book *Roman Life* (page 56, 1957 edition, published by Scott, Foresman, and Co.), this mosaic is divided into three sections, displaying the evolution of the ancient Italian society. The bottom portion shows a human hunter wearing a cloak made of a stag's skin, with a stag's head upon his own. He is pictured sneaking up on his prey, and herding them into a trap that he has prepared.

Above this scene, in the center of the mosaic, is a crude encampment where people are tilling the soil with primitive tools, employing various animals for some of the labor. In the upper portion of the mosaic, we find a classic Roman structure; the people are dressed in classical Roman attire and the animals are all of the domesticated variety. Of particular interest in this last section is the portrayal of a stag and a wolf, which are fleeing the more modern part of the human community. Captured here in this mosaic is the story of our ancestors, and the story of the stag and the wolf, who were gradually driven out of our communities and out of our religion.

It is interesting to note, in this same book, a picture of a Lare shrine in which two Lare hold up drinking vessels which are adorned with a stag head. Lare were originally deities of cultivated fields and later came to represent the spirits of Roman ancestors. In any agricultural society, the presence of deer pose a threat to the crops, and it would be unlikely that agricultural cultures would hold the stag in reverence (at least on the surface it would seem unlikely).

Why would the ancients have depicted the Lare holding drinking cups symbolizing a stag? The answer is contained within the imagery itself. A drinking cup is used to contain the essence that it receives, and serves to pass this essence on to whoever drinks from it. The stag cups represent the original connection with the Horned God of the forest, who later became the Slain God of the harvest, a remembrance of the origin of the "essence" of the Old Religion.

As stated earlier, the Goddess Diana is often depicted in art accompanied by either a stag or a hound. In some art forms we also find her with the God Pan. Here again we see the domesticated version of her earlier consort, the stag. In one of the legends concerning Diana we find the story of Actaeon. In the public Greek myth, Actaeon comes upon Artemis while she is bathing in the woods and stops to admire her beauty. He is noticed by one of her followers, and, in her anger at being seen nude by a mere mortal, Artemis turns him into a stag. His hunting dogs then turn upon him and kill him.

It is interesting to note that Actaeon was said to be the son of Artisaeus (who was the Horned God of Thessaly, being very much like Pan) and Autonoe, the daughter of Cadmusn. According to legend, Aristaeus was the son of Uranus and Gaea (or Apollo and Cyrene). He was brought up by the centaur Chiron and instructed in the arts of medicine and soothsaying. He was considered the protector of flocks and agriculture.

There is another Mythos concerning Diana and Actaeon that is much older, and more closely related to the Mystery Tradition of the Old Religion. In this myth, Diana fell in love with the god Actaeon, but because of her reputation as a chaste goddess she sorrowed for a love she felt she could never experience. An adversary of the god Actaeon discovered Diana's secret and plotted against the god. In the guise of a friend, the adversary went to Diana and told her to change Actaeon into a stag when he entered the forest, saying that she could then proclaim her love to him and no one would take notice.

Diana agreed with the plan and set out to seduce Actaeon. Knowing his usual hunting places, Diana decided to bathe nude in a forest stream so that Actaeon would encounter her. When Actaeon finally saw Diana, she transformed him into a stag and left her bath to go to him. In the course of the Mythos they became lovers, and Actaeon remained in the forest as a Stag God.

Unfortunately, one day as Actaeon intended to surprise Diana during her bath, he encountered a pack of wolves and fled to escape them. He was overrun by them and perished, having been brought down by the leader of the wolf pack (which is what his adversary had planned all along).

In *The Goddesses and Gods of Old Europe*, Dr. Marija Gimbutas writes:

> *The Lady of free and untamed nature and the Mother, protectress of weaklings, a divinity in whom the contrasting principles of virginity and motherhood are fused into the concept of a single goddess, was venerated in Greece, Lydia, Crete and Italy. She appears as Artemis and under many local names: Diktynna, Pasiphae, Europa ("the wide-glancing one"), Britomartis ("the sweet virgin") in Crete, Laphria in Aetolia, Kallisto ("the beautiful") in Arkadia, or Agrotera ("the wild"), and Diana in Rome . . . The stag is her standing attribute in plastic art; she is called "stag-huntress" in the Homeric Hymns.[2]*

In her conclusions, Dr. Gimbutas writes:

> *The teaching of Western Civilization starts with the Greeks and rarely do people ask themselves what forces lay behind these beginnings. But European civilization was not created in the space of a few centuries; the roots are deeper—by six thousand years. That is to say, vestiges of the myths and artistic concepts of Old Europe, which endured from the seventh to the fourth millennium b.c. were transmitted to the modern Western world and became part of its cultural heritage.[3]*

When we research the mythos of the stag and the wolf, we find a widespread legend connecting people from Eurasia, through Italy, and up into France and the British Isles. It seems quite reasonable to conclude that there was a common origin to this ancient totem concept, and that we can all trace our Traditions back to one common belief system.

An altar set with stag horns awakens a common spiritual mentality in all Pagans, Witches, and Wiccans. It is there in our very Being; it is part of us. The wolf also speaks to us, and the memory of its place in our mysteries is now hidden in the association of werewolves and the occult.

The werewolf legend, though altered by Christian revisions (as is common with most Pagan images), still contains elements of the Wolf Cult that was once a part of the Old Religion. This cult was the early warrior society in which men first came to understand their own mysteries. They were fearful and dangerous, but were controlled by the matri-archal priestesses before the male cults rose to power.

It is curious that only a silver sword or bullet could slay a werewolf (silver being a lunar symbol), and that a full moon transformed a person into a werewolf. Curious also that a pentagram appeared on the body of one who was a werewolf (a tattoo to symbolize membership in the ancient cult?). All of these ancient symbols are still associated with Witchcraft, and are ingrained in the human psyche. These ancient memories call to us, beckon us, and bid us awaken to the Old Ways.

THE LORD OF MISRULE

The Winter rites of the Old Religion, in Italy, are connected to the ancient rites of the Roman Saturnalia and Lupercalia. The "Lord of Misrule" found in the Saturnalia, and the "Wolf Cultists" present in the Lupercalia, are still aspects of Italian Witchcraft today. These characters are mainly visible in the daytime festivals and celebrations of the Old Ways, but glimpses of them can be found in the "Night Rituals" which make up the majority of ritual material in the Aridian Tradition. The Lord of Misrule and the Wolf Priest of Lupercus are responsible for the antics that follow their respective rites.

Even in public festivals of the common people today, there are remnants of these ancient practices. In Italy one can still observe the Carnevale, or Carnival. With the old season dying, and a new one being born, the Carnevale is the last party of the year. The Carnevale is an occasion for masked balls, processions, feasts, and ancient rituals to assure an abundant harvest in the time ahead.

During the Middle Ages, the Carnevale was marked with obscene songs and erotic dances. Games of chance and outrageous acts were performed, all under the protection of masks worn by those who joined in the festivities. The celebrations often ended in an orgy brought on by the sexual themes of the songs and dances. The intent was magickal in nature, and was designed to "impregnate" the earth, where the seeds were waiting for the season of growth. Pregnant women joined in the celebrations as well, in hopes of stimulating the growing "seed" within their wombs.

Today, the Carnevale begins with a fife and drum procession on the morning of Epiphany, January 6 (also the festival time of Befana). The Carnevale festival continues on for a week, consisting of street dances, parades, pageants, and feasts. People join in the celebrations as much as possible, napping for an hour or two whenever possible. A fava bean is baked into one of many pastries, which are placed before those who wish to partake in the "choosing."

Whoever finds the fava bean is proclaimed the King of the Carnevale, and may then choose anyone as his Queen. The couple will then "rule" over the festival for the entire week. The Carnevale ends with a candlelight procession in which an effigy of the King is carried. Behind the effigy, the man who portrayed the King carries a sword, the tip of which he allows to "scrape" along the walkway. The procession is silent, except for this sound.

It is dark by this time, and a bonfire is lit. The effigy is then "sacrificed" upon the bonfire, and the celebration concludes with a great deal of wine drinking and merrymaking. Later on, with the sounds of revelry fading in the night, and the flickering of thousands of candles, Carnevale ebbs away. With the rising of the Sun, Carnevale is dead.

This is an ancient theme, recounting the days when human sacrifice was offered in Pagan worship. This theme is well documented in such books as *The Golden Bough* by Frazer, and *Western Inner Workings* by William Gray.

THE CULTS OF THE CAVALLINO AND LUPERCI

During the parade of the Carnevale comes the appearance of the Cavallino. The origin of this brotherhood goes back to the days of antiquity, and there are striking similarities between the group and the ancient cult of the Calusari (addressed in *Ecstasies; Deciphering the Witches Sabbath*, by Ginzburg). In the Middle Ages, the Cavallino's public ceremonies consisted of dances, pantomimes, healings, and processions bearing swords and flags.

The Cavallino assembled under the banner of a queen who they called Erodiade, and sometimes gave her the title of "Mistress of the Fairies." Before they were eradicated by the Plague, the Church hunted them down as heretics who worshipped Diana, goddess of the Pagans.

The Society of the Cavallino has an interesting history. It was exclusively a society of men; women were not allowed at any of their private meetings/celebrations. It is believed that they were a homosexual Tradition, in very much the same manner as were the female worshippers of Bona Dea. The Cavallino always gathered in odd numbers, usually in groups of seven, nine, or eleven.

They dressed in women's clothing, feigned female voices, and painted their faces white. They were organized in a paramilitary fashion, and had various offices of authority, including a chief. The Cavallino bore flags in their procession, and carried ritual "vegetable weapons," such as fennel stalks and sidearms of garlic and absinthe. In their ritual practices they wore animal disguises and took on the characteristics of the animals that they portrayed.

Their animal disguises featured a horse's head on a pole, with a long flowing mane. These they "rode" about on during the processions. In pre-Christian times, the Cavallino were accompanied by a dancer masked as a stag (and still earlier as a wolf). The Cavallino cult can be traced back to the days of the Lupercalia, when they were priests called

Luperci. The Luperci were priests of the Wolf God and Goddess, whom they secretly called Martius and Lycisca (Faunus was officially worshipped at the Lupercalia, and, under the name Lupercus, he had a temple on the Palatine).

Their cult was associated with the constellation called Lupus (named the "wild beast" by early Romans), in the Stellar Mysteries. Although very ancient, Lupus is inconspicuous, lying partly in the Milky Way—south of Libra and Scorpio, and east of the Centaur. The wolf, Lupus, was said to be placed in the heavens as a reminder of the religious nature of Chiron, the Centaur, who is depicted as spearing the wolf in order to offer it as a sacrifice. It is interesting to note that the word "Cavallino" means "little horses," and that in their processions we can envision them as "centaurs"—part human, part horse.

In the constellation myth, we can see the connection between the wolf and horse as religious symbols. In star magick/astrology, Lupus has an acquisitive nature: grasping, aggressive, prudent, and treacherous, with a keen desire for knowledge, and strong "ill-regulated" passions.

The Luperci were present during the ancient Lupercalia, at which time they formed into two groups. One was called the Quinctiales and the other the Fabiani. As part of the ritual, they would run naked through the streets, carrying straps of hide.

Roman tradition says that these were straps of goat hide, but in their earlier form they were most likely wolf or stag. Women who desired fertility would gather in the streets, to be flogged by the Luperci as they ran past. Three strokes of the strap were believed to make a women fertile. When the spirit of the Lord of Misrule came upon the Luperci, they were known to chase women of various ages (innocent bystanders) around the town, much to the delight of the crowds that gathered for the spectacle.

During the height of the Roman worship of Olympic-class gods (usually within the cities), a parallel worship was taking place among Pagans who lived in the less-developed areas. The "sophisticated" city dwellers looked down upon the "uneducated" country dwellers. It was from this attitude that the term "Pagan" actually arose. The word pagan comes from the Latin words *paganus*, meaning someone who lives on uncultivated land (i.e., the heath, a heathen) and *pagus*, meaning country dweller (a peasant or rustic).

It was there, among the rustics, that the worship of the oldest gods and goddesses was being preserved, even at a time that we now think of as ancient. Many of these deities were unknown to the classic writers, and their names have never been recorded in the popular tales of Roman mythology. It is from these rustics that the Witch Clans are descended.

In the Aridian Tradition, the name of Lupercus has been preserved along with the mythos of the God. The festival of Lupercus takes place on February 2, in contrast to the Lupercalia, which was observed in ancient Rome on February 15. The priests of the Wolf God held their secret ceremonies on the second day of February, and the public rites on the fifteenth. This is why the dates seemingly do not coincide. February was the month of purification, and was sacred to Februus, the God of the Dead (also known as Dis, among the Etruscans). This is a time of personal renewal and purification. It is a time in which the primal nature is awakened, and the ritual participants draw from their most ancient roots. It is an atavistic experience. It is the Time of the Wolf.

The ritual, itself, is a drama play concerning the birth of Lupercus and the quest placed before him. He is the Golden Wolf who banishes the Wolves' Night. He is the new Sun God of the year and must prove his worthiness to rule in the heavens. At the conclusion of the ritual everyone is released from the circle and all join in the rite of "shape-shifting."

It is through this atavistic resurgence that one is transformed, and merges with these forces of Nature. It is in the "becoming" that a person is purified of the stain of domestication, and is "one" with the Time of the Wolf. This is the seed of freedom which dwells in the heart of all true Witches. It is what governments, rulers, and organized religions all fear. It is personal power, personal empowerment, and personal freedom. It is one of the reasons why Witches were hunted down by the Inquisition as a threat to Christianity. It is one of the reasons why men have suppressed the sexuality of women, while keeping the empowerment for themselves.

The wolf stalks its prey in Winter, a time which offers little sustenance. Decline is everywhere, and the world waits for renewal. In our own lives, perhaps, we find that it is through the loss of "things" or "situations" that we are truly freed. It is our fears that imprison us, and hold us hostage to the desires and demands of others.

The Holy Strega says that Witches must be "free," and it is in the message of Lupercus that one comes to understand her words. For when a person "tames" us, or "domesticates" us, then this person loses that part of us which attracted them to us to begin with (and we lose ourselves in the process). When one keeps company with wolves, one must run with wolves.

A wolf is a beautiful creature, worthy of admiration, but a wolf makes a poor dog, and neither the wolf nor the owner can be very proud of the situation. Wolves were meant to be free, and it was this type of freedom of which Aradia spoke when she said "and you must be free . . . " It was also this type of freedom which caused the Church to focus its attention upon the Witches of the Old Religion.

THE BENANDANTI AND MALANDANTI

In the latter part of the sixteenth century in Italy, the Church first encountered an ancient society that called itself the Benandanti. From the records of the Inquisition concerning the Benandanti (covering 1575–1647) we can draw a profile of the Benandanti and their beliefs. Professor Carlo Ginzburg recorded much of the story of the Benandanti in his book *The Night Battles; Witchcraft & Agrarian Cults in the 16th & 17th Centuries.* Although interpreted mainly through the eyes of the Christian Church, the "confessions" of the Benandanti contain a great deal of information which confirms the existence (and theology) of the Witch Cult as a surviving Tradition from pre-Christian European roots. In the opening of the foreword to Ginzburg's book we find these statements:

> *Some time in the late 16th Century the attention of a perplexed Church was drawn to the prevalence of a curious practice in the region of the Friuli, where German, Italian and Slav customs meet . . . Carlo Ginzburg argues that theirs was a fertility ritual once widespread throughout central Europe, but by this period perhaps flourishing only in marginal regions such as the Friuli (and Lithuania, whence a strictly similar institution of benevolent werewolves is recorded from the late 17th century), and suggests Slav or even Ural-Altaic influences, which must be left to the judgment of experts in popular religion.*

On March 21, 1575, a priest named Don Bartolomeo Sgabarizza appeared before Monsignor Jacopo Maracco at the Monastery of San Francisco di Cividale with an amazing account of a local practice in the village of Iassico. He related the story of a man named Paolo Gasparutto who had a reputation as a magickal healer. Upon questioning, Paolo admitted that he belonged to a society called the Benandanti (good-doers). He then revealed that the Benandanti would fall into trances on certain nights of the year (called the "ember days"), and that their souls would leave their bodies. Then they would engage in ritual combat with the Malandanti (evil-doers) over the fate of the harvest.

The Malandanti fought with sorghum stalks and the Benandanti fought with stalks of fennel in a ritual joust. In a recorded "confession" by a man named Battista Moduco we find these words:

> *In the fighting that we do, one time we fight over the wheat and all the other grains, another time over the livestock, and at other times over the vineyards. And so, on four occasions we fight over all the fruits of the earth and for those things won by the Benandanti that year there is abundance.*[4]

That the Benandanti did exist is quite clear from the continued discoveries of their society and trial transcripts, which span almost 100 years as recorded in the archives of the Inquisition. The information is consistent and does not seem to be designed by the Inquisitors, as it rarely plays into the hands of the Christian Church in its attack upon the Old Religion. In fact, the Benandanti at first deny that they are Witches but insist that they are an army for Christ in the war against evil. Obviously it would have been extremely dangerous and quite foolish for them to have professed to be "good Witches" at that particular time in Italian history. They give accounts of the banners which they carry into battle: their banner being white and bearing a gilded lion, and the Malandanti banner being red and bearing four dark angels. In time, the confessions begin to contain contradictions, and eventually the Benandanti confessions are seen as evidence that they are indeed Witches, but that they fight on the side of good against evil.

Of particular interest to Witches today is the background information which the trial transcripts contain. This information unintentionally gives support to the long-claimed practices of Wicca/Witchcraft. We have already mentioned that the Benandanti address the issue of "leaving the body" (astral projection), but there are other aspects to their practices which connect to the Old Religion as well.

In the confessions of Paolo Gasparutto and Battista Maduco, we find that the Benandanti and the Malandanti (referred to as witches in their confessions) gathered for seasonal rites associated with the fertility of crops and animals, and held feasts and played games, and performed marriages and dances. These are all things that speak of a community and a structured set of practices and customs. Since marriages were performed at these gatherings, we can assume that the society had priests and/or priestesses to perform the rites, and that a marriage rite would seemingly imply the existence of a religious or spiritual tradition behind it all.

Professor Ginzburg relates the rites of the Benandanti to an older tradition which be believes was once widespread throughout most of Europe. In chapter one (page 24), Ginzburg writes:

> *It may be supposed that this combat re-enacted, and to a certain extent rationalized, an older fertility rite in which two groups of youths, respectively impersonating demons favorable to fertility and the maleficent ones of destruction, symbolically flayed their loins with stalks of fennel and sorghum to stimulate their own reproductive capacity, and by analogy, the fertility of the fields of the community. Gradually the rite may have come to be represented as an actual combat, and from the uncertain outcome of the struggler between the two opposed bands would magically defend the fertility of the land and the fate of the harvests. At a later state these rites would cease to be practiced openly . . .[5]*

Ginzburg goes on to associate the struggle between the Benandanti and the Malandanti as an analogy of the rites of contest between the waxing and waning year. The use of fennel and sorghum represent the plants of winter and summer which are seen as the symbols of conflict and resolution. Here we see not only the ancient passing of power in a seasonal sense, but also the classic struggle of good against evil. Stories abound of villages during the Middle Ages whose people burned effigies of evil incarnate, and symbolically drove off evil-doers with rods and staffs out beyond the village's boundaries. Many of these accounts can be found in *The Golden Bough* by James Frazer and many other works.

Today, Witches may face a very similar situation to that of the Benandanti. Satanism is on the rise, and appears to be spreading quite rapidly across the United States. Many subcults of Satanism are forming, whose actions toward other people and animals can certainly be defined as evil. Once these subcults become skilled in magickal practices, then all hell is likely to break loose (so to speak). The social and political reasons for this are too intricate to be covered here, but suffice it to say that the reasons are many and varied.

Modern Witches continually have to deal with the erroneous label of "Satanists" attributed to them by Christian fundamentalists. The danger to Witches comes not only from Christians, but also from "spin-offs" of the actual Satanic groups themselves. This is not readily apparent on the surface, and many Witches and Satanists would probably not agree. However, "evil" is a thing which seeks to banish "good," and in the final analysis has no friends or allies.

I think it is not at all unlikely that Witches in the near future will be faced with protecting their communities from the destructive energies of an evil which is surely coming. Nor is it unlikely that Witches will take the blame for these misdeeds, as we have since the Middle Ages.

The Benandanti fought against negative and destructive thought-forms and cleansed the collective consciousness of their communities. Theirs was a battle against evil forces personified in a war between the armies of Light and Darkness. The Benandanti Tradition was a shamanistic society working behind the forces of Nature, reaching directly into the supernatural fibers that animate and direct physical Nature. It might be wise for Witches today to clear some garden space for a bit of fennel.

ENDNOTES

1. *The Goddesses and Gods of Old Europe*, by Marija Gimbutas, pages 171 and 174. University of California Press, reprint 1990.

2. *The Goddesses and Gods of Old Europe*, by Marija Gimbutas, page 198.

3. *The Goddesses and Gods of Old Europe*, by Marija Gimbutas, page 238.

4. *The Night Battles; Witchcraft & Agrarian Cults in the 16th & 17th Centuries*, by Carlo Ginzburg, page 6. Penguin Books 1985.

5. *The Night Battles; Witchcraft & Agrarian Cults in the 16th & 17th Centuries*, by Carlo Ginzburg, page 24.

Figure 11
A Tuscan Witch

9

Leland, Gardner, and Frazer

. . . and when I visited the villa of the mysteries at Pompeii I realized the great resemblances to the cult. Apparently these people were using the witches' processes . . . I showed a picture of these frescoes to an English witch, who looked at it very attentively before saying: "So they knew the secret in those days."

Gerald Gardner
Witchcraft Today

Most Wiccans readily acknowledge Gerald Gardner's role in the establishment of Wicca as a religion in modern times. During Gardner's time there were others whose interests were in a similar vein to his own. Two of them are worthy of mention for their influence upon Gardner and his development of Craft theology. These are, of course, Charles Leland and James Frazer.

What follows here is a brief look at three men whose love of ancient lore and religious thought focused the public eye firmly upon the Old Religion. Gerald Gardner will probably always be remembered for his contributions, but lest the world forget where Gardner's inspiration came from, I offer these biographies and commentaries.

LELAND

Charles Godfrey Leland was born in Philadelphia in 1824, and died in Florence, Italy in 1903. He was buried in Philadelphia at the Laurel Hill Cemetery. During his lifetime, he wrote and published more than seventy-three books. He was also an accomplished craftsman in wood, leather, and metalworking. These talents he put to use in the reconstruction of ancient Italian Witch charms and amulets.

Leland was the founder and first president of The Gypsy Lore Society, whose membership included the author and scholar, James Frazer. Leland was also an excellent scholar and attended Princeton as well as the Universities of Heidelberg and Munich. In addition to English, he also spoke German, Italian, Spanish, and French, and was familiar with Algonquian Indian dialects, Celtic, and the Romany language.

In 1869 he moved to England, where he began a study of British gypsies. He eventually became an authority on them, having lived among them for several years. In the later part of the nineteenth century, Leland published two books concerning the gypsies. One of these—*The English Gypsies and their Language*, published in 1873—is still considered a classic on the subject.

In 1880 Leland moved to Italy, where he spent the rest of his life researching Italian Witchcraft. Sometime during the year of 1886, Leland met an Italian woman named Maddalena. She was working as a fortuneteller in Florence, Italy when they met. Maddalena claimed to be an Italian Witch, and Leland quickly gained her confidence with his knowledge of folklore. Over the next year or so, he paid Maddalena to gather Italian folklore for his research material. On January 1, 1887 Maddalena presented Leland with the material that eventually became his book *Aradia; Gospel of the Witches*, published in 1899.

Leland went on in 1892 to publish *Etruscan Roman Remains*, which became a classic, rocking the world of scholars in his time. Until the advent of his book, people had not considered the idea that Witches still existed and continued to practice their ancient arts. They certainly did not have knowledge of what Leland proved in this text; namely, that Italian Witches were alive and well in Italy and were worshipping the Goddess Diana.

It was Charles Leland who laid the framework for what became the modern religion of Wicca. In his works, Witches worship a God and Goddess, gather nude beneath the Full Moon for their ceremonies, and work magick. Over half a century later, Gerald Gardner began to write on these same themes. (See appendix for additional information on Charles Leland.)

GARDNER

Gerald Brosseau Gardner was born in 1884 in Great Crosby on Merseyside, in the northwest part of England. He died in 1964 on a cruise ship off the coast of North Africa, while returning to England from a winter spent in Lebanon. During the 1950s he authored the now-famous books *Witchcraft Today* and *The Meaning of Witchcraft*. Many people today consider Gerald Gardner to be the "father" of modern Wicca. His influence upon the growth of this religion cannot be dismissed, and he was indeed an important figure in the Neo-Pagan movement.

Reading contemporary books on Wicca, however, one quickly comes upon the erroneous concept that Gerald Gardner was the source from which all things have sprung. Realistically, Gardner was simply one man, in one country, who set out to investigate the antiquity of Witchcraft. Some say that he made contact with a cult of Witches whose Tradition survived from ancient times. Others say that he made up the whole thing from fragmentary folklore and personal fantasy. This may be due to the fact that Gardner associated with the infamous Aleister Crowley, and some claim that it was Crowley who worked with him to create the *Gardnerian Book of Shadows* (see my Second Edition Preface and the Introduction).

A few writers even conclude that if Gardner made no contact with surviving Traditions, then they must not have existed. This conclusion is unsound, at best. If he found nothing, then it only indicates that he failed to find what he searched for. If Gardner made up his "Tradition," it does not prove that Witchcraft never survived or pre-existed. It only suggests that what he taught was not what he claimed it was. Personally, I dismiss these accusations against Gardner, and I feel that he was basically relating what he believed to be the truth.

I wonder if anyone has stopped to consider that if secret covens existed prior to Gardner's search, perhaps they still remain secret today! Clearly, no one has researched every country and every remote village on the planet, before proclaiming (as fact) that the Old Religion never survived anywhere. Yet, many people do proclaim just this very thing. I personally know of two surviving Traditions who purposely maintain their secrecy to avoid the offensiveness of being examined by people seeking to discredit claims of antiquity.

Many people feel that if a non-Gardnerian Tradition contains any Gardnerian material, then it is obviously a fabricated system. Perhaps what it really means is that someone in that Tradition admired a passage or two, and simply added it to their own material. Even systems of great antiquity enjoy the refreshing addition of new material from time to time. The Triad Traditions of Italy, for example, claim an unbroken line, back to the late fourteenth century, but do incorporate new material as deemed appropriate.

Evidence of the Witch cult in Italy is abundant, and easily traced back through the centuries. Records clearly show a long-standing association between the Goddess Diana and Witches, as reflected in trial transcripts. Despite torture and relentless Inquisitors, Italian Witches consistently maintained that they worshipped the Goddess (Diana, Herodias,

Abundia, etc.) and not Satan. In other parts of Europe, tracing the cult becomes quite a burden. Whatever the truth behind Gardner's material may be, it is of little consequence to the actual Witch cult of Italy.

Unfortunately (and unjustly), in the Craft community today, if your Tradition contains any Gardnerian material, then the rest of your material is rendered null and void, regardless of where the bulk of it originated. This perception is much like a person's reaction to a fly in their soup: it ruins the whole thing. It is curious why this isn't simply viewed as "imitation is the sincerest form of flattery."

The well-known "Charge of the Goddess" and the "Legend of the Descent" are also apparently considered to be of Gardnerian origin, and essentially modern pieces of literature. Many people even believe that Doreen Valiente authored these now-famous verses. It seems clear that the version appearing in Gardnerian Wicca might well be modern, but what many people are unaware of is that they are actually embellished versions of much older, non-Celtic material. In point of fact, the foundation of the "Charge"[1] comes from Italy, as recorded by Charles Leland in his book *Aradia, Gospel of the Witches,* published in 1899 (Gardner's version appears to have been written during the 1950s).

Leland claims to have received The Charge in 1887 from the Italian Witch, Maddalena. At the end of chapter one in Aradia's Gospel we find these words:

> *Whenever ye have need of anything, once in the month and when the moon is full, ye shall assemble in some secret place, or in a forest all together join to adore the potent spirit of your queen, my mother, great Diana. She who fain would learn all sorcery yet has not won its deepest secrets, them my mother will teach her, in truth all things as yet unknown. And ye shall be freed from slavery, and so ye shall be free in everything; and as a sign that ye are truly free, ye shall be naked in your rites, both men and women also . . .*[2]

As anyone familiar with the Charge can see, the earlier Italian verses are almost identical to the Gardnerian version written over half a century later. Although Gardner's text is greatly embellished, it is historically important to note that the original charge was Italian. Many people also claim that Gardner introduced nudity into Witchcraft, but it clearly appears in Leland's works over half a century earlier.

The Legend of the Descent, now claimed to be another modern Gardnerian text, is actually quite a bit older and appeared in the mythology of Italian Witchcraft long before the writings of Gardner or Valiente. The basic theme of the Goddess descending to the Underworld, being challenged, and encountering the God, can be found in the myth of Inanna from Sumerian mythology. The greatest influence on the Roman Mystery Cults in Italy came from the east, the cults of Tammuz and Mithras being examples. Therefore, this particular mythos would have been passed into Italy thousands of years ago.

Franz Cumont (scholar of comparative religions in classical antiquity), in his book *Oriental Religions in Roman Paganism*, addresses this and other influences of Eastern religions upon Roman religion. The Syrian cult of the Great Mother of the Gods was first brought to Rome from Syria around 204 B.C. The ecstatic cults of Syria, the mysteries of Egypt, the dualism of Persia, and the magick of the ancient Near East were well established in Italy long before northern Europe had ever even heard of them.

It is not surprising, therefore, to find a basic mythos similar to the Sumerian descent legend in Italian Witchcraft. In chapter seven of his book *Witchcraft Today*, Gerald Gardner writes of his visit to Pompeii:

> . . . *and when I visited the villa of the mysteries at Pompeii I realized the great resemblances to the cult. Apparently these people were using the witches' processes . . . I showed a picture of these frescoes to an English witch, who looked at it very attentively before saying: "So they knew the secret in those days."*[3]

Yes, Gerald, we knew the secret in those days.

I think we would all do well to be more flexible about eclectic and traditional material. If someone wants to add Gardnerian material or Italian material to his or her Tradition, then so be it. A hereditary Italian spell or ritual, in a Gardnerian Book of Shadows, does not render that Gardnerian coven a non-Celtic system. A Gardnerian verse in an Italian hereditary book does not make it a hodgepodge Gardnerian rip-off. People do add things into their systems that they find appealing, and try to incorporate them in a practical way. When an organism stops growing, then it begins to die.

In the Italian Tradition, it is proper to add to your material, but you can never delete anything. Everything that is added must fit completely within the established magickal and ritual correspondences. We do not add anything on a whim, but only add material when it appears to benefit the system as a whole. In this way, the Tradition can adapt to the times without losing the traditions of the past.

I would expect to find similarities in most Craft Traditions; it would be strange not to. We are all practicing the same religion seen through the eyes of different cultures. I think that we can all share aspects of our culture and our material between our traditions without compromising the integrity of our respective systems.

FRAZER

Sir James George Frazer was born in Glasgow in 1854, and died in Cambridge in 1941. He was a British anthropologist, folklorist, and classical scholar. His outstanding position among his colleagues was well established with the publication of *The Golden Bough; a Study in Magic and Religion*, in 1890. This work addressed the evolution of magickal thinking into religious thought. Frazer popularized the theme of the Divine King that is an integral part of Western Occultism.

Widely acclaimed by his peers for his research and insight into the ancient mysteries, Frazer is now overlooked by modern writers on Wicca, although his works were originally quite popular among Wiccans in the 1950s and 1960s. Since *The Golden Bough* deals largely with ancient Paganism in Italy, it is possible that the Celtic interests of most modern Wiccans have diverted their attention as well.

Frazer emphasized the relationship between the well-being of the community and the vitality of the Divine King. The King was slain at the peak of his power in order to transfer his vital essence back into the land (Nature). The abundance of plants for the harvest, and animals for the hunt, was long associated with the status of the Divine King, known also as the Slain God. As the old saying goes: "The Land and the King are One." This is one of the fundamental teachings in the Western Mystery Tradition. There is little doubt that *The Golden Bough* greatly influenced the works of Gerald Gardner.

Italian Paganism was planted in Britain by the conquering Romans, and became absorbed into Celtic religion over the course of 400 years of Roman occupation. Therefore, Frazer's writings appear to reflect many religious concepts now associated with Celtic religion, no doubt serving to confirm and expand Gardner's own Wiccan beliefs. After all, Gardner himself noted, in his book *The Meaning of Witchcraft* (chapter six), that the mysteries of Wicca may have been brought to Britain by the Romans. For a detailed account of how this was actually the case, I refer the reader to my book *The Wiccan Mysteries*.

ENDNOTES

1. It is interesting to note that Stewart Farrar, in his book *What Witches Do* (Peter Davies, Ltd., 1971), mentions that he copied the Charge from an Alexandrian Book of Shadows, and then goes on to give the text in "the original Italian."

2. *Aradia; Gospel of the Witches*, by Charles Leland, page 6. Phoenix Publishing, Inc. 1990 reprint of 1890 original.

3. *Witchcraft Today*, by Gerald Gardner, pages 82 and 88. Citadel Press. 1973 reprint of original 1953 text.

Part 2
The Workbook

The Tools of Witchcraft

10

The Tools and Symbols
of Stregheria

Many people have noticed the resemblance of the Witches' tools to the armor and weapons of a Knight. There is a definite connection, and any true Witch must (to some degree) be a Spiritual Warrior. This is equally true of anyone who walks a magickal path in life.

from the text

Humans have always used tools, from the days of throwing stones and swinging clubs to the current age of push-button destruction. In this chapter, we will examine the purpose, and the evolution, of Witchcraft's ceremonial/Magickal tools in humankind's quest to gain a balance with Nature. The earliest of Strega's tools was the wand, which was closely followed by the shell or gourd (depending upon the region). Over the centuries, other tools appeared, and today we have the Wand, Cup (chalice or grail), Sword (Spirit Blade), and Pentacle. The earliest appearance of these four tools displayed together in a magickal context originated with the fifteenth-century Italian Tarot now knows as the Cary-Yale Visconti deck. In some magickal lodges, these tools are given the following correspondences: Wand of Intuition, Cup of Sympathy, Blade of Reason, and Pentacle of Valor. Considered of equal importance, the Strega also include the ritual bowl and the Nanta Bag among their primary tools.

Many people have noticed the resemblance of the Witches' tools to the armor and weapons of a Knight. There is a definite connection, and any true Witch must (to some degree) be a Spiritual Warrior. This is equally true of anyone who walks a magickal path in life. In a metaphysical sense, the sword is necessary to maintain a stable mind, and to "cut through" deception and delusion. The chalice or cup serves as a reminder of compassion as one grows in personal power. The wand focuses the intuitive mind so that one can discern and realize what one perceives. The shield (pentacle) of valor is often left out in most texts of this nature, but it should be stated that one must carry their valor before them to serve as a protection against fear (the great enemy). A person of magick must hold true to their own set of values and codes of conduct, for one can only be as strong as their most vulnerable weakness.

As we continue with this chapter, we will take a look at each tool, its history, and its preparation as a magickal tool. Let us begin now with the primary tools.

THE PRIMARY TOOLS

The Wand

In early times, humankind observed that the branches of trees brought forth life. From season to season, the trees issued leaves, flowers, and fruits. Trees were held to be Sacred Beings, who gave life and provided food and shelter. These Beings were rooted in the Earth and reached upward into the sky. They were bridges between the Underworld and the Overworld. It is not surprising, then, that the ancients chose to "borrow" some of the tree's power by incorporating a part of it into a tool. Thus was born the wand (or staff) which became a magickal tool as well as a symbol of power (usually carried by the tribal shaman).

In reverence to the tree, strict procedures were adopted for the taking of a branch. First, offerings had to be made to the spirit (or Numen) of the tree. These were usually "first fruits" of the harvest or "nectar" which was made up of wine, honey, and milk. The wood was taken from the bend in the branch, out to the fork. This represented the human arm from the elbow to the tip of the middle finger, because the extending branch of a tree resembles a human arm and hand. Over the course of time, a measure was established. Wands were to measure from the inside of the elbow to the tip of the middle finger. Staffs were to measure to the height of the person, plus the measure of his or her wand (so that the staff was taller than the person; i.e., more powerful).

Figure 12a
The Wand

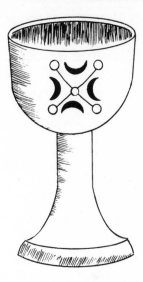

Figure 12c
**The Chalice
(Cup or Grail)**

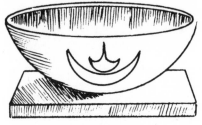

Figure 12b
The Spirit Bowl

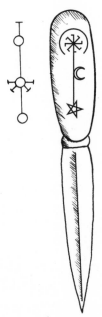

Figure 12d
The Spirit Blade

Figure 12e
The Pentacle Symbol

Once formed and prepared, the wand became a tool of Nature's inner magick. The wand is a tool which is used to request rather than demand, and it is gentle with power. This request possesses great influence, for its source is the Divine itself. It is used for calling upon the gods and nature spirits. It is a symbol of the element of air, and is associated with the east. Magickally it is often used for healing, divination, and astral workings.

The Ritual Wand Procedure—Choose a tree of the fruit-bearing variety, as these are best. If you wish, however, you may use oak or willow (even rose wood is fine). These woods have magickal associations to ancient cults, and many people prefer them for that reason. The wood of a tree that bears fruit is actually superior for a wand of general use.

Before sunrise, go before the tree and pour (or place) an offering. Tell the spirit within the tree what you wish to do, and why. Wait a few moments, and then proceed, unless you feel that the spirit has rejected your request. If you are going to take the branch, do so quickly. Wrap it up in cloth and return home. Trim the wood smooth, removing the bark, and shape the tip so that it resembles a phallus. Allow the wood to dry for nine days before carving or painting symbols upon it.

On the night of the Full Moon, place the symbols of the art upon it. Present it to the east quarter and declare it to be a wand of magick, and a power over the element of air. At midnight (or 9 P.M. if necessary) go out beneath the Full Moon, hold the wand up toward it, and say:

> *My Lady, Mistress of Night and of Magick,*
> *You who rule the star-filled heavens,*
> *bless and empower this Wand,*
> *that all may see, and know Thy Greatness.*
> *Wherefore, do I consecrate and dedicate this Wand*
> *to you, Great Mistress of Magick.*

After completing this, set a bowl out beneath the Moon. Place equal portions of the following herbs into the bowl: pennyroyal, rosemary, hyssop, and acacia. Pour boiling water into the bowl, and steep for three minutes. Strain the mixture through cheesecloth, and then add this liquid potion to a half-filled bowl of fresh spring water. To the spring water add nine drops of almond extract. Then drop three moonflowers (or white jasmine flowers) into the bowl. Pause a moment, and look up at the Moon. Raise the wand up to Her, and then lower it into the bowl. Bathe the wand in the liquid briefly, and then remove and dry it. It is now ready to use.

The Spirit Bowl (Shell)

One of the oldest ritual tools in Witchcraft is the shell or bowl. Originally, large shells were used to contain seawater for blessings, and various works of magick. The Moon has long been associated with the tides of the ocean, and for this reason seawater was considered to contain the essence of the Moon's power.

These shells were placed upon stone altars (or sometimes upon fallen trees) with the open end up. Normally these shells were the size of a common bowl. Seawater was then poured into the bowl, and a small white shell was placed in the center of the bowl. In this manner, the worship of the Moon could be carried out, even when the Moon was not visible in the night sky (or even indoors, if necessary).

The shell also symbolized the womb of the Great Goddess, and the shell within symbolized the "Child of Promise." The Child was the promise of prophecy, and the mediator between humans and gods. With the shell in place, the priestesses were assured of the divinatory powers of the Moon bowl. A series of small white shells were also placed around the bowl, forming a crescent shape just below the bowl. As the stones were placed, left to right, the name of the goddess being invoked was chanted. At the conclusion of the rite, the shells were removed, one at a time, from right to left.

In time, in the interior parts of Italy, this shell was replaced by a gourd or wooden bowl, and later still by a ceramic bowl. By the time the Temple of Diana stood on the shore of Lake Nemi, the use of the Moon bowl had changed. Instead of seawater, an alcohol-like fluid was placed in the bowl. The shell was no longer set in the bowl, but was replaced by a flame, burning on the liquid's surface. The flame represented the presence of Deity, and so the shell fell out of usage, at least in the temple setting. The Moon itself reflected off the waters of Lake Nemi, where the Temple of Diana stood. This seemed a natural replica of the old Moon bowl. The use of the flame was a step in the evolution of the Cult.

Today, in the Triad Clan's System, the bowl is called the Spirit Bowl and is set in the center of the altar. An alcohol-based liquid (such as Strega Liquore) is poured into it, and lighted. This is done with a series of gestures and verbal incantations that aid to empower the flame. Once established, the flame is considered to be the presence of Deity, within the ritual setting. Traditionally, a woman will tend the altar and renew the liquid, so that the flame will not die out.

The Chalice (Cup) or Grail

Having studied in other Traditions/Systems, I think it possible that the common Chalice may have originated from the shell or gourd. In the Aridian Tradition, we also use a chalice and it does have the same "womb" associations as does the bowl. In effect, the chalice serves as a type of Grail. Ancient lore addresses the legend of the Grail, which was a vessel of transformation.

In time, this Grail legend was adopted by Christianity, and the Grail itself became the chalice from which Christ drank at the Last Supper. Here he said that the wine was his blood (contained within the cup), and bid everyone to drink of it. The cup then becomes the vessel of transformation, and carries with it the very essence of the Divine (from which nourishment is drawn).

The Grail legend originates with the Moon bowl, which serves as a meeting place for humankind and Deity. The liquid within the bowl symbolized a state of existence between matter and Spirit (physical and yet not physical). It is here that we connect to the source of our existence upon the Earth. Traditionally, seawater was the fluid within the bowl. Since many people believe that we evolved from life within the ocean, perhaps this practice stemmed from an ancient memory of our own beginnings.

Today, in the old system, the shell (as a moon bowl) is used only in private devotional rites. This is not to say that it can no longer be used in group celebrations, for indeed it can, but a metal bowl has taken its place, because of the use of fire. Some Strega, however, have taken a large abalone shell and filled it with sand, and then placed a small metal bowl upon the sand. In this manner, the spirit flame can still be kindled within the shell/Moon bowl with no damage to the shell or risk of fire spreading, should the shell crack. Technically, there is no real preparation of the bowl other than a simple blessing and a dedication of its service to the God and Goddess.

The Spirit Blade (Sword)

One of the most common tools associated with the practice of the Craft today is the *athame*, or dagger (in the Aridian Tradition it is called a Spirit Blade). This section will cover the ritual preparation for the dagger as performed in the Nemaic System of Witchcraft. I created the Nemaic System myself as an "outer-court" system in 1980, and it is based upon the Old Italian Tradition. Please bear in mind that this particular technique is an eclectic modern work based upon an old tradition.

Preparation of the Blade—Three nights before the Moon is full (the third night being the Full Moon), dig a small hole in the earth which is as deep as your hand is long. Then take equal portions (about a handful) of the ground herbs: rue, vervain, and fennel.

Add them to the soil from the hole which you dug, and mix this all together. Then replace the soil in the hole. Leave this until the night of the Full Moon. On the night of the Full Moon, boil some water (about eight ounces), to which you will add three pinches of salt. Then go outdoors and pour the boiled water out (slowly) on the area where you dug the hole. Next mark out a triangle around the hole. Then place nine drops of liquid camphor (Campo-Phenique will do, in a pinch) directly upon the center of the hole. At this point grasp the dagger in both hands, with the blade pointing down, and raise your arms up to the Moon, saying:

> *O Great Tana, bless me with Power.*

Then push the blade down into the soil (directly centered in the hole) up to the handle base. Next, draw power down from the Moon as follows. Kneel before the Moon, hands upon your thighs, and say:

> *At will, I make swift streams retire*
> *To their fountains, whilst their banks admire;*
> *Sea toss and smooth; clear clouds with clouds deform.*
> *With spells and charms I break the viper's jaw,*
> *Cleave solid rocks, oaks from their seizures draw,*
> *Whole woods remove, the lofty mountains shake,*
> *Earth for to groan, and ghosts from graves awake,*
> *And Thee, O Moon, I draw. . . .*

(As you begin the last verse, raise your left hand and "cup" the Moon.) Then quickly close your hand in a grasping manner, seemingly closing the Moon within your hand. Do not look up at this point, but bring your closed hand down (as if drawing or pulling) and grasp the knife handle. Next place your right hand firmly over your left and concentrate upon the knife, and imagine it glowing with power. After a few minutes, remove the knife from the soil, and clean it off with a white cloth. The knife is then ready for the symbols to be placed upon the handle. All that remains is to charge the knife with the four elements, and to dedicate it to the service of Tana.

The Pentacle

The original ritual pentacles were flat rocks employed to mark the center of the "sacred space" in a ritual setting. Later the rock was engraved with etchings to denote the four cardinal points comprising this space. The ancients believed that the rock itself contained a spirit, and so the marked pentacle represented the four elements of creation held in balance by the spirit of Nature. When humans became more proficient at using tools, pentacles were often made from sacred woods associated with the Deities of the cult artisans.

Today, the pentacle can be made from any natural substance, and bears a pentagram image on its surface. This five-pointed star represents the four elements, overseen by the fifth element of spirit. We see in this symbolism that the original concepts were retained up into modern times. Generally speaking, the pentacle does not require any special preparation after the pentagram is set upon it. This is because it is a natural substance, and as such is filled with the spirit force of Nature. A general blessing and anointing with the names of the God and Goddess will serve quite nicely.

The Nanta Bag

The Nanta Bag is a very old tool, appearing in various forms as it is traced back through the Ages. The form in which we have it today comes to us from fifteenth-century Italy. The purpose of the Nanta Bag is two-fold. First, it is designed to keep its wearer in harmony with the forces of Nature. Second, it serves as a carrier for the tools of the Craft, so that a Witch can perform his or her magick anywhere or any time. The original followers of Aradia carried them as they traveled from village to village, and soon they became a symbol of being a Priest or Priestess of the Old Religion.

Within these bags were miniature representations of the ritual tools, along with elemental symbols and objects of personal power. Typically the bag would contain a thimble (chalice), a needle or pin (ritual blade), a coin (pentacle), and a twig (wand). Also included would be a stone (earth), a feather (air), a flint stone (fire) or a match today, and a shell (water) or vial of liquid. Finally, the bag would contain a symbol for the God and Goddess, along with objects of personal meaning. If someone was given a small token by one whose power they respected, then this also would be added to the Nanta Bag.

The principle of "contagion" magick was the foundation for empowering the bag. Basically, this means that objects absorb power and have an energy field around them. When one object is placed in contact with another, then these objects are joined and influence one another. The Nanta Bag, in turn, has a contagion influence upon the person who carries it (in direct proportion to the items it contains). The following list is a basic example of the items that might be contained within a functional Nanta Bag:

A small stone, smooth and rounded

A small feather, blue or very light in color

A small portion of ash (wood or coal)

A small vessel of pure water

A small coin, with a five-pointed star etched upon it

A small twig (fruit or nutwood)

A pin with a black head (or needle)

A thimble

A portion of incense

2 small white candles

A piece of marking chalk

A measure of cord (nine feet)

A small finger-sized bowl (cup or dish)

A symbol of the God: (an acorn, small pine cone, piece of horn, etc.)

A symbol of the Goddess: (a seashell, string of beads, nutshell)

A personal power object (a lucky piece, a crystal, etc.)

A portion of salt

A small vessel of anointing oil

Collect these items and make a bag of leather or cloth large enough to contain them. You may wish to add some healing herbs or other desired items. For example, use a stone for earth, a feather for air, etc. The first four items are to be gathered in a manner that brings you into contact with the element represented.

Finally, take the completed bag and consecrate it in the manner of the altar tools, charging by the Elements and Gesture of Power (see "The Gesture of Power," Figure 14). Then say over the completed bag:

> *O Great Nanta bag, be thou a natural focus*
> *and a bridge to Power.*
> *I am linked to thee and thou art linked to Nature.*
> *We are One from Three.*
> *We are the Triangle manifest.*
> *In the names of Tana and Tanus, so be it.*

THE SECONDARY TOOLS

The secondary tools of Stregheria are all Folk Magick tools, and are associated with the hearth and home. They are, therefore, tools of the Matriarch and symbolize her power. It must be remembered that Italian women were (and still are) very powerful forces in the family. The association of domestic tools with women, in the Strega tradition, is not an insult but rather a remembrance of when women ruled.

The Broom

The broom was not publicly associated with Italian Witches, as a symbol, until around the later part of the eighteenth century. Strega were always portrayed as riding to the

Treguenda (Sabbat) on the backs of goats, unlike Witches of northern Europe, who were portrayed as flying on broomsticks. There is a similarity in this mythos, in as much as the goats provided flight in the same manner as did the broomsticks.

As a ritual tool, the broom can be used for protection and banishment, and it also serves as a symbol of the Goddess when turned brush-side up. As a tool of protection, the broom is laid across a doorway or entry way of any sort. When a ritual "doorway" is opened in a ceremonial circle, the broom can be set across the opening, while members exit and re-enter the circle. Ritual blades can also be used for this same purpose.

In banishment, the broom can be used to sweep salt (scattered around the affected area) out through the front door or entry area. The sprinkling of salt to remove negative energy is a very ancient practice. It can also be used to "thrash the air" in any setting to purify the area. Typically this involved censing the place with incense smoke, and then swinging the broom through the smoke.

The broom can also be set, brush-side up, near a ritual gathering site to represent the presence of the Goddess. This symbolizes the fertile and sexual power of the Goddess. Traditionally, a new broom was given to a bride on her wedding day as a symbol of her own power within the home and family. In ancient times, this was meant to honor her for nurturing and supporting the family structure. The entire family was dependent upon her, and through this she was given a great deal of respect and authority.

The Scissors

Another domestic tool wielded by the women of the home was a simple pair of scissors. In the Folk Magick of the Strega, scissors are used to break spells and sever magickal or astral connections. This is accomplished by acts of either cutting, slashing, or actually dropping the scissors. Cutting up a picture can sever the connection with that person, as can cutting up a piece of their clothing.

Olive oil drops can be placed upon the surface of a bowl of water, to represent whatever needs banishment. The scissors can then be jabbed into the drops while visualizing the problem. A person believed to be under a spell can be freed by sneaking up behind them and dropping the scissors to the floor. I suppose that this is similar to curing "hiccups" by scaring the person.

A charm in the image of a pair of scissors can also be worn for protection, or hung in a window, or over a doorway. The same is also true of a horseshoe, key, or a piece of horn. These, of course, are Folk Magick beliefs.

The Cauldron

The cauldron is used primarily for offerings with a ritual setting. This can be either an offering to deities or spirits. Typically the cauldron is set at the appropriate directional quarter of the ritual circle, which symbolizes the powers or forces whose influence is sought.

Offerings to the spirits of earth would be performed at the north quarter. Spirits of air receive offerings at the east quarter, spirits of fire to the south, and spirits of water to the west. Most deities are given offerings at the north, but occasionally this may be performed at either the east or west. In such a case it would involve aspects of Deity associated with either the Sun or Moon, since those are the quarters of rising and setting.

The Lare House (or Lasa Shrine)

Although not truly a tool per se, the Lare house is so integral a part of Stregheria that all Strega must possess one. Each one resembles a temple roof supported by two columns set upon a landing. Typically, this landing section extends out to form a ledge upon which offerings can be placed. This shrine is a focal point for the old spirits to commune with the Strega. The Lare are associated with ancestor worship in classical Roman religion, but this is quite different from the Strega practice.

In northern Italy, the Strega view the Lasa as beings who have already lived as humans and are now moving up the scale to demi-god status. Tuscan Witches call upon them for help in all matters and work very closely with the Lasa. In central and southern Italy, these entities are called Lare and are viewed more as the "collective consciousness" of former Strega. They can be called upon for assistance in the same manner as are the Lasa.

During important family occasions, offerings are made at the Lare house, which typically is set in the east or west of the home. Originally Lasa shrines were set in the west and Lare houses set in the east. Celebrations of birthdays, marriages, and other events call for the lighting of votive candles upon the shrine, as well as an offering of nectar.

When the Lare house is first established in the home, it is blessed in the names of the God and Goddess. A figure is usually added to the shrine depicting the Lare. Some Strega use a small figure of an angel in the Lare house, and, since Lasa were always depicted with wings, this is quite appropriate. To complete the shrine, a small offering bowl is set in place, along with a fava bean. The fava is symbolic of the "Otherworld" and was considered a plant sacred to the Underworld by ancient Greeks and Romans.

The Symbols

Before humans had invented an alphabet, as we understand one, they used symbols to communicate. Hunters used animal tracks as symbols of their prey and later as sigils of their power. The difference between a symbol and a sigil is that a symbol represents something else, but a sigil is the thing itself (or at least the essence of the thing). This is why sigils are used for invocations, and symbols are used to mark tools and equipment, but not to actually call upon an entity.

The following are the most common symbols and sigils used in Italian Witchcraft (Figures 13a–c, pages 106–108):

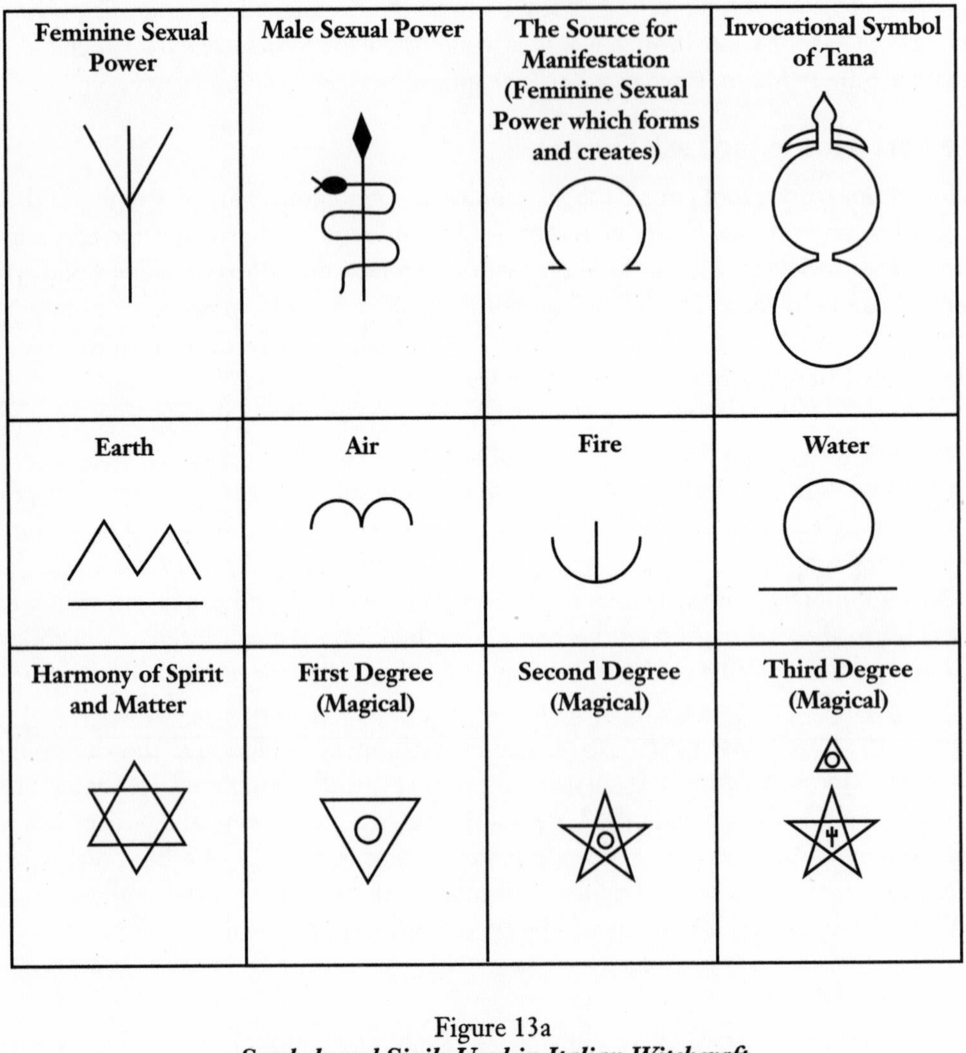

Feminine Sexual Power	Male Sexual Power	The Source for Manifestation (Feminine Sexual Power which forms and creates)	Invocational Symbol of Tana
Earth	Air	Fire	Water
Harmony of Spirit and Matter	First Degree (Magical)	Second Degree (Magical)	Third Degree (Magical)

Figure 13a
Symbols and Sigils Used in Italian Witchcraft

The Source of All Things	The Goddess	The God	The Elements of Creation (Spirit, Earth, Air, Fire, and Water)
The Power	Power of the Goddess	Power of the God	Wheel of the Moon
Power of the Union of the God and Goddess	The Goddess Manifest (the Moon Cross)	Tanus (light)	The Spirit of Aradia (The Teachings)
Guardian of the North	Guardian of the East	Guardian of the South	Guardian of the West

Figure 13b
Symbols and Sigils Used in Italian Witchcraft

107

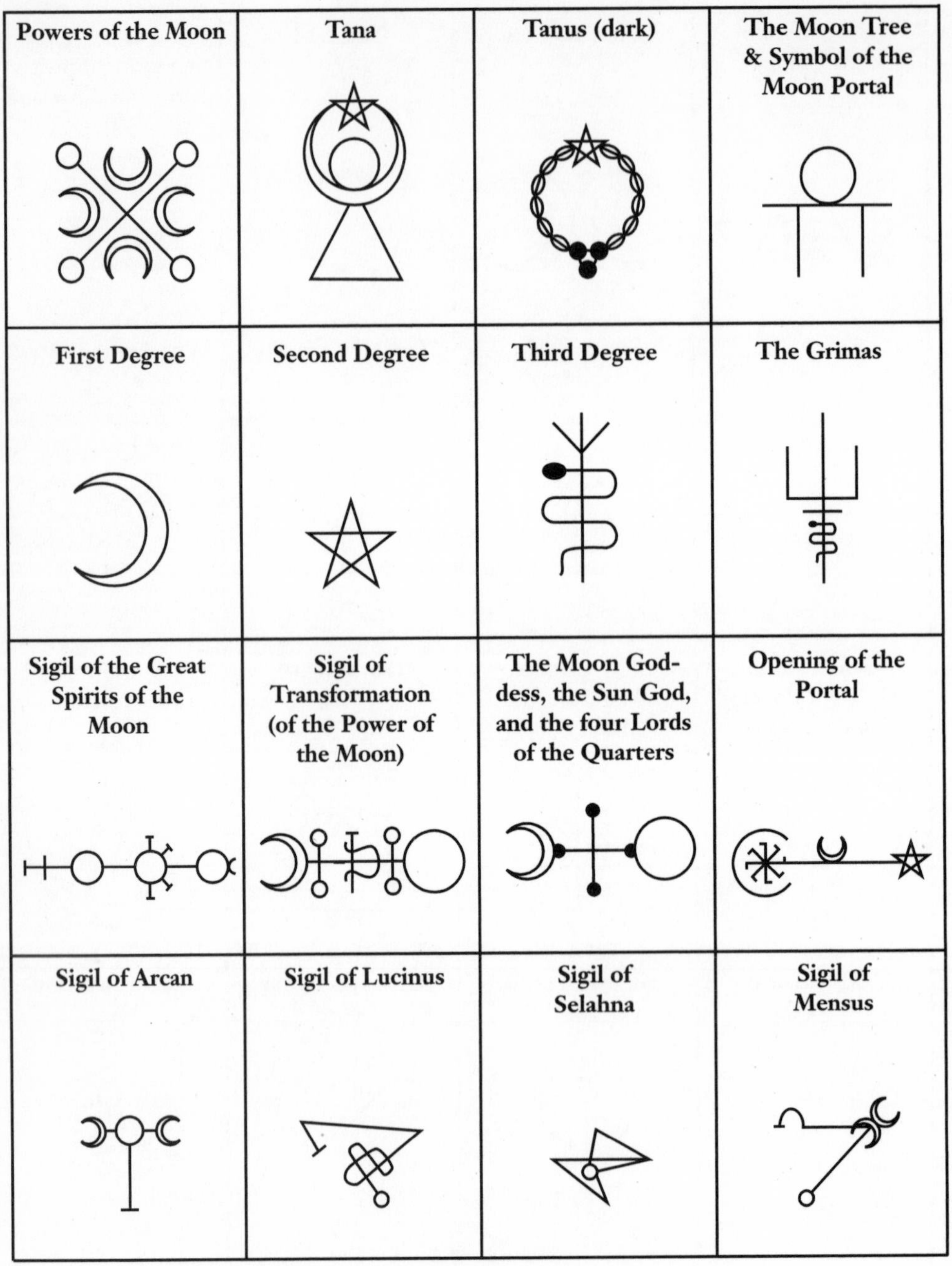

Powers of the Moon	Tana	Tanus (dark)	The Moon Tree & Symbol of the Moon Portal
First Degree	Second Degree	Third Degree	The Grimas
Sigil of the Great Spirits of the Moon	Sigil of Transformation (of the Power of the Moon)	The Moon Goddess, the Sun God, and the four Lords of the Quarters	Opening of the Portal
Sigil of Arcan	Sigil of Lucinus	Sigil of Selahna	Sigil of Mensus

Figure 13c
Symbols and Sigils Used in Italian Witchcraft

108

11

Raising and Drawing Power

It is interesting to note that the medical symbol of the caduseus, symbolizing perfect health, is itself a symbol of the God and Goddess currents flowing in balance along the spine.

from the text

The attraction, accumulation, and direction of power is essential in the magickal arts. Presented here are several of the most common forms of raising and drawing energy for magickal purposes in the Strega Tradition. Also presented here are the centers of power within the human body. To begin this chapter, it is important to become familiar with the Spirit Flame, which is the foundation for establishing magickal power.

The Spirit Flame represents the presence of the gods as well as the Spirit of the Old Ways. Aradia taught that fire came from divinity and she used it as a symbol of the teachings (of the Old Ways). All that the Strega do, whether magickally or ceremonially, is drawn from the Spirit Flame. It is one of the most powerful tools that a Strega can possess.

THE SPIRIT FLAME

In the Aridian System, the focal point of the altar is called the Spirit Flame. A bowl is placed upon the center of the altar, and is filled with a special liquid that will burn with a blue flame. Many Strega use an Italian liquore called Strega Liquore, but rubbing alcohol works nicely, as does any good-quality cologne. The appearance of the blue flame represents the presence of Divinity within the ritual setting. The use of fire as a sacred symbol is one of the most ancient of practices.

In ancient times, fire was a mysterious force. It provided warmth and protection, and was an extremely valuable possession. When people lived in villages and towns, crude lamps were used to provide light. Fuel for these lamps was expensive, and therefore had to be used sparingly. Light was only used at night for short periods, and was a time for family gathering. Today, with the convenience of modern lighting, it is difficult to appreciate how precious light (and heat) can really be. In time, light became a symbol of all that was positive in human life.

Aradia associated the flame as the "soul" of the Old Religion. Among her followers, the Spirit Flame image became a symbol of the Old Ways. Even today, its symbol appears as a sacred sign of our religion. It is an essential part of setting up the altar, and prescribed gestures and words of evocation are used to empower it as a vessel for Divine presence. Traditionally, the bowl, which will bear the flame, is placed upon the pentacle. The four elemental tools are then placed around the bowl, at each of the cardinal positions. The altar candles, which represent the God and Goddess, are set to the far left and right corners of the altar. Together with the Spirit Flame, they will form a triangle of light.

If you are interested in experiencing the spirit flame, try the following: Obtain some good quality cologne (or Strega Liquore) and pour it in a small bottle, preferably of green glass, and set it out under the Full Moon for several hours (three is fine). Be sure that the bottle is well sealed. When you bring it in, pour out what you will use into a small bowl, filling it about halfway. Extinguish all the lights, then trace a crescent over the fluid with your ritual knife, and say:

> *In the name of Tana, and by this sacred sign, be thy essence of magick!*

Now the fluid is ready to ignite. Perform the Gesture of Power (see Figure 14) with a lighted candle, and just before you light the fluid (position 3) say:

> *I call now, upon the Source of All things, and pray Thee impart thy essence into this most sacred flame!*

A beautiful blue flame will gently appear, and dance upon the surface of the liquid. Now simply sit, and look upon the flame. Do not extinguish it, but allow it to go out on its own. Experience it. The various uses for the flame can be found throughout this book. We consider the flame to be sacred and we use it to bless objects, empower tools, and create sacred space. Feel free to experiment with it, but remember to treat it with respect.

THE GESTURE OF POWER

The Gesture of Power, which appears in this chapter, can be used as a tool for evocation and for "charging" objects. It can also be used to open and close a ritually-cast circle. Read through the instructions carefully, so that you understand this technique completely before performing it in actuality (see Figure 14).

Hold the wand in your left hand, and the dagger in your right. Extend both arms out to your sides, position 1. Next move the tools down, in a circular manner, to position 2. Each tool will be tracing a separate crescent. Bring both together, and crossed, up to position 3, just above your head. Finally, concentrating strongly, bring the tools down to position 4, imagining that you are drawing down power. Position 4 must bring the tools to touch upon the object being charged, or the area to which the evocation is being directed.

To open a circle that is presently established, go to your point of exit and cross the wand and blade, assuming position 3. Move them down to position 4, then to 2, which will uncross the tools. Move to position 1, in circular motion, then assume the arms-outstretched posture. This will unseal your circle. To close again, simply perform the original procedure of 1 through 4, at the opening that you created.

Each time you perform the gesture, you will be tracing out the symbol as pictured in the illustration. Look at the symbol, and practice following the outline of it. Do not move outside of the image as you pass through the positions. With practice, I think you will find this technique quite useful. You may wish to enhance it by visualizing the symbol glowing as you trace it in the air.

For charging, you may wish to condense the image (mentally) into a glowing sphere, and then transfer it into the object being charged, as the tools are brought down upon it.

THE CENTERS OF POWER

Within the human body are located various centers of power (see Figure 15). In Italian Witchcraft there were originally only three acknowledged, but with the advent of Eastern Mysticism four others were added. In the modern structure, the first center is the Energy Center, also called the Fire Center or Serpent Center, which operates within the genital region. This is the Seat of Power, where concentrated life energies and psychic energies dwell. It is essentially a transmitive center.

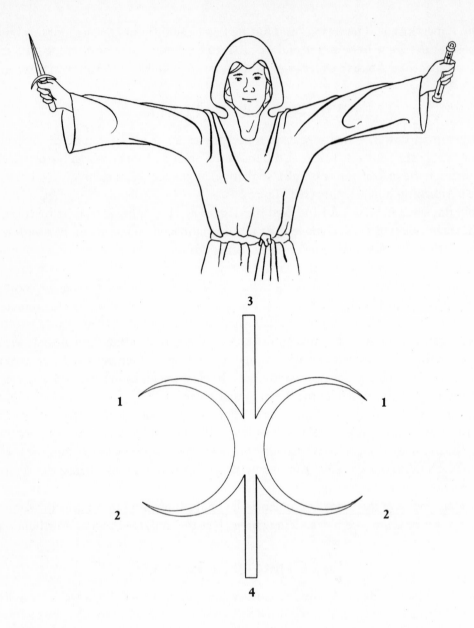

Figure 14
The Gesture of Power

The second center is known as the Personal Center. This center is both receptive and transmitive, and deals with astral energies. It is one of several gates through which the astral body of the individual can exit from the physical flesh. Great amounts of energy can be drawn in or sent out from this area, which is used extensively in shamanistic practices.

The third center is the Power Center. This center is also transmitive and receptive and deals with life energies. Through this center, both physical and astral bodies are nourished.

The fourth center is called the Emotional Center. This center is basically receptive, but it is transmitive as well. The Emotional Center deals with human feelings and ethics. This center enables us to sense another person on an emotional level.

The fifth center is the Vibrational Center. It is transmitive and deals with causing actions and reactions. It is the most physical of the nonphysical centers. The sixth center is the Psychic Center. It is basically receptive, but functions in a transmitive manner as well. This center is also called the Third Eye and the Purity Center. It is a very active psychic center and another exit point for the astral body. The seventh center is the Divine Center. It is receptive and transmitive and deals with "Deity-Consciousness." This is our higher self and our place of union with that which created us.

On a physical level, these centers function to maintain the body and its organs. The Energy Center governs the reproductive organs. The Personal Center governs general health: specifically, the liver, pancreas, and spleen. The Power Center governs the adrenal glands. The Emotional Center governs the thymus gland. The Vibrational Center governs the thyroid gland. The Psychic Center governs the pineal gland. The Divine Center influences the pineal gland.

There are two currents of energy, known as the God and Goddess currents (see Figure 16) flowing through these centers within the body. These currents issue forth from the Energy Center and cross at the Emotional Center, then cross again at the Psychic Center. They directly influence our sexuality and gender preference through the "frequency" of their energy patterns, and define our inner nature. In Judaic-Christian cultures, usually only one of these currents is fully functional, rendering people either heterosexual or homosexual. Both currents operating in balance align one with the natural bisexual state. It is interesting to note that the medical symbol of the cadeusus, symbolizing perfect health, is itself a symbol of the God and Goddess currents flowing in balance along the spine.

DRAWING DOWN THE MOON

This technique is designed to draw upon lunar energy, or astral energy, with which to empower a spell or work of magick. It can also be used for psychic development and meditation. In the Strega practice, drawing down the Moon is not the same thing as invoking

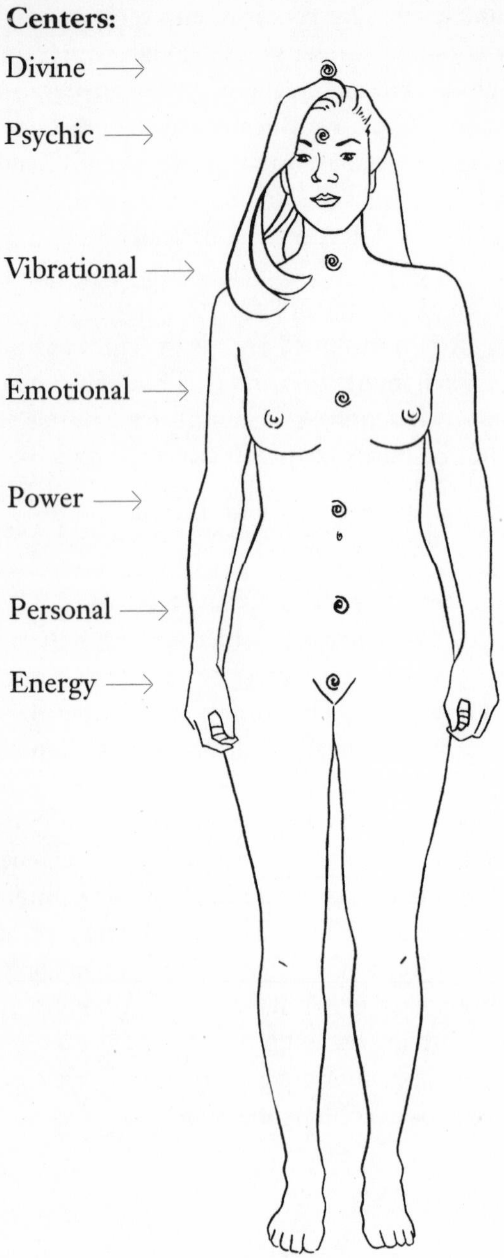

Centers:

Divine $\longrightarrow$

Psychic $\longrightarrow$

Vibrational $\longrightarrow$

Emotional $\longrightarrow$

Power $\longrightarrow$

Personal $\longrightarrow$

Energy $\longrightarrow$

Figure 15
Power Centers of the Human Body

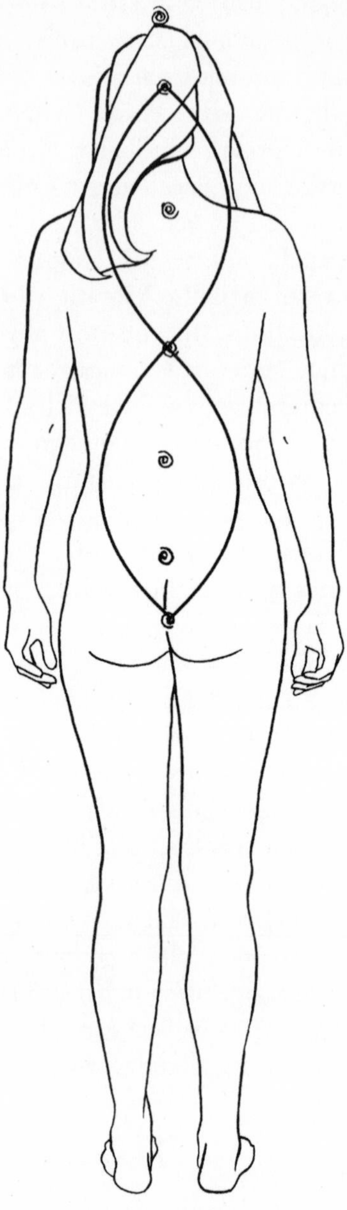

Figure 16
*God and Goddess
Currents of Power*

114

the Goddess. When we invoke the Goddess upon the High Priestess, we refer to it as "calling down the Goddess." The first act is connecting with the Moon, while the second act is connecting with the Goddess. The Moon and the Goddess are not the same thing, though admittedly they are difficult to separate.

Technique 1: Drawing Down the Moon

Sit quietly and visualize the Full Moon above you (see Figure 17). Mentally bring the Moon down to each of your body centers, visualizing each one glowing with the Moon's light. Concentrate on each center for at least a minute before moving on to the next.

Technique 2: Drawing and Raising Power

Sit comfortably, close your eyes, and imagine a white sphere of light about six inches above your head (see Figure 18). Imagine it flowing down through your head, neck, shoulders, chest, arms, and so on. Let this energy flow through every inch of you. Let it completely saturate the inside and cover the outside. Imagine that your entire being is glowing. At this point you are in touch with power, and you may proceed with healing or other works of magick.

Figure 17
Drawing Down the Moon

Figure 18
Drawing and Raising Power

Technique 3: Grounding Exercise

There are times when it is necessary to drain off excess energy from ritual or magickal work, and to regain a sense of balance. Sit directly upon the bare earth with your legs folded in front of you, and the palms of your hands pressed down upon the ground.

Imagine your arms to be hollow (like two hoses) and mentally pour the excess/unwanted energy out into the soil. Slow, deep breathing is helpful in this technique. Once you feel the energy is drained, then quickly get up and leave the area. It is best not to return there for a few hours. The earth will neutralize the energy, and the area will be as it was before you employed it.

Technique 4: Raising the Energy Sphere

This is a basic exercise for raising personal power. It will be the foundation for works of healing, charging, and magick. To raise a sphere of power (see Figure 19), place your hands in front of you, about six inches apart (palms facing), and begin to move them slowly back and forth (like playing an accordion). Experience the sensations of warmth, pressure, and magnetism.

Once a sphere of power has been established, you can pass a mental sigil into it, or project a thought-form, thereby giving the sphere its purpose. Then mentally visualize the sphere entering the object that you wish to charge.

To increase this energy, use your concentration and imagination. You can visualize a glowing force of power. Do not allow your hands to touch while performing this exercise. Once you have accomplished this method, then begin putting your hands around various objects and feeling their energy fields. Soon you will discover many other uses for this basic ability.

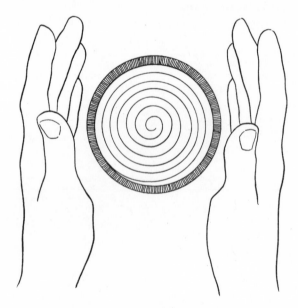

Figure 19
The Sphere of Power

116

Technique 5: Cleansing and Repairing the Aura

This is a simple technique for cleansing and repairing the aura which surrounds the body (Figure 20). First, raise your sphere of energy. Next, slowly glide your hands along the form of the body being treated. Avoid touching the person; keep your hands about four or five inches away.

Starting at the head, completely cover it with graceful sweeps of the hands, moving downward. When you complete this area then shake your hands toward the ground (as though you were shaking off some water).

Continue down the body a section at a time. You may have another person assist you if you desire. Move along the natural curves as you proceed. Remember to "shake off" after finishing a section; this helps to remove astral debris. After completing the general sweep of the body, run your hands along the aura, sensing for "gaps" in the structure. If you sense any, then raise a sphere and "patch" it into the gap. Let your intuition guide you as you go along.

Figure 20
Cleansing and Repairing the Aura

117

THE WEB OF POWER

This technique is employed in order to connect a group of individuals with either an invoked/evoked entity, a charged object, other participants within a ritual, or the facilitator of the rite itself. In this method, a "web of light" is visualized as extending out from the object or person that is the focal point of the joining. A single beam of light is imagined for each participant, and then pictured as extending out from the focal point to each person's forehead. To end this method, simply cease the visualizations and this will disconnect the participants from the focal point.

12

The Aridian Rituals

Establishing the altar is an important part of any ritual and is performed with concentration upon the inner meanings as each item is placed on it. In effect, as you set up an altar and cast a circle, you are creating your own microcosm of the Universe (from which you will create your own reality).

from the text

The rituals that follow in this chapter are taken from the modern Aridian system of the Strega Tradition. The Old Religion was originally a fertility cult, and the rites were quite sensual and sexual. Procreative energy was the "battery" which empowered the rituals and most works of Magick. This is still very much a part of the old Strega Tradition.

In the rites presented here, the sexual aspects have been replaced with symbolic representations. This is due, in part, to health issues associated with sexuality in modern times, but also because of sexual attitudes and inhibitions that many contemporary people carry. Modern elements have also been added to the rituals in keeping with the times.

To begin, we shall look at the Rite of Dedication, basic altar set-up, and the method of casting a ritual circle. The chapter will conclude with the Full Moon Ritual and the Seasonal Rites.

THE RITE OF DEDICATION

This is a simple rite based upon one that dates from the fifteenth century in Italy. If you wish to become a Strega, then perform the following rite. Feel free to modify this rite as you need to. It is the intent that is important here, but I would advise keeping it as traditional as possible.

At midnight, when the Moon is full, go out into an open field or a clearing within the woods, and take with you a vessel of water, another of wine, and a mixing bowl. Take also a small red bag containing a sprig of rue as your amulet, and a pinch of salt.

Pour some wine and water into the bowl and add the pinch of salt. Remove your clothing and kneel beneath the Moon. Dip the sprig of rue into the bowl of liquid and anoint yourself with it, in the manner of the pentacle: forehead—right nipple—left shoulder—right shoulder—left nipple—forehead. Then cup the sprig of rue in your palms and lift it up toward the Moon, saying:

> *I kneel beneath the same Moon*
> *that all the Witches of old*
> *have knelt before.*
> *And I am one with them*
> *in this sacred light.*
> *Hear me O Diana, goddess of the Moon, Queen of all Witches,*
> *for I bear the symbols of the Old Religion.*
> *hear me then,*
> *and think yet even for a moment*
> *upon this worshipper who kneels before you.*
> *For I have heard the Strega's story,*
> *and I believe the words of the Holy Strega.*
> *When she spoke of your beauty in the night sky,*
> *when she bid us seek and find you above all others.*
> *Here as the Full Moon shines upon me,*
> *receive me, O Diana.*
> *Receive me as your child*
> *and grant me the powers of those who follow you.*
> *For I believe in the gifts of Aradia*
> *which you promised to all who follow in the Old Ways.*

Anoint yourself again with the rue dipped in the bowl and say:

> *Diana, beautiful Diana,*
> *Goddess of the Moon and beyond,*

Queen of all Witches,
goddess of the dark night and of all Nature,
if you will grant me your favor
then I ask a token sign from you.
Let there be heard the sound of a dog,
the neigh of a horse,
the croak of a frog,
or the call of a bird.

Anoint yourself a third time with the sprig of rue, saying:

In the name of Diana, so may it be.

Gather up the items and place the rue back into the red bag. Sit quietly beneath the Full Moon and listen to the sounds of the night. If you hear any of the sounds requested, then Diana has granted you her favor, and you are one of the Strega. If you do not hear them, it is not a rejection, but simply means the time is not yet right.

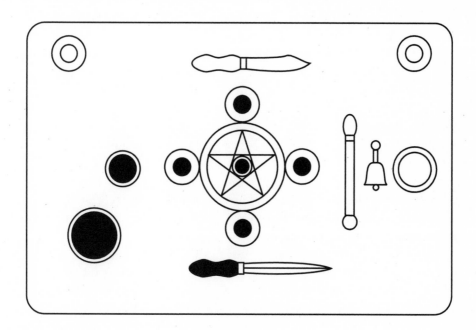

Figure 21
Altar Arrangement

Traditionally, the sound had to be heard before the Sun rose. If it was not, then the person could try again on the next Full Moon. Sometimes the sound was heard while sitting beneath the Moon, and sometimes it was heard while returning home.

Once a person became a Strega, then the rue was a potent charm granting him or her the powers promised by Aradia (see appendix F: "Gifts of Aradia").

THE ALTAR ARRANGEMENT

The altar is always oriented to the north quarter of the ritual setting. The north is considered the "place of power," and all practitioners face this direction as they stand before the altar. Traditionally the altar is round, but a rectangular or square table may be used as well. Establishing the altar is an important part of any ritual and is performed with concentration upon the inner meanings as each item is placed on it. In effect, as you set up an altar and cast a circle, you are creating your own microcosm of the Universe (from which you will create your own reality).

A black cloth is laid over the table to symbolize the darkness of "procreation" from which all things manifest. Candles symbolizing the Goddess and God are placed to the northernmost part of the altar; the goddess candle is set to the northwest and the god candle to the northeast. Icons of the Goddess and God are placed next to the candles. This represents their presence as they "oversee" the process of creation.

The altar pentacle is placed on the center of the altar, and upon this is set the spirit bowl containing a flammable liquid. This liquid is the spirit fluid which will burn a beautiful blue flame, representing the presence of Divinity. Then elemental bowls are placed around the pentacle, representing the creative materials from which all things are made manifest.

The bowl representing earth is set in the north position and contains sand or small stones. To the east is the bowl containing incense (smoking) to represent air, to the south is a bowl with a votive candle for fire, and to the west is a bowl with purified Water (see Figure 21).

The ritual wand is set upon the altar, next to the air elemental bowl. The Spirit Blade (athame) is placed to the south by the votive candle, and the chalice to the west by the bowl of water. With this arrangement the altar is now complete. Mundane tools may also be placed on the altar now: a utility knife, candle snuffer, and so on.

PREPARATION OF THE RITUAL CIRCLE

When casting a circle by group participation, the following items are required:

4 white quarter candles (to be placed at the cardinal points)

2 white altar candles

1 length of rope slightly over 14 feet long (for 9-foot diameter circle)

6 candle holders

1 object to serve as altar (set in center of circle, oriented to north quarter)

1 black altar cloth (large enough to fully cover altar)

1 God and Goddess statue or symbolic representations

4 elemental bowls (filled with associated material unique to each element)

1 incense burner (a censer with chain) and matches or lighter

1 silver bell

1 candle snuffer

1 bottle of spirit fluid (Strega Liquore)

1 metal bowl to contain the spirit fluid (must be able to hold fire)

1 bottle of red wine (at least) and ritual cakes or cookies for celebration

Ritual tools: spirit blade, wand, chalice, pentacle, summoning horn.

When the time is proper (Full Moon or Treguenda), then shall you seek a meadow or a clearing within the woods. It is best that this clearing have flowing water, and stones so as to mark your ritual circle.

To mark the place of power in the north, set your ritual circle before a tree or a boulder. The tree must be true, without a gnarled branch or twisted trunk.

1. Mark the place where you will establish the circle, set the quarter candles, and purify the area with consecrated water (three pinches of salt to one cup of water).

2. Set the altar as is proper, and light the Spirit Bowl, reciting the invocation: (with gesture of power):

   Awaken now, O Spirit of the Old Ways.

3. Light the altar candles once the blue flame is established, and give altar calls:

   (To the Goddess): Beautiful Tana, goddess of the Moon and beyond, think even for a moment upon we who gather in your name.

(Bella Tana, dea della luna e del di la pensa per un momento a noi reunite qui nel tuo nome.)

(To the God): Tanus, god of the Sun and beyond, think even for a moment upon we who gather in your name (Tanus, dio del sole e del di la pensa per un momento a noi reunite qui nel tuo nome).

4. Conjure the elementals: ring bell over each elemental bowl thrice, beginning at the north, and recite:

   I call out into the mist of Hidden Realms, and conjure you spirits of earth and air and fire and water. Gather now at this sacred circle, and grant us union with your powers.

5. Ring altar bell over elemental bowls again thrice, then tap each bowl thrice with the Spirit Blade.

6. Place the Spirit Blade into the Spirit Flame and mentally draw out the blue flame into the blade.

7. Beginning at the north, tread the circle, laying out the blue power along the edge of the circle (visualize the blue flame pouring out through the blade into the circle's rim as you walk) and recite:

   In the names of Tana and Tanus, and by the Old Ones,
   I conjure this circle of power become a sphere of protection,
   a vessel to contain the power
   which shall be raised within,
   wherefore do I charge you, and empower you.

8. Quarter candles are lit from the Spirit Flame and charged with an element, then each is placed at the proper quarter.

9. **Conjuration of the Grigori:** One Grove member swings a censer of incense back and forth three times at each quarter, as the name of the Grigori of that quarter is called out. Another member accompanies and sounds the horn of summoning three times, once the name is called out (or rings a bell if a horn is unavailable).

   Invocation (by High Priest[ess] at the altar):

   We call to You O Ancient Ones!
   You who dwell beyond the Realms,
   You who once reigned in the Time before Time.
   Come! Hear the Call!
   Assist us to open the Way, give us the Power!

Open wide the gates to the Realms of the Gods
and come forth by these names:
TAGO! BELLARIA! SETTRANO! MEANA!

High Priest(ess) declares circle to be cast, and raps wand three times upon the altar.

BANISHING A CAST CIRCLE

A circle must be dissolved when the ritual is completed. This is done as follows:

1. Beginning at the north quarter, give ritual salute and recite:

   Hear me, Old Ones, we honor You for Your attendance and bid You now depart to
   your secret Realms.
   With peace we say now; Ave, Vale!

   Grove members respond:

   Ave, Vale!

2. Repeat the above action at each of the quarters (moving west, south, east, and north again).

3. Point the Spirit Blade down toward the circle and tread the same direction as above, mentally drawing the blue power back up from the circle perimeter, into the blade. Once the circle has been tread then put the tip of the blade into the Spirit Flame and visualize the power flowing back into the bowl. Allow the Spirit Flame to diminish on its own, until it has departed. Dissolve the elements within the elemental bowls by "snapping" your fingers over them three times each.

4. Extinguish all quarter torches and all other ritual flames, then depart the area. The circle is dissolved.

THE RITE OF UNION

This rite is performed to the sunrise in adoration of the God (through observance of his symbol) and to the Full Moon in adoration to the Goddess (through observance of her symbol). It may also be done at any other time, or setting, when you feel "Union" would be appropriate. (Positions are illustrated in Figures 22 and 23).

1. Standing or kneeling before the light (or symbol) raise hands as in position 1, saying:

   Hail and adoration unto Thee, O Source of All Enlightenment. I pray Thee impart
   to me Thy Illumination.

Position 1   Position 2   Position 3

Position 4   Position 5

Figure 22
The Rite of Union Postures

2. Lower arms to position 2, saying:

   And enlighten my mind that I may perceive more clearly, all things in which I endeavor.

3. Lower arms to position 3, saying:

   And illuminate my soul, imparting Thy essence of Purity.

4. Lower arms to positions 4 and 5, saying:

   I reveal my Inner Self to Thee and ask that all be cleansed and purified within.

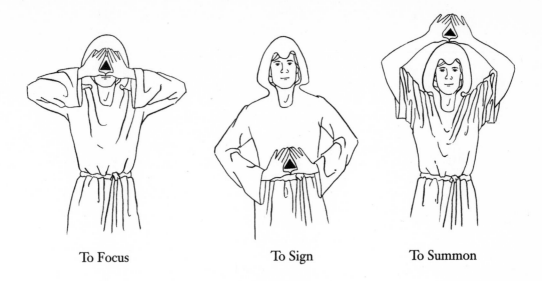

To Focus   To Sign   To Summon

Figure 23
Gestures to Focus, Sign, and Summon

FULL MOON RITUAL

1. Cast the circle in the usual manner.

2. The Grove assembles before the altar. High Priestess or High Priest (based on season) gestures the Moon Altar hand position (Figure 24) to the Full Moon, and addresses the Grove members (all members enclose the Moon with the same gesture):

   We gather on this sacred night of our Lady, beneath the Full Moon, to adore Her symbol, which She has placed among the stars. And we gather to give due worship unto the Great Goddess, for this is the appointed time which the Holy Strega bid us observe. As it was in the time of our beginning, so is it now, so shall it be.

   Grove responds:

   Hail and adoration unto You O Great Tana.

   High Priestess (signs the Triangle of Manifestation, Figure 24):

   Hail and adoration unto You O Great Tana. Hail Goddess of the Moon, and of the Night. You have been since before the beginning, You who caused all things to appear, Giver and Sustainer of Life, Adoration unto You.

127

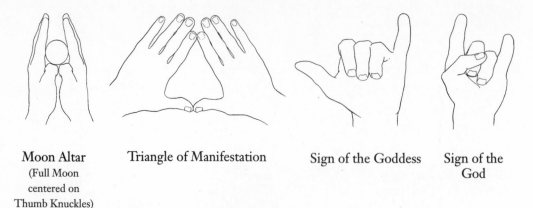

Moon Altar
(Full Moon
centered on
Thumb Knuckles)

Triangle of Manifestation

Sign of the Goddess

Sign of the
God

Figure 24
Magickal and Ritual Gestures

Grove responds:

Hail and adoration unto You, O Great Tana.

Grove members perform the Rite of Union (Figure 22), facing the Full Moon (if indoors, face High Priestess or a symbol of the Full Moon).

3. High Priestess or High Priest (seasonal) addresses Grove members:

    Let us now sound the ancient name of Power, and join ourselves, one to the other, and unite us with Her Holy Emanation.

4. High Priestess or High Priest (seasonal) directs Grove members to sit in a circle, then he/she spreads the web of power over them. The chalice filled with wine is set in the center of the group. High Priestess/High Priest begins the chant, focusing on the wine as the chant builds. Once the linking is complete, the Grove is signalled to cease the chant, then the wine is passed for all to drink (thus is the essence passed to all, and all are joined together).

5. Offerings are now made to Tana by all (at the west quarter). Grove will sing or chant as each member goes to the west, one at a time.

6. High Priestess or High Priest (seasonal) speaks from the altar:

    O Great Tana, think yet even for a moment, upon we who gather in Your name. Beneath the Sun do men toil, and go about, and attend to all worldly affairs. But beneath the Moon, Your children dream and awaken, and draw their power. Therefore, bless us, O Great Tana, and impart to us Your mystic Light, in which we find our powers.

Grove responds:

Bless us, O Great Tana.

7. High Priest directs the Grove to draw down the Moon (summon the light, Figure 17). All gather in a circle, and center themselves as invocation begins:

O Ancient Wanderer of the Dark Heavens, Mystery of the Mysteries, emanate Your sacred essence upon we who gather below at this appointed time. Enlighten our inner minds and spirits, as do you lighten the darkness of night.

(High Priest directs a mental journey designed to provide magickal/mystical experiences for the Veglione event. High Priest later signals the end to the summoning after mental journey is completed. Everyone shares his or her experience of the episode.)

8. After this, High Priest has everyone sit quietly within a circle, and he recites the Veglia:

Once, long ago, our people worshipped in the open fields and upon the ancient sites. And our chants were carried upon the winds. Our prayers were received upon the smoke of our incense by the Old Ones. But in time, we were enslaved by the worshippers of a jealous god, and our villages were given over to cruel lords. The Old Ways were forbidden and we were forced to accept the ways of our oppressors.

For us now, it is a time of gathering in the shadows. We have suffered persecution for our beliefs, and many of us have died. Yet we have been reborn among our own again. Always has it been that the cycles of life pass and return again. All things are remembered, and all things are restored.

We are the hidden children of the Goddess. From generation unto generation have we passed the knowledge and kept to the Old Ways. And so for us, it is a time of remembrance. We gather this evening, beneath the Full Moon, to honor our past, secure our future, and receive the essence of the Old Ones. As it was in the time of our beginning, so is it now, so shall it be.

9. High Priestess or High Priest (seasonal ruler) blesses the wine and cakes for the union:

Blessings upon this meal, which is as our own body. For without this, we ourselves would perish from this world.

Blessings upon the grain, which as seed went into the Earth where deep secrets hide. And there did dance with the elements, and spring forth as flowered plant, concealing secrets strange. When you were in the ear of grain, spirits of the field came to cast their light upon you, and aid you in your growth.

Thus through you we shall be touched by that same race, and the mysteries hidden within you, we shall obtain even unto the last of these grains.

High Priestess gestures the symbol of union (Figure 22) over the wine, saying:

By virtue of this sacred sign, be this wine the vital essence of the Great Goddess.

High Priest gestures the symbol of union (Figure 22) over the cakes, saying:

By virtue of this sacred sign, be these cakes the vital substance of the Great God.

High Priest or High Priestess addresses the Grove members:

Through these cakes and by this wine, may Tana and Tanus bless you, and give you inner strength and vision. May you come to know that within you which is of the gods. Blessed be all in the names of Tana and Tanus.

Grove members now come forward, one at a time, to receive the Union through cakes and wine. A toast is given to Aradia, with wine from the chalice, in memory of her name.

10. High Priestess recites "L' incarico di Aradia" (The Charge of Aradia):

Whenever you have need of anything, once in the month when the Moon is full, then shall you come together at some deserted place, or where there are woods, and give worship to She who is Queen of all Witches. Come all together inside a circle, and secrets that are as yet unknown shall be revealed.

And your mind must be free and also your spirit, and as a sign that you are truly free, you shall be naked in your rites. And you shall rejoice, and sing; making music and love. For this is the essence of spirit, and the knowledge of joy.

Be true to your own beliefs, and keep to the Ways, beyond all obstacles. For ours is the key to the mysteries and the cycle of rebirth, which opens the way to the Womb of Enlightenment.

I am the spirit of Witches all, and this is joy and peace and harmony. In life does the Queen of all Witches reveal the knowledge of Spirit. And from death does the Queen deliver you to peace and renewal.

When I shall have departed from this world, in memory of me make cakes of grain, wine, and honey. These shall you shape like the Moon, and then partake of wine and cakes, all in my memory. For I have been sent to you by the Spirits of Old, and I have come that you might be delivered from all slavery. I am the daughter of the Sun and the Moon, and even though I have been born into this world, my race is of the stars.

Give offerings all to She who is our Mother. For She is the beauty of the Green Wood, and the light of the Moon among the stars, and the mystery which gives life, and always calls us to come together in Her name. Let Her worship be the ways within your heart, for all acts of love and pleasure gain favor with the Goddess.

But to all who seek her, know that your seeking and desire will reward you not, until you realize the secret. Because if that which you seek is not found within your inner self, you will never find it from without. For she has been with you since you entered into the ways, and she is that which awaits at your journey's end.

11. **Calling Down the Moon** (invoking the Goddess, Figure 17): (only performed in times of need). The High Priestess stands at the west, facing east. High Priest kneels before her (performing the act of invocation) touching her with the wand as follows: right breast nipple, left breast nipple, pubic area, right breast nipple.

Invocation:

Tana, beautiful Tana, Goddess of the Moon and beyond I invoke you and call to you with an upraised voice. (Tana, bella Tana, Dea della Luna e del di La, a te invoco e te chiamo ad alta voce.)

Tana, beautiful Tana, You are as beautiful as you are good, so I praise you much with joy. Beautiful Tana, Goddess of the stars and of the Moon, the most powerful Queen, appear now before us! (Tana, bella Tana, che tanto bella e buona siei, e tanto ti e piacere ti ho fatto. Bella Tana Dea delle stelle e della Luna, La Regina piu potente, Appari di fronte a noi!)

Silence and concentration is observed as the High Priestess receives the Goddess. Once this is accomplished she will speak, then requests may be made of her.

12. High Priest or High Priestess (seasonal) recites closing prayer:

O Great Tana, Queen of all Witches, hear our song of adoration. Hear our voices as we speak Your praises. Receive our words as they rise heavenward, when the Full Moon brightly shining fills the heavens with Your beauty. See us for we gather before You, and reach our arms up towards You. As the Full Moon shines upon us, give us all Your blessings.

O Great Goddess of the Moon, Goddess of the Mysteries of the Moon, teach us secrets yet revealed, ancient rites of invocation that the Holy Strega spoke of, for I believe the Strega's story; when she spoke of Your timeless glory, when she told us to entreat You, told us when we seek for knowledge to seek and find you above all others.

Give us power, O Most Secret Lady, to bind our oppressors. Receive us as Your children, receive us though we are earthbound. When our bodies lie resting nightly, speak to our inner spirits, teach us all Your Holy Mysteries. I believe Your ancient promise that we who seek Your Holy Presence will receive of Your wisdom.

Behold, O Ancient Goddess, we have gathered beneath the Full Moon at this appointed time. Now the Full Moon shines upon us. Hear us. Recall Your Ancient Promise. Let Your Glory shine about us. Bless us, O Gracious Queen of Heaven. So be it done.

13. Spirit Blades are now recharged through the ritual embrace technique (members embrace, pressing the blade between their breasts, one blade at a time). Three works of magick may be performed before the circle is closed, if desired. Close with celebration of cakes and wine. Banish the circle and give libations to the Earth and the Moon when celebration is completed.

God Posture   Goddess Posture

Slain God Posture
(not shown) Same as God Posture, but with head bowed.

Figure 25
Postures of the God and Goddess

SHADOW FEST — a Festa Dell' Ombra
October 31

Items required (in addition to standard altar items):

>   1 vial of essence oil (God scent)
>
>   2 red candles for altar
>
>   4 black candles for quarter points
>
>   1 human skull (replica/symbol) placed at the west quarter
>
>   Winter treguenda incense
>
>   Root of rue plant
>
>   Small white candle for each person attending
>
>   Dried leaves (oak leaves or pine needles)
>
>   Personal offerings to the God
>
>   Large blanket (optional)
>
>   Cauldron

1. Cast the circle in usual manner.

2. Place skull at the west quarter. High Priest stands before the Grove and assumes the Slain God posture (Figure 25). Grove members perform Rite of Union (Figure 22) facing High Priest.

3. High Priestess sounds altar bell thrice, saying:

   O ancient gods of our ancestors, bless this sacred gathering, that we who worship in your ways may be protected from the coming powers.

4. High Priestess stands at the west quarter and reads the "Myth of the Descent of the Goddess" to the assembled Grove:

Myth of the Descent of the Goddess

Tana, our Lady and Goddess, would solve all mysteries, even the mystery of Death. And so she journeyed to the Underworld in her boat, upon the Sacred River of Descent. Then it came to pass that she entered before the first of the seven gates to the Underworld. And the Guardian challenged her, demanding one of her garments for passage, for nothing may be received except that something be given in return.

And at each of the gates the goddess was required to pay the price of passage, for the guardians spoke to her: "Strip off your garments, and set aside your jewels, for nothing may you bring with you into this our realm."

So Tana surrendered her jewels and her clothing to the Guardians, and was bound as all living must be who seek to enter the realm of Death and the Mighty Ones. At the first gate she gave over her scepter, at the second her crown, at the third her necklace, at the fourth her ring, at the fifth her girdle, at the sixth her sandals, and at the seventh her gown.

Tana stood naked and was presented before Dis, and such was her beauty that he himself knelt as she entered. He laid his crown and his sword at her feet saying: "Blessed are your feet which have brought you upon this path." Then he arose and said to Tana: "Stay with me I pray, and receive my touch upon your heart."

And Tana replied to Dis,: "But I love you not, for why do you cause all the things that I love, and take delight in, to wither and die?"

"My Lady" replied Dis "it is age and fate against which you speak. Thus I am helpless, for age causes all things to whither, but when all die at the end of their time, I give them rest, peace, and strength. For a time they dwell within the Moon's light, and with the spirits of the Moon; then may they return to the realm of the living. But you are so lovely, and I ask you to return not, but abide with me here."

But she answered: "No, for I do not love you." Then Dis said: "If you refuse to embrace me, then you must kneel to death's scourge." The goddess answered him: "If it is to be, then it is fate, and better served!" So Tana knelt in submission before the hand of death, and he scourged her with so tender a hand that she cried out: "I know your pain, and the pain of love."

Dis raised her to her feet and said: "Blessed are you, my Queen and my Lady. Then he gave to her the five kisses of initiation, saying: "Only thus may you attain to knowledge and to joy." And he taught her all of his mysteries, and he gave her the necklace which is the circle of rebirth. And she taught him her mysteries of the sacred cup which is the cauldron of rebirth.

They loved and joined in union with each other, and for a time Tana dwelled in the realm of Dis. For there are three mysteries in the life of man which are: birth, sex, and death (and love controls them all). To fulfill love, you must return again at the same time and place as those whom you loved before. And you must meet, recognize, remember, and love them anew. But to be reborn you must die and be made ready for a new body. And to die you must be reborn, but without love you may not be born among your own.

The God with a Lasa

135

But our Goddess is inclined to favor love, and joy, and happiness. She guards and cherishes her hidden children in this life and the next. In death she reveals the way to her communion, and in life she teaches them the magick of the Mystery of the Circle (which is set between the worlds of men and of the gods).

5. High Priestess stands at the west quarter and addresses Grove members:

    Tana dwells now in the Realm of the Dread Lord of the Shadows. The world grows cold and lifeless. But let us not sorrow for this harsh season, for all is as it must be. Therefore, let us draw close to the Dark Lord and embrace Him. Let us find comfort in the knowledge of His Essence. Blessed be all in the name of the God.

    Grove members respond:

    Tanus protect us.

6. High Priest moves to the north, assuming the Slain God Posture (Figure 25, page 132).

7. A female who has been chosen as a "love offering" to the God is now presented to the High Priest. Female kneels beside the High Priestess at the north quarter.

8. High Priestess kneels, and touches High Priest on the shoulders and phallus with her left hand (tracing a triangle from his right shoulder, to left shoulder, then to phallus, and back to right shoulder).

    High Priestess says:

    O Ancient One, Lord of the Shadows, approach and receive this sacred gift of love. Come you now among us! For now it is your Time of Power, O mighty Horned One. Lord of our Passions and Desires, come you among us!

    We freely offer this lovely woman to you, for you delight in the beauty of womanhood. We welcome you with love and with trust. O Ancient One, come you among us!

    There is now a moment of silence, as the God prepares to receive the female through the High Priest. They embrace, kiss, and hold each other for a few moments. Grove members will sing or chant during this time. High Priest will then release the female, who will anoint the High Priest's wand with essence oil, and then she will return to the assembled Grove.

9. High Priest assumes God Posture (Figure 25) in the north. High Priestess goes to him and lays her symbols and tools of rank at his feet, saying:

    My Lord, I give my reign over to you, for I know now the pains of love.

    High Priest takes up the symbols of the High Priestess and kisses them, then places them down at the north quarter. High Priest recites the Charge of the God:

Hear you all, the words of the God. By the fallen temple stone or in a forgotten glen, there shall you gather, all who seek to know my secret mysteries. I am He who guards and He who reveals all of these things.

I am the Lord of earth and sky, of rocky cliffs, and forests deep and darkened. I was there when the world was new, and I taught you to hunt and to gather plants for food. Look within yourselves, for I am there. I am that strength upon which you draw in times of need. I am that which conquers fear. I am the hero and the fool. I am your longing to be free, and your need to be bound.

In my love for you, I give up my life. I die, but rise up again. I prepare the path upon which you journey, going always on before you. For it is in becoming as you, that you may become as me.

Hear the thunder, there am I. See the hawk and the raven soar, there am I. See the great wolf and the stag appear in the forest clearing, there am I. Close your eyes at the end of your days, and there am I, waiting by the temple stone.

An assistant places the High Priestess' tools near the altar pentacle.

10. High Priestess, in Goddess posture (Figure 25) at the altar faces the Grove from the north and addresses them:

    The wheel of the year has turned, Cycle unto Cycle, Time unto Time. I have journeyed to the Hidden Realm of the Shadows; there to prepare a place for you. The harshness of the season I leave behind me; kindle for yourselves a fire of love within, and I shall remember you, and return to you. For you are the Keepers of the Flame, and all who kindle the flame I shall never abandon.

    By the changing of the harsh season shall you know that I draw near you again. And I shall return then the greenness of plants and trees; then will you know that I have come.

11. Each Grove member now comes forward to the altar and receives a white candle. Grove then moves to the High Priestess who lights each candle from the "goddess candle" on the altar.

12. High Priestess kneels before the High Priest at the north quarter, lifts up the chalice (filled with wine) to him. High Priest charges the wine and places his wand (tip down) into the wine within the chalice.

13. High Priestess offers wine to each Grove member, one at a time saying:

    Accept now the Essence of the God.

14. Each member now goes to the High Priest at the north quarter, bearing the lighted candle that they received from the altar.

    High Priest addresses each Grove member as they stand before him:

    This is the light that you bore, from the season before. Accept now my Essence.

    High Priest then snuffs out the member's candle, and bids them to taste a small piece of rue root, which he first dips in the wine.

15. Grove moves around the circle and back to the High Priest. All females will embrace and kiss the High Priest, all males will give the ritual salute.

16. The cauldron is filled with the dried leaves, lit, and set where it can be seen by all, preferably in the north. All Grove members then place their offerings in front of it. High Priest then addresses the Grove:

    Behold the womb of the Goddess of Night, which kindles the Child of the coming year. O symbol of the Mystery by which we return, we honor your Essence, and the magick that emanates from Union with you.

    Grove members respond:

    O bring to us the Child of Promise.

17. High Priestess addresses Grove:

    Let us be secure in the protective power of the God. We shall not be in want, nor shall we suffer, for we are in his care. Let us therefore feast and celebrate, all in his praise.

    Grove responds:

    Blessed be all in the God. Tanus protect us.

18. Grove assembles in a circle, standing along the perimeter line of the ritual circle. Beginning with the High Priestess, everyone will go around the circle and give the opposite sex a kiss and an embrace, saying, "Many blessings," as they do so.

19. Celebration of wine and cakes concludes the ritual.

20. Ritual circle is closed, candles are snuffed.

WINTER SOLSTICE — La Festa dell' Inverno

Items required (in addition to usual ritual items):

Evergreen wreath

Small log of oak

Small "newborn god" candle for the "God-flame"

Cauldron for offerings

1. Cast the ritual circle in the appropriate manner.

2. High Priestess, at the altar, addresses the coven:

   We mark now, with this sacred gathering, the rebirth of the Sun God. It is the Great Mother who gives him birth. It is the lord of life born again. From the Union of our Lord and Lady, hidden in the Realm of Shadows, we receive now the Child of Promise!

3. High Priest stands at the north quarter in the God posture (Figure 25) as High Priestess addresses the Quarters. Grove members perform Rite of Union (Figure 22) to the God Form:

   We call forth now into the Portal of the Northern Power. We call to the Ancient God, He who brought forth the beasts of field and forest. We call upon the Ancient God, He who was beloved of our ancient tribes.

4. High Priest (in God Posture) is addressed by High Priestess:

   My Lord, we greet You O Horned One, horned with the rays of the Sun, by whose blessings and grace shall life always be born again. Behold, Your Witches are gathered! Bless them, and the days before them! These gifts do we give you . . .

5. A vessel is set before the High Priest, with the Grove members making the gesture of manifestation (Figure 24). High Priestess places an offering within, followed by each member.

6. High Priestess recites prayer:

   O most ancient provider, Lord of Light and Life, We pray You grow strong that we may pass the Winter in peace and fullness. Emanate Your warmth and Your Love that the cold and harshness of Winter not dwindle Your followers.

   O Ancient One, hear us! Protect us and provide for us in the harshness of these times. We give You adoration and place ourselves in Your care. Blessed be all in the God!

   Grove responds:

   Blessed be all.

7. High Priest now goes to each Grove member, anoints them with the oil, and gives them the prepared ruta (sprig of rue), saying:

   Blessed be in my care.

8. High Priest and High Priestess enact the "Myth of the Season" with four of the Grove members, as the Grove observes the drama play (which takes place at the northeast quarter).

Narrator:

Now the time came, in the Hidden Realm of Shadows, that Tana would bear the child of the Great Dark Lord. And the Lords of the four corners came and beheld the newborn God. So it came to pass that the Great Lords were brought before the throne of the Dark One. And they spoke, saying: "Do we find You here, O Janus?" And the Great One replied: "Yes, it is I. Now you have truly seen my two faces."

Then Tana spoke to the four Lords, saying: "Take my son who is born of Janus, that he might bring life to the world. For the world has grown cold and lifeless." So the Lords of the four corners departed to the world of men, bearing the new Lord of the Sun. And the people rejoiced, for the Lord had come that all upon the earth might be saved.

The New Sun God

Ritualists now proceed with the drama play:

The Drama Play

I. High Priestess takes the posture for giving birth. High Priest kneels between her legs and produces a flame (lighted candle) in the manner of delivering a baby. The lords surround the High Priest and High Priestess, slightly obscuring the view of the Grove members.

II. Once born, the flame is taken by the Lord of the east, who carries it to the east quarter. Here the Lord presents the flame to the Grove members, saying:

Hail, behold the newborn Sun.

Grove responds:

Hail Janus, Hail Lupercus, Hail Lord of the Sun.

Each Lord, in turn (south, west, north) will perform the same act at his associated quarter, with the same Grove response.

III. The east Lord will tread the circle (from east quarter) to the north, taking the god-flame from the north Lord and making one full pass around the circle again (holding up the God-flame).

Upon returning to the north, the east Lord will raise the flame to this quarter and then to the assembled Grove. The east Lord will then carry the God-flame to the east and repeat the last act.

IV. The God-flame is now carried to the altar and set upon it.

V. High Priest addresses Grove members:

Let your spirits be joyful and your heart despair not. For on this sacred day is born He whose Light shall save the World. He has come forth from the Darkness and His Light has been seen in the east. He is Lord of Light and Life.

(High Priest gestures the Horned God sign with hand, toward the God-flame.)

Behold the Sacred One, the Child of Promise! He who is born into the World, is slain for the World, and ever rises again!

VI. Now the sacred evergreen wreath is brought out and placed before the altar. The small oak log is set in the center of the wreath. The God-flame is then set on top of it (symbolic of the Lord of Light and the Lord of Vegetation, being as one and the same).

9. High Priest addresses assembled Grove members (palms held above the god-flame):

> *Behold the God whose life and light dwells within each of us. He is the Horned One;*
> *Lord of the Forest, and the Hooded One; Lord of the Harvest, and The Old One;*
> *Lord of the Clans. Let us therefore honor Him.*

Grove members place gifts for each other before the sacred evergreen, in recognition of the Divinity within each person. The ritual is then concluded with the meal of cakes and wine. Celebration of the season may continue within the circle, or be taken to another location. Traditionally bonfires are set either on hilltops or upon the beach. Grove members may leap the fire, or simply toss items into the flames to "encourage the light."

LUPERCUS — Festa di Lupercus
February 2

Items required (other than usual ritual items):

> Wolfskin cloak (symbolic)
>
> Deerskin or goatskin strap (for scourge)
>
> Small fur or skin piece for charging chalice (traditionally wolf, or goat)
>
> Small candle for each Grove member
>
> Lupercus torch or candle (for presentation)

1. Circle is cast in the usual manner.

2. High Priest addresses Grove members:

> *We gather at this sacred time to give due praise and worship to the Lord of Light.*
> *He who was Janus has risen again, and enters into the world that all the people of*
> *the Earth might be saved. We mark now, at this appointed time, the waxing splen-*
> *dor of the young god. He who is Lupercus, Lord of Light, Banisher of Darkness, the*
> *Great Golden Wolf.*

3. High Priest lights a torch from the altar and treads the circle from the north, returning north again, as the High Priestess addresses the Grove and members perform the Rite of Union (Figure 22):

> *Behold the Lord of Light, He who mastered the twelve labors of the Great Lords.*
> *He who causes the world to rejoice in his rising. He whose Light brings Salvation*
> *to the earth.*

142

4. High Priestess kneels at the east quarter and begins the invocation to the God. At this point the High Priest moves before her at the east quarter, assuming God posture (Figure 25) as High Priestess summons (employing the tonals of the Luperci):

   Vorte tu apro Osa datae Lupercus! Orphae il athe daei aldus ayeo kae aeto. Nigla gai avato kiel nada omnae, arae il athe okri maedeta, doma akaes lae il ba!

5. At this time everyone is given a torch. Each member will move to the north, pause, then proceed to the south, where they will light their torch, and then move to the east and place an offering to Lupercus.

   High Priestess at the altar recites (as members are circling):

   O Ancient One, rayed in splendor and horned with power, embrace us, for without You we shall surely perish. It is now the appointed time and we offer You our worship. Warm now the sleeping seeds that lie beneath the cool Earth, within the womb of the Great Mother. Comfort us and renew our strength! Behold this circle of Your children; we have lit the ancient fires, and do faithfully serve you. We await Your emanation of warmth.

6. High Priestess goes to the east and gives the chalice of wine to the High Priest, which he then charges (wrapping chalice in fur piece and twisting it sunwise [clockwise] while visualizing the newly kindled Sun rise as he gazes into the wine).

7. High Priest addresses Grove members:

   Behold the cool drink of Immortality. For herein is the Essence of Life, and the Giving of Life. Let your hearts now be joyful, and come unto me and drink of the Light of Rejuvenation. Receive this into your blood, and be fulfilled.

8. Grove members move to the High Priest and receive the wine, one at a time.

9. High Priestess recites the final address:

   Let us now give due praise and adoration unto the Lord of Light. For he is the symbol of the Mystery by which we are reborn again. Let us always rejoice in His rising, for by this we are joined to the Essence of Rejuvenation, and Rebirth.

   Grove members respond:

   Hail and adoration unto You, O Lord of Light.

10. Chanting and drumming begins now as Grove members form a circle, sitting before the altar. High Priest moves away and adorns himself with the wolf cloak. High Priestess begins to extinguish all torches, except those of the altar, and opens

a gateway out of the circle. Members drink prepared wine from the chalice passed among them.

11. High Priest appears in the north quarter as Lupercus (dressed in wolf cloak) before the Grove, and is given the strap by the Maiden. High Priest addresses Grove members:

> *Come now and awaken to the lash of the God. Thus shall you be purified and rise anew from within.*

The Lord of Misrule

High Priestess moves to stand beside the High Priest. Everyone removes their robes and comes forward to the north quarter, in procession one at a time. Each member moves before the High Priest and High Priestess and is lashed by both (no one is to be harmed by this, as the force of the lash is meant to sting only). The breasts, back, and buttocks are struck on each person as they pass. After being lashed, each person leaves the circle through the gateway and crouches outside the circle, watching and waiting.

When everyone is outside, the High Priestess approaches them and says: "It is the time of the Wolf!" Grove members then disperse, and romp as wolves: running, howling, etc. They may chase and wrestle with each other, or go off and run the woods alone. Often this was a time for mischief-making on nearby villages.

Traditionally everyone will regather around a fire later, and when the sun rises they perform the Rite of Union to the Sun. If people will not be returning after the romp, then the circle must be closed beforehand.

SPRING EQUINOX — Equinozio della Primavera

Items required (other than usual):

Cauldron

Torch to represent the "God-light"

Torch to represent the Goddess' returning light

Offerings for the Goddess

Small cloth (hand size)

Small white cloth with a red stain (originally a wolf pelt)

Body oil

Pouch to hold offerings

Pouch of soil (worn by the High Priestess)

Pouch of seed (worn by the High Priest)

Seeds intended for planting (to be blessed)

1. Circle is cast in the usual manner.

2. High Priest addresses Grove members:

   We mark now with this time of gathering, the beginning of the Ascent of our Lady from the Hidden Realm of Shadows. For this is the time of Her desire for the light

and life of the world. We mark also the death of the Wolf God, and the splendor of
the new young God, rayed in power, Lord of the Sky.

Grove performs Rite of Union (Figure 22) to the altar (gazing upon the statues or
symbolic torches). High Priest and High Priestess place the seeds upon the white
cloth stained with a red mark, and bless the seeds for planting:

*Blessed be these seeds in the names of Tana and Tanus. May they grow strong and
abundant, providing a bountiful harvest for all.*

Grove responds:

In the names of Tana and Tanus, so be it done.

3. Maiden addresses Grove members:

*Now it came to pass that Tana longed for the light of the world, and for Her many
children. And she departed from the Hidden Realm, in secret, leaving the Dark
Lord in His solitude.*

Maiden reads the Ascent Myth:

The Myth of the Ascent

*Now the time came in the Hidden Realm of Shadows that Tana would bear the
Child of the Great Dark Lord. And the Lords of the Four Corners came and beheld
the newborn god. Then they spoke to Tana of the misery of the people who lived upon
the World, and how they suffered in cold and in darkness. So Tana bid the Lords to
carry Her son to the world, and so the people rejoiced for the Sun God had returned.*

*And it came to pass that Tana longed for the light of the world, and for Her many
children. So She journeyed to the world and was welcomed in great celebration.*

*Then Tana saw the splendor of the new god as He crossed the heavens, and she
desired Him. But each night He returned to the Hidden Realm and could not see the
beauty of the Goddess in the night sky.*

*So one morning the Goddess arose as the God came up from the Hidden Realm, and
She bathed nude in the sacred lake of Nemi. Then the Lords of the Four Corners
appeared to Him and said: "Behold the sweet beauty of the Goddess of the Earth."
And He looked upon Her and was struck with Her beauty so that He descended
upon the Earth in the form of a great stag.*

*"I have come to play beside your bath," He said, but Tana gazed upon the stag and
said: "You are not a stag but a god!" Then He answered: "I am Kern, God of the
Forest. Yet as a I stand upon the world, I touch also the sky, and I am Lupercus, the*

Sun, who banishes the Wolf Night. But beyond all of this, I am Tanus, the first born of all the Gods!"

Tana smiled and stepped forth from the water in all Her beauty. "I am Fana, goddess of the forest, yet even as I stand before you I am Diana, goddess of the Moon. But beyond all this I am Tana, first born of all Goddesses!"

And Faunus took Her by the hand, and together they walked in the meadows and forests, telling their tales of ancient mysteries. They loved and were One, and together they ruled over the world. Yet even in love, Tana knew that the God would soon cross over to the Hidden Realm and Death would come to the World. Then must She descend and embrace the Dark Lord, and bear the fruit of their Union.

4. High Priest speaks (from the north quarter):

   Where is my Lady?

5. High Priestess, beginning at the north, moves to each quarter bearing a lit torch, then (passing the north) stops at the east quarter.

6. Maiden replies to High Priest:

   O Dark One, Your Lady comes to us and we welcome Her with great rejoicing. All living things do know that She is near, and the world stirs with life again. Our Lady journeys now to meet us and Her Essence is upon the forest, field, and glen.

7. High Priestess calls out:

   Hear me, for now I draw near! Hear me, all who sleep from Winter's embrace, awaken unto rebirth, come forth now. Receive now my essence and be full with life, and the desire for life.

8. Maiden speaks to High Priestess:

   O Great Goddess of the earth, return to us in Your fair nature, lovely Maiden of youth, and joy and love. Only You can break the spell of Winter, and enchant the Earth with Your Essence. Hail to the Great Goddess!

High Priestess disrobes and assumes the Goddess posture (Figure 25). Maiden ties pouch of soil to waist cord of High Priestess, so that it is suspended over her pubic area.

Grove responds:

   Hail to the Great Goddess. All praise be to Tana!

Everyone then comes forward to the High Priestess and welcomes the Goddess by invoking the triangle of manifestation (Figure 24) upon her body with their fingertips (touch right breast, left breast, and pubic area) and then embracing her, saying:

Blessed be all in Tana.

Maiden then opens the pouch on the waist of the High Priestess, pours a small amount of wine into the pouch, then removes some of the damp soil, placing it on a small cloth. Maiden then sets the cloth into the cauldron.

9. Everyone comes forward and places an offering into the cauldron, which the Maiden places before the High Priestess. Prayers, requests, or blessings may be offered now. High Priestess remains in Goddess posture the whole time. When completed, High Priestess moves to the west quarter.

The Goddess Departing the Underworld

10. High Priest takes a lighted torch and treads the circle to all points, thrice, beginning at the north. As he begins the third pass, four Grove members (representing the Grigori) stop him at the east quarter and present him to the High Priestess, who now stands at the west quarter.

11. A "Grigori" addresses the High Priest:

    Behold the Beauty of the Goddess, She who is Fana, Lady of the Earth; She who is Jana, Mistress of the Moon; She who is Tana, Ruler of the Universe!

12. High Priest addresses High Priestess:

    You are truly the beauty of all things. You are the Earth, the sky and beyond.

13. Maiden goes to High Priest and ties the pouch of seeds upon his waist cord, so that it is suspended above his pubic area. Then a "Grigori" addresses the High Priestess:

    Behold the Power of the God. He who is Faunus, Lord of the Earth; He who is Janus, Master of the Heavens; He who is Tanus, Ruler of the Universe!

14. High Priestess addresses High Priest:

    You are truly the Power in all things. You are the Earth, the sky, and beyond.

15. High Priestess and High Priest anoint each other with the triangle of manifestation (Figure 24), and say to each other:

    Blessed be the Plow, the Seed, and the Furrow.

    Grove members repeat this upon a partner of the opposite sex.

16. High Priest disrobes, followed by all Grove members. Grove then forms a circle and all of the opposite sex exchange an embrace and a kiss.

17. While this is taking place, the Maiden goes to the High Priest, and opens the pouch of seeds. She takes out a small handful and then places them upon the cloth of soil within the cauldron.

18. The celebration concludes with wine and cakes, singing, feasting, etc.

    Afterward, the items within the cauldron are collected and placed within a pouch or bag. Grove members will later bury the pouch in a planting field (for increase of crops) or will suspend it from a tree within the woods (for an abundant hunt). In ancient times the entire Grove would copulate with one another upon the tilled soil or within the woods, to charge the area with fertile energy.

TANA' S DAY — La Giornata di Tana
May 1

Items required:

    Crown wreath of flowers

    Small candle for each member

    Bottle of body oil

    Fresh flower (picked by the High Priestess)

    Ritual sword

1. Circle is cast in usual manner. All members are nude within the circle.

2. High Priest addresses Grove members:

   We gather at this joyous time and welcome the return of our Lady. That which began in the Time of Shadows has come to its fullness. Cycle unto cycle, time unto time, age unto age.

   As it was in the time of our beginning, so is it now, so shall it be.

3. At the southern quarter, the High Priest calls down the Goddess upon the High Priestess (who assumes the Goddess posture [figure 25]), as the Maiden addresses the Grove:

   By and by all things pass, season unto season, year unto year. Our Lady has come again to Her Hidden Children of Time. And our Goddess ever bestows love and peace, and guards and cherishes Her Hidden Children in life.

   In Death She teaches the way to Her Communion, and in this world She teaches them the mystery of the magick circle, which is placed between the worlds of men and of the gods. And for this our Lady descended, in times of old, into the Realm of Shadows.

   And the Lord of the Shadows was bewitched by Her Beauty. And He taught Her the mysteries of Death and Rebirth. And in love He bowed before Her and gave Her all of His Power.

   Grove members perform the Rite of Union (Figure 22) to the High Priestess, who stands in Goddess posture (Figure 25).

4. High Priest kneels before the High Priestess and lays down his sword, saying:

   My lady, I give all my power to You, for this is so ordained. And with love I submit to You, and I give my reign over to Your hands.

150

The Goddess Tana

5. High Priestess takes up the sword and gives the Charge of Aradia:

> *Whenever you have need of anything, once in the month when the Moon is full, then shall you come together at some deserted place, or where there are woods, and give worship to She who is Queen of all Witches.*
>
> *Come all together inside a circle, and secrets that are as yet unknown shall be revealed. And your mind must be free and also your spirit, and as a sign that you are truly free, you shall be naked in your rites. And you shall rejoice, and sing; making music and love. For this is the essence of spirit, and the knowledge of joy.*
>
> *Be true to your own beliefs, and keep to the Ways, beyond all obstacles. For ours is the key to the mysteries and the cycle of rebirth, which opens the way to the Womb of Enlightenment. I am the spirit of Witches all, and this is joy and peace and harmony.*
>
> *In life does the Queen of all Witches reveal the knowledge of spirit. And from death does the Queen deliver you to peace.*
>
> *When I shall have departed from this world, in memory of me make cakes of grain, wine, and honey. These shall you shape like the Moon, and then partake of wine and cakes all in my memory. For I have been sent to you by the Spirits of Old, and I have come that you might be delivered from all slavery. I am the daughter of the Sun and Moon, and even though I have been born into this world, my race is of the stars.*
>
> *Give offerings all to She who is our mother. For She is the beauty of the Green Wood, and the light of the Moon among the stars, and the mystery which gives life, and always calls us to come together in Her name.*
>
> *Let Her worship be the ways within your heart, for all acts of love and pleasure are like rituals to the Goddess. But to all who seek her, know that your seeking and desire will reward you not, until you realize the secret. Because if that which you seek is not found within your inner self, you will never find it from without. For she has been with you since you entered into the ways, and she is that which awaits at your journey's end.*

6. High Priestess moves to the east quarter, setting the sword before the altar as she goes, and assumes the Goddess posture (Figure 25). High Priest gives address:

> *Hail and adoration O Great Tana! You who are the Great Star Goddess, Queen of Heaven, Lady of the Earth, we welcome You, and rejoice in Your presence.*

Maiden then places the fresh flower into the waist cord of the High Priestess, inserting the stem so that the flower is positioned above the pubic area.

All males and females will come forward and embrace the High Priestess, saying:

Blessed be all in the Goddess.

7. High Priest then takes a chalice of wine to the High Priestess. Everyone will then go before the altar and chant "Tana" as the High Priestess charges the wine (breathing out upon the surface of the wine, then dipping the flower from her waist into the chalice).

   High Priest then leads the Grove to the east quarter to receive the wine (essence of the Goddess) of which they all drink.

8. High Priest will take a crown (of flowers) and place it upon the head of the High Priestess. They will then kiss and embrace. All Grove members will then come forward and embrace the High Priestess also (one at a time). Each person will receive a torch (token of the Life Force), which is lit from the Goddess-candle. Candles may be set aside for continuation of rite.

9. The Grove will then form a circle along the ritual circle's perimeter line, facing inward. Each person will then go around the circle, kissing and embracing each member of the opposite gender.

10. Ritual celebration continues with cakes and wine. In ancient times the Grove joined in sexual union to affirm life and fertility.

SUMMER FEST — La Festa dell' Estate

Items required (in addition to standard ritual set-up):

Flowers for procession

Symbol for God and Goddess

Cauldron

Libation fluid (nectar/ambrosia)

4 small bowls for libation (at quarters)

Offerings (one for deities and another for Nature spirits)

Fennel stalk

Sorghum stalk

1. Cast circle in usual manner, then open a threshold at the northeast.

2. Grove members form a line, making a corridor (at the northeast) into the circle.

3. High Priest and High Priestess pass through the corridor into the circle. All members toss flowers about them as they walk.

4. All enter the circle behind them, and then the threshold is sealed.

5. High Priestess gives address (at the altar) to the Grove members:

> *We gather now on this sacred night of Summer's Eve, and join ourselves to the powers and forces of this mystical season. On this night the Folletti gather, as do all those spirits of Nature to which we are kindred. For the Witch and the Fata are of a similar race. So it was in the time of our beginning, so is it now, so shall it be.*

The Union of Dianus and Diana

6. Symbols of the God and Goddess are placed before the cauldron, which is set at the southern quarter.

High Priest addresses the Grove:

Here is the Divine Couple, whose Union gives Life to the World.

Grove responds:

Blessed be all in the God and Goddess.

Grove performs Rite of Union (Figure 22) facing the symbols.

7. Grove members now come forward and place Deity offerings in the cauldron, at the south quarter.

8. Appointed members then go to each of the four quarters and pour a libation of nectar into the bowls set there for libation.

9. All Grove members now place Nature spirit offerings at the four quarters.

10. High Priestess speaks from the altar:

O spirits of the Elemental forces, hear me, and receive our blessings. O spirits of the Earth, O powers that be, hear me and receive our blessings. Assist us on this sacred night to maintain the natural balance which keeps vital the essence of the earth. Let there always be clear, flowing water, freshness in the air, fertility within the soil, and abundant life within the world.

11. High Priestess and High Priest direct the drama play of the struggle between the forces of Light and Darkness. The fennel stalk represents the powers of Light and the sorghum stalk represents the powers of Darkness. Ritual combat begins at the east quarter and continues around the circle, ending at the north. At the completion, the sorghum stalk is broken, the fennel stalk is raised in victory, and is then presented at each quarter. Grove responds with cheers of approval.

12. Grove then assembles in a circle to raise the Cone of Power. (Concerning the Cone of Power: Grove members form a circle around the High Priest or High Priestess [whichever is directing]. The Grove stands, the director sits or kneels. The method may be performed with cords or wands. Grove moves in a circle sunwise, around the director. The chant should be simple, using a Deity name or a word of power. When the signal to release is given, the members drop to the ground and the director quickly rises up and hurls the Cone upward.) High Priest or High Priestess addresses Grove members as they prepare themselves:

We form this Cone of Power to be a positive force, whereby we charge You, O Sacred Ether of our world. Be free of all evil and negativity. We charge you for the good of all life within our world.

Grove is then directed to raise the Cone of Power.

13. Once formed, the High Priestess, or High Priest, signals the release of power, and directs the Cone up into the ether of the community.

14. End ritual with celebration of cakes and wine. Close circle. Leave libation bowls out overnight for the nature spirits.

It is said that on the night of Summer's Eve, all the spirits of nature are in celebration. Fairies, elves, and all the "little folk" gather in meadows, forests, and any secret or hidden place. If you see them or can find any evidence of their celebration the next day, then you will receive a special blessing. Should you come across any of their gathering sites, be sure not to disturb anything. Leave everything as you found it.

CORNUCOPIA
July 31

Items required (other than usual ritual items):

  1 cornucopia icon

  Offerings for the harvest

  Body oil/massage oil

  Cornucopia incense

1. Circle is cast in the usual manner.

2. High Priestess addresses Grove members:

   We gather now on this appointed day in anticipation of plenty. Now do we acknowledge the Grace of the Earth Mother and the Sky Father. From Him have we received the Sacred Emanation, which the Mother has nurtured, and delivers unto us.

   Grove members perform Rite of Union (Figure 22) to the altar torches/symbols of God and Goddess.

3. Grove members are directed to give offerings at the south, as High Priestess addresses:

Let us now go forth and give offerings to the Great God and Goddess. And let us be thankful of all that we have which is good in our lives. For the Great Ones provide for us, and we must always remember Them and give thanks.

Chanting or singing is performed during the offerings.

4. High Priest lights cauldron, following the offering, at the south quarter and places a token of his needs/requests in the flames. Grove members come forth, one at a time, and do the same (requests may be written on parchment or cloth, and burned in the cauldron fire).

5. High Priestess speaks at the altar, as High Priest pours sweet herb incense into the cauldron flames:

   I call out to You, O Tana and Tanus, and pray that You receive our wishes and desires as they rise up to you on the smoke of our incense. We ask that You grant our requests and bring them to their fullness, even as You bring forth the fruit from the seed.

   Grove members reply:

   So be it done.

6. High Priestess addresses Grove from the altar.

   Now hear the words of Aradia: "Know that every action brings forth another, and that these actions are linked together through their natures. Therefore, whatsoever you send forth, so shall you receive. A farmer can harvest for himself no more than he plants. Therefore, let us consider what is good in our lives, and what is full. Let us also consider what is bad and what is empty. And let us meditate upon the reasons for all of these things."

7. High Priest and High Priestess bless the ritual cakes and wine: High Priestess kneels with chalice of wine before the High Priest. High Priest lowers his wand into the wine, saying:

   Herein is the Essence of the union of Tanus and Tana, wherein all things are renewed and made vital.

   High Priest kneels before the High Priestess holding up the ritual cakes to her. High Priestess makes the sign of Union (Figure 22) with her hand over them, saying:

   Here is the substance of the Union of Tanus and Tana, wherein all things are established and renewed.

8. Grove members come forth to receive the cakes and wine, one at a time. As each one is given the chalice and drinks of the wine, the High Priest or High Priestess says:

   In the names of Tana and Tanus, blessed be.

9. Ritual ends with celebration of the coming harvest. High Priest holds up the wand, High Priestess holds up the chalice (or small cauldron). High Priestess speaks:

   Blessed be the Plow, the Seed, and the Furrow.

Grove members then pair off male and female, and move together. Females brush the males' chest with the palms of their hands, and down their arm muscles.

The Ripe Harvest

Females say:

> *Blessed be your strength.*

Males then brush the females' womb areas with their palms, and say:

> *Blessed be your mysteries.*

Females lift up the wand, saying:

> *Blessed be the plow.*

Males then lift up the chalice, saying:

> *Blessed be the furrow.*

Females then touch wand to males' pubic areas, saying:

> *Blessed be thy ripened grain.*

Males then place the chalice upon the center of the females' chests saying:

> *Blessed be thy place of nurture.*

High Priestess speaks:

> *Blessed be the Plow, the Seed, and the Furrow.*

Traditionally everyone slipped away into the fields and engaged in sexual activity, laying among the crops, to conclude the ritual.

If any females are visibly pregnant, they are brought forward and their bodies are oiled by selected Grove members (oil olive or any safe massage oil). Then they are presented to the four quarters, with the High Priestess saying:

> *Behold the Earth Mother, the fullness of Her harvest to come. Blessed be She who bears fruit.*

AUTUMN EQUINOX — Equinozio di Autunno

Required items (other than usual ritual items):

Candle or torch to represent the "God-flame"

Ruta (sprig of rue)

Small vessel to receive grain "essence"

Cauldron for offerings

Grain and pouch

Loaf of bread

Red cord to tie around God-candle on altar

Oak leaves and vessel to contain them

1. Circle is cast in the usual manner.

2. High Priest at the altar says:

> *We gather at this sacred time to rejoice for the abundance which has come into the world. Yet also do we honor Kern, our Lord who is sacrificed for our sake. The time has come when all things have grown into their fullness, and are gathered by hunter and fieldsman. As it was in the time of our beginning, so is it now, so shall it be.*

3. High Priest stands to the east, then moves to the west, bearing the God-flame candle or torch. High Priestess addresses him at the west (giving him a chalice filled with the wine of farewell, containing also a sprig of rue. The rue is taken from the whole plant of which two pieces are used at the Autumn Equinox, and the rest dried and saved for Winter Solstice. It is the symbol of death and rebirth, waxing and waning; it is the god-root plant. This plant is grown from the seed planted at the Spring Equinox):

> *Farewell, O Janus, Lord of Two Faces, who stands in the Light and within the Darkness. The Hidden God who ever remains, and ever departs to the Hidden Realm through the Gate of Shadows; Ruler of the heights and of the depths. Farewell O Faunus. Lord of the Earth. Within You is the union of men and Gods. You dwell within the Sacred Seed, the seed of ripened grain and the seed of flesh. You are hidden in the Earth, and You rise up to touch the stars.*

Maiden ties pouch of grain to waist cord of High Priest, positioning it to hang above his pubic area.

Grove performs Rite of Union (Figure 22) to the High Priest, as he stands in the God posture (Figure 25) with ritual wand and God-flame.

4. Female Grove members go to each quarter (beginning north) and dance from quarter to quarter. When they come to the High Priest, they ritually seize him by the arms. The maiden then takes his ritual wand in her hand and, with the other females, leads him back around each quarter, returning to the west.

Then the Maiden embraces him, gives him a kiss of farewell, removes the pouch suspended from his waist, and places it in the vessel set within the cauldron of offering. Maiden then hands him a sprig of rue and extinguishes the High Priest's flame.

5. High Priestess addresses Grove members:

> *The God has departed from His shining abode in the heavens, for the season has come. And Death shall come to the world for the Winter draws near. The Lord of Light now becomes the Lord of the Shadows.*

6. A vessel is brought out and placed in the west. Everyone will come forward, one at a time, and place some oak leaves within it. Then they will taste some of the grain that is placed beside the vessel.

7. High Priestess recites a portion of the Mythos:

> *In the earliest times, our Lord and Lady lived in the ancient forest of Nemi. Now our Lady seduced the Lord and there did She receive the sacred seed from which all things spring forth.*
>
> *But our Lord knew not the secret which only the Goddess understood, for She had drawn the life from Him. And the World was abundant with all manner of animal, and that which grows from the Earth.*
>
> *Now there came a time when all things grew to their fullness, and were to be gathered by hunter and fieldsman alike. And in that time was the God slain and drawn into the Harvest.*

8. High Priest is brought to the north. He is fully cloaked and his hood is drawn up over his head (which is bowed down). Female attendants hold him on each side. High Priestess leads the Grove from the south past him twice. Grove members salute as they pass each time.

9. The Hooded One assumes the God Posture (Figure 25) at the west quarter. The High Priestess goes and stands before the Hooded One, and they begin the sacred dialogue:

> (Goddess) *I have come in search of Thee, is this where I begin?*
>
> (God) *Begin to seek me out, and I shall become as small as a seed, so you may but pass me by.*
>
> (Grove) *Then we shall split the rind, crack the grain, and break the pod.*
>
> (God) *But I shall hide beneath the earth, and lay so still, that you may but pass me by.*
>
> (Goddess) *Then I shall raise you up in praise, and place upon you a mantle of green.*

(God) *But I shall hide within the green, and cover myself, and you may but pass me by.*

(Grove) *Then we shall tear the husk, and pull the root and thresh the chaff.*

(God) *But I shall scatter, and divide, and be so many, that you may but pass me by.*

(Grove) *Then we shall gather you in, and bind you whole, and make you One again.*

10. Maiden comes forward to the altar, passing first each quarter from the north, carrying the sacred loaf.

Embracing the Slain God

11. High Priestess addresses Grove members (holding ritual dagger, pointed at the loaf upon the altar):

   Behold the Harvest Lord.

   Grove responds:

   Blessed be the Lord of the Harvest.

12. High Priestess cuts the loaf into pieces, one for each Grove member.

   Everyone then comes forward and receives a piece of the loaf. When everyone has one, the High Priestess says:

   Behold the Lord, the Green Man, the Stag King, the Hooded Man. Let us take Him within us, and be as one.

   Everyone eats a piece of the loaf but leaves a small portion. (Traditionally a piece of each loaf slice is placed within the cauldron. It is then ground into crumbs and distributed into the fields, forests, lakes, or hills.)

13. High Priestess passes the chalice of wine, and bids all to drink, then speaks:

   Behold, you are now as one, you are of the blood. That which was, at the time of beginning, is now, and always shall be.

Grove responds:

   As it was in the time of our beginning, so is it now, so shall it be. Blessed be all!

Celebration concludes with cakes and wine, music and merriment!

Three Aspects of Life

13

The Rites of Community

*For there are three mysteries in the life of man which are: birth, sex, and death
(and love controls them all). To fulfill love, you must return again at the same time
and place as those who loved before. And you must meet, recognize, remember,
and love them anew.*

from the text

A sense of community permeated all aspects of life in the early days of the
Clan. The birth of a child, the wedding of a man and woman, and the
death of a member were all integral parts of tribal existence. This cycle
was just as much a part of the understanding of life as were the cycles of
Nature. It is only natural that rituals were created to acknowledge these
aspects of human experience, and that each was interwoven with the religious and magickal practices of the Clan.

The following modern rites of community are derived from three separate traditions of Italian Witchcraft. The ceremony to bless a child is
from the Tuscan witches of northern Italy. The marriage rite is from the
modern Aridian Tradition in the United States, and the burial rite is from
the coastal region of central Italy. Although these are essentially a blend

of Janarric and Tanarric rites, it is common to the Triad Traditions as a whole. I have added modern material to this section in order to make its use universal. Some readers may find certain older elements of the child blessing a little disquieting, but alternative methods are provided to accommodate personal inhibitions.

BLESSING OF A CHILD OF THE CLAN

This is a ceremony for a child born into the Clan, or adopted in whatever manner. Traditionally the parents will chose someone to be "of the Fata" for the child (either an individual or another couple). This is someone who will see to the child's spiritual well-being, should the parents become absent in the child's life. The term "of the Fata" dates back to the early belief that the Strega were, in some way, related to the Nature spirits (or more specifically to the Fay, or Fairy Race). In this rite is preserved the ancient Etruscan ceremony in which someone is adopted into the family by suckling on the mother's breast.

Traditionally, the ceremony is performed on the first full moon following the birth of the child.

1. A ritual circle may be cast in the usual manner, or a circle may be marked out with flowers or leaves. Traditionally the leaves are from laurel boughs and the flowers are rosolaccio blossoms (rose-lace, also known as red poppy or cornflower).

2. The child is blessed by the High Priest(ess), who anoints the soles of the child's feet and forehead with olive oil, using a sprig of rue:

   May the Lord and Lady look upon you always with great favor, and may your days be filled with all that is good in life. In the names of Tana and Tanus, so be you blessed.

3. High Priest(ess) addresses parents:

   You have been chosen by our Lord and Lady to raise and care for this child. May your days be filled with all that is good in life, and may Tana and Tanus bless you and watch over you.

4. High Priest addresses parents:

   Have you chosen someone to be "of the Fata"?

   Parents reply:

   We have chosen (name of person).

   High Priest(ess) addresses the chosen one:

Is this your wish to be of the Fata for this child?

Fata parent replies:

It is.

5. High Priest(ess) addresses parents and Fata parent:

You must then be joined together through the link of Mother and Child, and become of one family, intimately bonded to blood and clan. You must be nurturer and nurtured. As it was in the time of our beginning, so is it now, so shall it be.

6. Birth mother then suckles the child and the Fata parent with milk from her breasts. They may suckle together, or one at a time. In the case of an older child or a mother who has no breast milk, a cup of goat's milk can be substituted. In this case the mother will dip her nipple into the cup of milk and then the cup is offered to the child and the Fata parent. If the mother is lactating, but personal inhibitions prevent the suckling of her breast, then the cup method can be used with the mother's milk instead of goat's milk.

7. The child is then presented to the four Quarters by he or she who has been chosen to be "of the Fata."

8. Members of the family and friends may now come forward and offer tokens to the child which symbolize their wishes for the child as he or she grows. Upon presentation, the person will say the child's name, and then say:

I wish for you (name of virtue or wish, etc.).

These items will be kept for the child to be later placed in his or her Nanta bag. Some examples of tokens and their significance:

A shell: abundance and fullness in life

A raven's feather: wisdom, cunning, and a sense of humor

A flower: spiritual gifts of healing and cleansing

A stone: strength and fortitude, strong in nature

A hawk's feather: hunting skills and keen senses

A stag horn: virility and strong ties to Clan, personal power

A coin: prosperity

A rabbit's foot: good luck

9. Ceremony is concluded. Close circle and proceed with social occasion.

THE MARRIAGE RITE

Traditionally the bride wears a saffron-colored gown with a red veil. The groom is dressed in green. Around the waist of the bride is tied the Knot of Magick (by the parents of the bride), which the groom will later untie prior to the consummation of the marriage. On the day before the ceremony, the bride and groom will make a laurel cake together. This cake will symbolize the union of their lives.

Wreaths/garlands of myrtle with orange blossoms are worn by the bride and groom to the place of the ceremony. Traditionally there is a procession to the site by the wedding party, and flowers are strewn out before the couple, along with leaves of rosemary and bay. The flowers may be of any of the following: primroses, violets, daisies, or roses.

Traditionally the bride will offer three coins to complete the rite of marriage: One to the groom, one to the crossroad, and the last coin she will place upon the hearth, at the couple's place of dwelling.

1. A circle of flowers is laid out to mark the wedding site. The circle is cast by the High Priest(ess) and a doorway is left at the northeast.

2. Attendants form a walkway into the circle. The couple then follows the High Priestess and High Priest into the circle. Attendants toss flowers upon them as they pass.

3. High Priest(ess) and couple move to the altar. The ritual circle remains open.

4. High Priest(ess) presents the laurel cake to the gods at the north quarter. Couple proceeds around the altar to the face of the altar.

5. High Priest(ess) addresses couple (who are holding the cake):

> *(Groom's name) and (bride's name) you have come into this Sacred Circle, and before those assembled here this day, to join together your lives and your futures, so that they may become as one.*
>
> *This sacred cake, which you have made together, symbolizes the union of your love and your lives. Partake of this cake, and in the openness of your love for each other you shall be joined together.*
>
> *(Bride's name) is this your desire? (reply: It is.)*
>
> *(Groom's name) is this your desire? (reply: It is.)*
>
> *Partake then now of the Sacred Cake of Wedding.*

6. Bride and groom offer each other a bit of the cake. Bride offers to the groom first, and then the groom offers to the bride.

7. High Priest(ess) blesses the tokens (rings) of Oneness, and then addresses the couple:

Uni Suckling Hercules (the Adoption)

These are the symbols of your love, which you have chosen to wear, so that all may know of this special relationship between the two of you, and of the joining together of your love, your lives, and your paths.

8. High Priest(ess) presents bride's ring to groom and says:

Take this token and present it to your beloved (groom complies) and repeat after me: "This is a symbol of my love for you." (Groom repeats.)

Bride accepts the token upon her left hand (ring finger). High Priest(ess) addresses bride:

(Bride's name) repeat after me: "I receive this token of your love, and I will wear it always as a symbol of my love for you, and of your love for me."

9. High Priest(ess) presents the groom's token to bride and repeats the procedure in step 8 (reversing roles).

10. High Priest(ess) blesses the couple, and says:

In the names of Tana and Tanus I bless this Union. May your love make fruitful all of your desires, and may your future be prosperous, and may the gods grant you the best of fortune ever.

11. High Priest(ess) binds the right hand of the groom to the left hand of the bride with a wedding cord.

12. High Priest(ess) places a sprig of rosemary herb in the groom's right hand, and a laurel leaf in the bride's left hand, and says:

Where he is Lord, she is Lady.

13. High Priest(ess) taps bride and groom upon their chests with the ritual wand, and says:

(Bride's name) and (groom's name) in accordance with our ways, and before those who have gathered here, I now declare you husband and wife. (couple kisses.)

The ceremony is completed.

THE RITE OF PASSAGE FOR THE SOUL

Traditionally the body is cremated, although the Fanarra Clan was known to practice burial of the whole body in the forest. During the Middle Ages, the magickal practice was to cremate the body upon a structure of cedar, sandalwood, and juniper wood. The Janarra were known to have made a raft upon which these woods were piled. The body was then laid upon the wood and the wood was ignited. Then the raft was pushed out upon the lake, or the bay, symbolizing the journey to the Realm of Luna.

Preparation of the Body

The body should be anointed upon the forehead center, chest center, and just below the navel, with an oil of pennyroyal. The Clan mask should be painted upon the face, along

The Rite of Marriage

with the forearm and hand symbols. The body should be clad in either the ritual robe or some article of clothing which the person may have designated (or would have been known to have desired).

Placed with the body should be the cord of initiation, along with the person's book of the Old Ways. Their physical ritual tools may be included or passed down to another person.

1. At the site of the burial, High Priest(ess) addresses those assembled:

> *We have come to the time now when _____ must begin the sacred journey to the Realm of Luna. He/She knows now the Mystery that is forgotten in this life, and has therefore attained the greatest of all initiations. Let us not bind our friend to this world with our longing for him/her, nor burden his/her spirit with our sorrow. Let us release our friend with love, even as a parent must free a child who has grown.*
>
> *Blessed be _____ (everyone repeats), we wish you love and light to be with you on your journey, and happiness with the beautiful realms into which you pass. Blessed be.*
> *(all repeat).*

2. Ritual bell tolls thrice. High Priest(ess) then reads the "Myth of the Descent of the Goddess" aloud to all.

> *Tana, our Lady and Goddess, would solve all mysteries, even the mystery of Death. And so she journeyed to the Underworld in her boat, upon the Sacred River of Descent. Then it came to pass that she entered before the first of the seven gates to the Underworld. And the Guardian challenged her, demanding one of her garments for passage, for nothing may be received except that something be given in return. And at each of the gates the Goddess was required to pay the price of passage, for the Guardians spoke to her: "Strip off your garments, and set aside your jewels, for nothing may you bring with you into this, our realm."*
>
> *So Tana surrendered her jewels and her clothing to the Guardians, and was bound as all living must be who seek to enter the realm of Death and the Mighty Ones. At the first gate she gave over her scepter, at the second her crown, at the third her necklace, at the fourth her ring, at the fifth her girdle, at the sixth her sandals, and at the seventh her gown. Tana stood naked and was presented before Dis, and such was her beauty that he himself knelt as she entered. He laid his crown and his sword at her feet saying: "Blessed are your feet that have brought you down this path." Then he arose and said to Tana: "Stay with me, I pray, and receive my touch upon your heart."*

And Tana replied to Dis: "But I love you not, for why do you cause all the things that I love, and take delight in, to fade and die?"

"My Lady" replied Dis, "it is age and fate against which you speak. I am helpless, for age causes all things to wither, but when men die at the end of their time, I give them rest, peace and strength. For a time they dwell with the Moon, and the spirits of the Moon; then may they return to the realm of the living. But you are so lovely, and I ask you to return not, but abide with me here."

But she answered: "No, for I do not love you." Then Dis said: "If you refuse to embrace me, then you must kneel to death's scourge." The Goddess answered him: "If it is to be, then it is fate, and better so!" So Tana knelt in submission before the hand of death, and he scourged her with so tender a hand that she cried out: "I know your pain, and the pain of love."

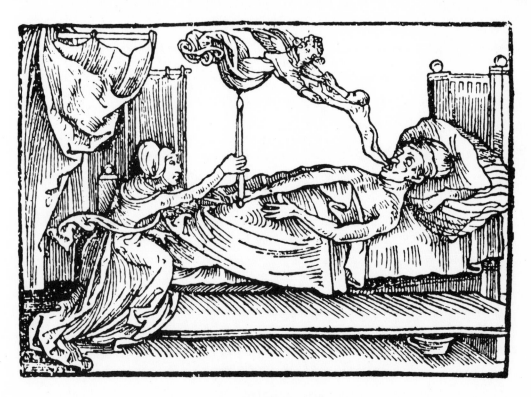

Passage of the Soul

Dis raised her to her feet and said: "Blessed are you, my Queen and my Lady." Then he gave to her the five kisses of initiation, saying: "Only thus may you attain to knowledge and to joy."

And he taught her all of his mysteries, and he gave her the necklace which is the circle of rebirth. And she taught him her mysteries of the sacred cup which is the cauldron of rebirth.

They loved and joined in union with each other, and for a time Tana dwelled in the realm of Dis.

For there are three mysteries in the life of man which are: birth, sex, and death (and love controls them all). To fulfill love, you must return again at the same time and place as those who loved before. And you must meet, recognize, remember, and love them anew. But to be reborn you must die and be made ready for a new body. And to die you must be born, but without love you may not be born among your own.

But our Goddess is inclined to favor love, and joy and happiness. She guards and cherishes her hidden children in this life and the next. In death she reveals the way to her communion, and in life she teaches them the magick of the mystery of the circle (which is set between the worlds of men and of the gods).

3. High Priest(ess) addresses the Gods:

We call upon you now, O Great Lord and Lady, to grant comfort and enlightenment to our friend. To forgive his/her offenses in this life, and to shorten the time of resolution which awaits him/her. For we trust in your love and compassion.

And when the time has come for our friend to return, grant him/her a healthy body and mind, and a good life among his/her loved ones. In your names, O Great Ones, so be it done.

(All repeat) So be it done.

4. Now anyone who wishes to speak about the departed may do so. Memories may be shared, deeds retold, and so on.

5. Each person attending may come forward now before the vessel containing the ashes and personally bid their friend farewell. Singing or chanting may begin at this time.

6. In conclusion the funeral prayer is recited:

We gather now in honor of our brother/sister who has crossed over and begun the sacred journey to the Realms of Luna. We wish you well on your journey, and send with you the emanations of our love, and our friendship. We know that the sorrow which we feel is of our own making. There has been no loss among us, for we shall meet each other again in a future life to come. And we shall remember, and know each other, and love again. We shall speak your name and remember you at Shadowfest. If it is that we shall see you, or speak with you, then let it be of your own desire. For it is not our wish that our desires should bind you to this life.

May the Great Lord and Lady receive you into their care, and may they comfort you and prepare you to be born anew.

May the realms of Luna give you all that you desire, and may you find peace and pleasure, and reunion with those who have gone before.

Farewell dear brother/sister, farewell dear friend. Blessed be.

The ashes are then scattered (or buried) and everyone may toss flowers or other tokens as the body is received by the Great Mother. If the body was set out on a raft upon the lake or ocean, then the tokens may simply be tossed into the water as the raft burns. It is completed.

An Angel Head

14

The Art of Magick

If the celebrants can then put themselves totally into the ritual moment, power can be generated and magick is created naturally.

from the text

Most people are aware of the definition of magick as "the manifestation of desire through will." More accurately, magick is the manifestation and directed focus of states of consciousness. I sort magick into the following categories, which we shall examine in this chapter: Natural Magick, Personal Magick, Spirit Magick, and Deity Magick.

Even though each level of magick is unique they are often combined in such arts as spell casting and ritual magick. When viewing a work of magick, it is important to understand that everything within its structure is designed to influence the state of consciousness. Every human possesses the "Divine spark" of their creator, and therefore has their own ability to create. The consciousness acts as the "hands of the potter," kneading and forming the "clay" of raw magickal energy. It is the will that gives the thought its form, and directs the current of energy to accomplish the work at hand. Let us now look at each aspect of magick.

NATURAL MAGICK

Natural Magick incorporates the mundane into a focused act of manifesting will or desire. These mundane things can be anything from crystals or herbs to oils, potions, and natural phenomenon. On a very basic level, let's take a look at something that you may never have thought of as magick. When getting ready for a date, or perhaps a job interview, we select certain clothes (incorporating color and design), which we feel make us more desirable.

We may then add a scent with perfume or cologne. Makeup, hair, and personal grooming complete the ritual. Usually a change takes place in our consciousness as we periodically look in the mirror to check our appearance. To a certain extent, this part of the process may be thought of as self-enchantment, and actually can serve to add additional power to the effect.

Once everything is perfect, we have created the necessary personality with which to carry out our desired influence. We look good and we feel good in proportion, thus we are generating energy outward. Should someone comment on our outfit, scent, or overall look, the "enchantment" then begins to take effect.

In a very similar manner, the setting up of a ritual circle also establishes a change in consciousness. As the area is marked, the altar arranged, candles set, there is a gradual air of magick established. Once the celebrants have robed (or disrobed) everyone is "transformed" from their everyday personality into something special. There has been a change of consciousness. This can be amplified by wearing crystals or other power objects. If the celebrants can then put themselves totally into the ritual moment, power can be generated and magick is created naturally.

Serpent of Magick

PERSONAL MAGICK

Personal magick is the ability to change one's consciousness at will, and to collect and focus energy. Usually this is acquired through much practice and devotion to the Arts of Magick. In some cases, certain individuals may naturally have access to these abilities with little or no effort on their part.

The basic components of Personal Magick are: imagination, visualization, will, and expectation. In many books these are symbolized by "the magickal triangle." Expectation (for some reason) is usually omitted in the average book on magick. It is important to note that if you do not expect any results, then there probably won't be any.

To activate personal power, one must employ the aspects of the triangle while establishing Personal Magick. This is often accomplished through acting, drama, or sexual stimulation, or anything that will serve to get you "worked up" or energized. Watch young children at play sometime, and you will see a very good example of personal magick. When a child is putting everything he or she has into being a "Super Hero," or a "Warrior," then in his or her mind, this becomes a reality. Fortunately for us adults, children lack the focus and will required to manifest their desires. However, every parent knows that children do possess another awesome set of powerful tools with which to manifest their desires. Simply observe them in any store or shopping mall. It's a lot scarier than most forms of magick.

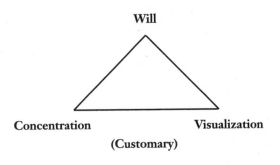

Will

Concentration   Visualization

(Customary)

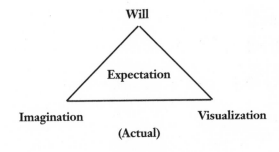

Will

Expectation

Imagination   Visualization

(Actual)

Figure 26
The Magickal Triangle

SPIRIT MAGICK

Spirit Magick is the attracting and drawing of spirit entities for the purpose of empowering a ritual or work of magick. Traditionally these would be spirits of the Elemental Forces of Earth, Air, Fire, and Water. Since these elements comprise all of creation, it is logical to incorporate elemental spirits into formation of any desired manifestation.

Spirits from any realm can be called upon for the purposes of magick. This would include elven or fairy spirits, along with various Astral entities. It is important that you provide an offering to attract the spirit, and an environment in which to draw the spirit. For example, you would not evoke a fire elemental into a bowl of water, or a water elemental into a bowl of soil. Well, at least you wouldn't be doing that for very long (karma is watching . . .). In other words, if you want a fish as a pet, you must provide it with an environment which will allow it to function as a fish. The same is true of any spirit which you call upon. If you do not do so, then these spirits will quickly disperse. Respect, trust, and rapport are essential to successful Spirit Magick. Make sure this foundation is solid.

DEITY MAGICK

Deity Magick is the ability to call upon the gods for assistance. This is essentially your spirituality and your rapport with Deity. One very common error people make in this relationship is that of trying to turn the gods into personal servants. Another mistake is lack of common courtesy. People often begin by requesting something from their deity, without any preliminary dialogue. It is important to first call upon the name of the deity and to express your feelings about them, or admiration of them. After this you may proceed with your needs.

When we phone a friend, we first exchange greetings and concern for each other's well-being, before we get to the point of the phone call. It would be rude to bypass the greeting and "how are you doing?" elements, and in the case of Deity it is absolutely foolish. Yet many people commonly do just that, and then wonder why things are not progressing the way they desired.

Another error commonly made is to not address Deity for months at a time, and then call upon them in time of need. Just like any relationship, you must keep in touch during the good times, if you expect any help in the bad times. Essentially, I'm addressing rapport with the Deity. Establish an altar, and greet your Deity each day. Give thanks, place offerings of flowers, show appreciation, be loving, be loyal.

THE FORMULA OF MAGICK

Now that we have looked at the components of magick, we must now understand how to make it work. The inner mechanism of magick is animated through a formula which is as follows:

1. Purpose or intent

2. Required objects or ingredients needed

3. Tools (to establish and direct magickal energy)

4. Symbols or sigils (to attract and focus)

5. Vehicle or element to "carry" the magick to its "target"

6. Direction or location of target

7. Proper setting and timing for the work of magick

8. Offerings for assistance

9. Release of energy

To serve as an example of this formula in action, I will use the sending of a letter as an analogy. The purpose of my letter will be to obtain a mail-order catalog. Knowing what my purpose is, I must consider what is required to accomplish my goal: I will need a pen and paper, an envelope, a stamp, and $3.00 for the catalog.

The pen and paper are my ritual tools. The words which I write will be sigils which are understood by both myself and the receiver (Celtic runes would be useless in addressing Italian deities). The envelope is the vehicle (or element) which will carry my magick. The address is the direction in which my desire abides. The stamp is an offering to the spirit who will assist my spell (the postal worker), and the $3.00 is an offering to attract the entities who possess the catalog, in hopes that they will respond to my desire.

Having collected all that is required, I must now set it into motion, or release it. If I do not do so, nothing will happen. Therefore I place the letter bearing the sigils of direction (the address) and the offering (stamp) out in the mail box (proper setting) so that the spirit (postman) will carry it off for me (proper timing). Failing to do any of these correctly could easily result in a lack of manifestation according to desire (no magick, no catalog).

Magick is an Occult science. It has its own laws and principles. Essentially, magick can be divided into the following categories: Earth Magick, Solar Magick, Lunar Magick, and Stellar Magick. Each of these can then be divided up into sub-categories (Earth Magick into herbs, crystals, and so on). Traditionally, magick can be thought of as being comprised of "raised magick" and "drawn magick." In other words, power is either raised (or generated) by someone or drawn from an outside source (whether from Nature or from Otherworld entities).

Just as the conscious mind must direct the actions comprising the formula of magick, the subconscious mind also plays its part. It is directly linked to the Plane of Forces and therefore to the Astral Plane. Anything that is received by the subconscious will affect the Astral. Whatever takes form in the Astral Realm will move toward manifestation in the physical dimension. The trick is getting it to take root there so that the desired effect can be realized.

When the conscious mind purposely creates a symbol or image and gives it to the subconscious mind, then its form is strong enough to draw an Astral response. The technique for this transference is typically accomplished through vigorous dance, chanting, or sexual stimulation (or a combination of these techniques). In some traditions wine is also used to alter the consciousness prior to employing these methods.

As the energy from the chosen technique begins to accumulate, then you proceed with the mental imagery of the sigil while giving yourself over to the stimulation. Once the conscious mind becomes fatigued, it will begin to lose its perception of the magickal work at hand. When that occurs, the subconscious will become active and receive the symbolism of the magickal intent.

The secret here is that the subconscious mind must be given sigils, because its language is one of images. Once the subconscious has received the image, then you must be careful not to consciously dwell upon the matter. The more you reflect upon the goal of your magick, the more you rob the subconscious mind of its link to the Astral. In so doing you will draw energy back through the conscious connection, and disperse the magickal effect.

THE INNER MECHANISM

Occult philosophy states that there are four worlds that comprise Creation, and seven dimensions within them. For the purposes of this chapter we will deal only with the inner dimensions since these function as part of the inner mechanism for magick.

Just as there is a physical dimension, or plane of existence, there are also Astral or spiritual dimensions. Each plane is thought to be a reflection of the one above it. An old Occult saying, "As above, so below" originates from this concept.

Essentially each descending plane manifests the "formed-thought" of the plane above it. In magick, one establishes his or her desire upon a higher plane so that it will return as the manifestation of that desire. The seven planes are listed as follows:

1. The Ultimate Plane

2. The Divine Plane

3. The Spiritual Plane

4. The Mental Plane

5. The Astral Plane

6. The Plane of Forces (Elemental Plane)

7. The Physical Plane

Immediately above the Physical Plane is the Plane of Forces, often referred to as the Elemental Plane. Everything that happens on the Physical Plane is directly linked to this plane. The dimensions react very much like a row of domino pieces: one triggers the other and a chain reaction takes place. This is the law of physics and also metaphysics (as above, so below), and this is how magick spells and religious prayers are transmitted.

This law is the essence of the working of the planes, each one vibrating in response to the next. Above the Plane of Forces is the Astral Plane, which is an etheric realm housing the formed thoughts of Collective Consciousness. It is here that all the heavens and hells of religious belief exist, fed by the minds of worshippers on the Physical Plane. In this plane we can form images of what we desire (as well as what we fear).

Since we all bear the Divine spark of that which created us, we also employ the same patterns. Our creative minds operate in the same manner as that which gave us creative consciousness, the main difference being that we are limited since we are but the spark, and not the source. The creative process, however, is much the same and we use it to create magick.

For example, if I decided to create a stand that will hold papers during a speech, I would first need to formulate the thought. This would go through several stages represented by the seven planes. The Divine Plane would receive the spark from the Ultimate Plane. The Spiritual Plane would conceive the plan, the Mental Plane would bring forth the visualizations, the Astral Plane would form the thought in etheric material, the Plane of Forces would carry the formed thought, and the Physical Plane would give it substance.

In simpler terms, the need arises (Ultimate Plane) and I begin to think of what I require to satisfy the need (Divine Plane). Eventually I form an idea (Spiritual Plane), and then refine it into something I can visualize (Mental Plane). Once I can see the object in my mind's eye, I draw it out and give it form on paper (Astral Plane). Then I gather the materials required and begin to assemble the object (Elemental Plane). Once the labor is finished I have the physical object required to accomplish my task (Physical Plane).

The magickal art is one of creation. The material that we use is the astral substance. The power to create from our thoughts resides within us, due to the divine spark. We create in accordance with the "Divine formula" of the planes. The stronger the emotion, the more exact the thought; so, too, is the corresponding Astral response.

In order to cause changes in the Physical World (magickally) you must first cause them in the Astral World. The purpose of ritual magick is to raise and direct the energy (containing the thought-form) off into the Astral Plane. The symbols, gestures, colors, and other ritual trappings are all methods of Astral communication. They also create the necessary mentality of all participants through which magickal images are communicated to the subconscious mind. Each one conveys its own vibration or energy and sets into motion subtle waves of stress and flow. Thought-forms can then begin to appear in the Astral dimension and become channels for the higher forces of the other planes.

The ritual energizes these forms, channels then open, like responds to like, and the forces become potent. Then, according to the work and its nature, raised energy will ascend to the Astral Plane or Divine energy will descend to the Physical Plane. The latter is the case in rituals that invoke Deity.

15

The Art of Casting Spells

*When creating your own spells, or embellishing ones that already exist, it is
important to consider any correspondences related to the work at hand.*

from the text

The art of spell casting incorporates many different aspects. Most spells
include the use of various types of candles, herbs, charms, oils, and so on.
Also common to most spells is the verse or incantation. In this chapter, we
will examine the spell itself and each of its ingredients, as they pertain to
the casting of spells.

THE SPELL

A spell is a simple, or basic, work of magick which incorporates the use of
personal power and/or "Otherworld" power (known also as drawn power).
In a spell, the mind is conditioned by each step or phase of the spell. This
allows the mind to draw upon its inner powers. The spell is a focus for the
mind and a catalyst. It enables the mind to create changes in the Astral
substance, which will then cause changes to occur in the physical world.

The forces that work together for the success of a spell are basically these: the trained mind, the magickal current, and the Astral substance. The mind is trained in visualization, concentration, and imagination. These are the keys to raising Personal Power. The magickal current is the Plane of Forces, and is sometimes called the Elemental Plane. It is a "current" flowing to and from the Astral Plane. Anything that enters the flow will manifest in the realm opposite its origin. The Astral substance forms around any energy that stimulates it. Thus does it transform the energy of mental/magickal images into formed thought.

Once a thought form is firmly established within the Astral Realm, a corresponding change will occur in the Physical Plane. When a spell employs the aid of a god or goddess, the formula is still the same. The deity involved simply uses the Astral Realm as a mediator and "responds" to the spell from another realm.

Spells can be used for many different reasons. They may be used to heal or to harm. They can bind a person from performing a certain act, or they may remove an obstacle to allow a person to accomplish a goal. The power of a spell is limited to the power of the spell caster, and to his or her own ability to formulate and direct the spell.

The Spell Book

The casting of spells involves the employment of the four elements. Candle wax is symbolic of earth. Oils represent water. Incense smoke is symbolic of air, and candle flames/ritual flames represent fire. The use of these elements serves as a "battery" of power. Together with the spell caster's own mental and emotional energies, this "battery" supplies the drive needed to accomplish the magick of the spell.

It is important to visualize your desire as you work the spell. Concentration is also very important, for it will "fix" and "bind" the spell. Symbolism is also essential in the art of spell casting. You must incorporate all colors, scents, images, personal links, and so on, which pertain to the person or situation for which the spell is intended.

In conclusion, you must symbolically release the power of the spell. An example would be to visualize a sphere of energy forming before you (or perhaps between your palms). Then mentally project the sphere off in the ether, or in the direction of the spell's "target." Finally, you must dispose of any melted wax, ash, or debris in a manner suitable to the nature of the spell. This is explained below.

There are four systems that are useful in the casting of spells. Each of these relate to the elements as follows:

Fire: acts through combustion

Air: acts through dispersion

Water: acts through evaporation (or mixture)

Earth: acts through decomposition

At the conclusion of a spell, you would dispose of the debris in accordance with its elemental action. This applies to the general cleanup, in most cases, and you may wish to dispose of various substances by combining ways for magickal influence. For example, you may wish to melt a wax candle in a pan, until it evaporates, to release its magickal charge.

If a spell covers a certain nature, then you may wish to dispose of the ritual materials accordingly:

Fire: motivation, passion, vitality, virility, force, etc.

Air: intellect, creativity, artistry, mental activity, etc.

Water: love, fertility, emotion, mutability, etc.

Earth: strength, endurance, fortitude, stagnation, etc.

These are only a few of the many possible associations. If the spell touches upon more than one element, you will want to employ them respectively.

Fire: burn in an open flame

Air: toss into the wind or evaporate

Water: drop into moving water

Earth: bury in the soil

The effect of this method is in the merging of the spell's energy with that of the Universal Elemental Energy. In the following section we will examine the various ingredients in spell casting.

Candles

Candles may be used in spells to represent the person or situation that the spell is designed to influence. In such a case the candle would be colored appropriately, linking its symbolic color to the nature of the work at hand. If the candle represents a person, then the color of the candle would reflect something about that person. The same is true of using symbols to represent any situation.

The candle may be made in the image of a man or woman, if the shapes help to focus your mind. Usually a standard candle is used and simply named after the person or situation at hand. To accomplish this you merely anoint the candle with an oil (or cologne) which symbolizes what the candle is to represent, and say, "I name you _____, you are _____." Or for a situation you might say, "Here is _____, this candle is now _____."

The way in which the candle is used for a spell varies. Sometimes a candle is notched into sections for the purpose of burning a section at a time. Each section will mark one day of the spell casting. Other times candles may be moved in some symbolic fashion, representing the goal of the spell. The examples that follow in this chapter will make this much clearer.

Incense

The use of incense is three-fold. It conditions the mind by stimulating the sense of smell (along with any physiological effects). It draws spirits through its magickal associations that aid the spell. Finally, according to ancient beliefs, it raises or lifts the spell up into the ether.

The type of incense burned must correspond to the nature of the spell itself. Most spells use an incense of planetary symbolism or deity association. Love spells incorporate an incense of Venus, binding spells an incense of Saturn, and so on.

Incense can also be used to add power to your candles by passing the candle through the incense smoke three times, in a circular clockwise manner.

Oils

Oils are somewhat similar to incense, inasmuch as they relate to the sense of smell. In addition to this (and more importantly), oils have the ability to hold magickal charges. When an object is anointed with a charged oil, the object then becomes charged as well. Traditionally, candles are anointed with oil that is then rubbed along the length of the candle. Concentration upon the intent of the charge is important at this point of the spell.

Scented oils correspond to planetary symbolism in the same manner as incense, so you will want to become more familiar with these correspondences.

The purpose of oils in spells is to add power. Therefore, the spell caster as well as the candles should be anointed (if it is appropriate to the spell).

Herbs

Herbs, like oils and incense, correspond to planetary symbolism. Yet they have a deeper level of influence than do the others. The herbal plant is a living vessel for a spirit or entity. This is similar to the relationship between our own spirits and bodies. When treated properly, the "consciousness" of the herb can work toward our needs.

Herbs may also be used in a spell for their physical properties, such as in potions and the like. In some cases, herbs have been used as offerings to spirits and deities, for some are considered sacred. Some spells incorporate herbs as charms to be carried or buried in a particular place. Often herbs are used to "charge" candles. In this method the base of the candle is hollowed out and the appropriate herb is placed within, then sealed over with melted wax.

Condensers

Condensers are similar to oils, but their influence and use is more diverse. A condenser can be any liquid substance that is magickally charged. The advantage of a condenser over an oil is that condensers can dry and evaporate with relative quickness. Condensers also blend better with other liquids, and are easily absorbed by dry substances. This makes them ideal for times when you wish no trace of the material left as evidence.

Condensers may incorporate more symbolical ingredients than oils and, therefore, are potentially more useful in magick. Oils, however, adhere to objects better and can easily be added to the wax when making candles. Use condensers as you would oils for magickal purposes.

Charms

Many spells incorporate the use of charms. The charm can be a natural object such as a root, or it can be something handmade. In the case of an handmade object, symbols may be engraved along with runes, or words of power, in an attempt to summon aid from spirits or deities. Natural objects are used when they resemble something pertaining to the spell (such as a heart-shaped stone for a love spell) or when they correspond symbolically (as in the case of herbs and incenses).

Verses

There are basically three different types of verses used in spells. The most common type is that of the rhyme. The advantage of the rhyme is that it allows the mind to easily memorize the verse. It also frees the mind, during the spell, from thinking about the verse on a conscious level. This helps the spell caster to focus his or her attention upon the rest of the spell.

The second type of verse is that of the free verse. The advantage here is that you may say exactly what you desire to say word for word, without seeking words that rhyme to convey your meaning. The last type of verse is the formula verse. This verse calls upon spirits or deities in such a way as to draw their response, seemingly through emotional rapport. The following examples will demonstrate these different verses.

The Rhyming Verse

> *Water to water,*
> *a Witches' spell.*
> *Cast I now to speed*
> *this well*
> *Forces and powers*
> *from out of the night*
> *gather within*
> *and give my spell flight.*

The Free Verse

> *Hear me, O Goddess of the Moon,*
> *hear me, and grant me success*
> *in the Ways of Magick.*

Send to my Spell,
Thy powers of Enchantment,
assist me in all my endeavors.

Hear me,
for I am a Child of the Moon,
grant me the ancient power.
For Thou art the Great Goddess,
Mistress of Magick, and I worship Thee!

The Formula Verse

1. Speak of the virtues of the deity or spirit that you call upon. Flatter as you go along.

2. Praise its power to influence things by its very presence and nature. Exaggerate.

3. Dispraise everything that is opposed to the nature of the deity or spirit.

4. Request (in a pleading manner) that your desires be granted, stating what it is your desire of the deity or spirit.

5. Condemn all that is opposed to your desire.

CORRESPONDENCES

Herbs

Unlike most of the other tools of magick, herbs often have several different associations or symbolic correspondences. An herb can be linked to a planetary influence by its color, scent, taste, smell, or appearance, all of which may correspond to a different planet. Therefore, it is the aspect of the herb being used in the spell that will determine its symbolism. The following list contains those herbs which are commonly associated (for a variety of reasons) with the planetary influences.

Sun: Peony, angelica, sunflower, saffron, cinnamon, laurel, wolfsbane

Moon: Selenotrope, hyssop, rosemary, watercress, moonflower, moonwort, garlic

Jupiter: Basil, mint, elecampane, henbane, betony sage

Venus: Lavender, vervain, valerian, coriander, laurel, lovage, foxglove

Mars: Wolfsbane, hellebore, garlic, tobacco, capsicum

Saturn: Dragon's wort, rue, cummin, mandrake, aconite, hemlock

Mercury: Fennel, mint, smallage, marjoram, parsley

In the above list, garlic is associated with both Mars and the Moon. In ancient times, garlic cloves were placed at the crossroads on the night of the Full Moon as offerings to the Goddess of Witchcraft. In this case it was most likely the white, Moon-like appearance of garlic that determined its symbolic correspondence. Garlic is also associated with Mars because of its strong taste and odor.

Wolfsbane is associated with Mars because of its leaves that grow in groups of five spike-like clusters (the number of Mars). Its flowers may be yellow, white, or blue which would link it to the Sun or Moon, or even Jupiter. Laurel is an herb sacred to Apollo, which would link it to the Sun, yet laurel leaves often appear in love spells, which would associate their uses with Venus as well.

Planetary Colors

Sun: Gold or yellow

Moon: White

Mars: Red

Mercury: Violet

Jupiter: Blue

Venus: Green

Saturn: Black

Color Symbolism (Candles)

White: Purification, protection

Pink: Love, friendship

Yellow: Drawing (pulling/compelling)

Green: Material success, abundance

Red: Passion, vigor, sexual energy

Orange: Concentration, psychic energy

Purple: Power over obstacles, magickal forces

Brown: Neutralizing

Gold: Drawing (strengthens other candles)

Blue: Peace, spirituality, spiritual energy

Dark Blue: Depression

Black: Crossing, suppressing, ending

Ritual Color Symbolism (Ceremonial Items)

White: Purity, transmitting

Green: Nature Magick, love, receptive fertility

Blue: Peace, spiritual forces

Red: Life force, sexual energy, vitality, active fertility

Brown: Earth Magick, neutralizing/grounding

Yellow: Mental energy

Black: Drawing, absorbing

Elemental Associations

Earth: (Yellow) Strength, fortitude

Air: (Blue) Intellect, healing, freeing, inspiration

Fire: (Red) Sexual energy, life-giving, cleansing, force, desire

Water: (Green) Emotion, subconscious, love, fertility, adaptability

Trees

Sun: Laurel and oak

Moon: Willow, olive, palm

Mars: Hickory

Mercury: Hazel

Jupiter: Pine, birch, mulberry

Venus: Myrtle, ash, apple

Saturn: Elm

Aromatics

Sun: Cinnamon, laurel, olibanum

Moon: Almond, jasmine, camphor, lotus

Mars: Aloes, dragon's blood, tobacco

Mercury: Cinquefoil, fennel, aniseed

Jupiter: Nutmeg, juniper, basil

Venus: Myrtle, rose, ambergris

Saturn: Myrrh, poppy, asafoetida

Numbers

Sun: 6

Moon: 9

Mars: 5

Mercury: 8

Jupiter: 4

Venus: 7

Saturn: 3

Stones

Sun: Diamond, topaz

Moon: Moonstone, opal, clear quartz crystal

Mars: Bloodstone, ruby, jasper

Mercury: Chalcedony, citrine

Jupiter: Amethyst, chrysocolla, chrysoprase

Venus: Emerald, green tourmaline, aquamarine

Saturn: Black onyx, jet, black jade

When creating your own spells, or embellishing ones that already exist, it is important to consider any correspondences related to the work at hand. Go over the lists in this chapter and work in as many items as possible. Also consider the numerical value of the planet that rules over the spell's intent. An example of this might be to add seven roses to a spell for love, since seven is the number of the planet Venus, and roses are sacred to the goddess Venus.

Remember that colors, scents, and symbols are all necessary, as they stimulate the senses of the person casting the spell. This stimulation creates a vibration, which then causes a reaction within the subconscious mind, then in turn within the etheric substance of the Astral plane. As we know from the law of physics, every action causes a reaction. So it is, too, with the law of metaphysics. Review the chapters in the workbook section of this book for further correspondences.

SPELLS OF THE STREGA

The spells appearing in this section are samples of the various types used among the Strega. Some are old traditional spells and some are modern eclectic. However, even the modern spells are based upon the Italian magickal system. A few of these spells are quite primitive and, in some respects, perhaps even a little crude. I include them here in order to preserve them and to provide the reader with something of true antiquity.

THE PROTECTIVE PENTAGRAM SPELL

1. On the night of the New Moon you shall construct an amulet of protection bearing the symbols of the Art. Draw or carve the pentagram symbol (Figure 27) upon any object or entrance you wish to protect.

   If this symbol is already formed as a piece of jewelry, etc., then trace it with your finger (left hand). Once the figure is established, proceed as follows:

2. On the night of the Full Moon, light the Spirit Bowl and suspend the amulet over the Spirit Flame, tracing the symbols with the tip of the Spirit Blade or finger: first the star, and then the circle.

3. Next, hold the amulet in your left hand, and with the tip of the Spirit Blade or your finger touch the first point and say:

   I call upon the Source of All Power to protect _____ against all that is evil, negative, or unbalanced.

4. Touch the second point and say:

   I call upon ye spirits and Guardians of the Western powers to protect _____ against all that is evil, negative, or unbalanced.

5. Touch the third point and say:

> *I call upon ye spirits and Guardians of the Southern powers, to protect _____ against all that is evil, negative or imbalanced.*

6. Touch the fourth point and say:

> *I call upon ye spirits and Guardians of the Northern powers, to protect _____ against all that is evil, negative or imbalanced.*

7. Touch the fifth point and say:

> *I call upon ye spirits and Guardians of the Eastern powers, to protect _____ against all that is evil, negative or imbalanced.*

8. Complete the spell by placing the tip of your right index finger upon the center of the pentagram, and say:

> *I bind here, by all of these powers and forces, this unyielding Pentagram of Protection. To thee thy course by lot hath given charge and strict watch, that to this (place or person) no evil thing approach or enter in.*

Figure 27
The Pentagram of Protection

9. You may wish to strengthen the spell by burning an incense of angelica, Solomon's seal, dragon's hood, dittany of Crete, and periwinkle.

10. Now draw the blue flame up from the Spirit Bowl (mentally) and form it into a five-pointed star. Visualize it merging into the pentagram. Next, dip the amulet into the flame three times, and present it to the North.

11. To conclude, hold the amulet in your left hand and place the tip of the Spirit Blade or finger against the power symbol, then say:

> *Henceforth art thou a pentagram of protection and a force of awesome power! In the names of Tana and Tanus, so be it!*

To Cure the Malocchio (Evil Eye)

One who has received the "overlook" (Malocchio) may suddenly and unexplainedly become ill. A severe headache preventing a person from going about their daily routine can be a sign of Malocchio (especially centered between the eyes and forehead). Becoming extremely tired and groggy without reasonable cause may also be a sign.

1. To test whether this is from natural causes place three drops of olive oil, one upon the other, into a bowl of water. If the drops remain together then the illness is natural. If the drops separate or smear across the surface of the water, then Malocchio is present.

2. To break the Malocchio spell, take two sewing needles and insert the tip of one needle into the eye of the other saying:

> *Occhi e contro occhi e perticelli agli occhi, crepa la invida e schiattono gli occhi. (Eyes against eyes and the holes of the eyes, envy cracks and eyes burst.)*

3. Then drop the needles into the water, on top of the oil drops. Next sprinkle three pinches of salt into the water. Take a pair of scissors and jab them into the water three times, through the oil drops. Take the scissors and "cut" the air above the bowl three times. The spell is then broken.

SPELL OF THE WITCHES' PENTAGRAM

The symbolism:

1. The Divine Totality
2. The God Energy
3. The Goddess Energy
4. The Astral Plane (or substance)
5. The Elemental Plane
6. Manifestation

If you desire to cause a change within yourself, then you will use your left hand to perform this spell. If you desire to cause a change within another person, or a situation, then you will use your right hand.

Preparation: Draw a five-pointed star, enclosed by a circle (Figure 28) large enough to accommodate the tips of four fingers and the thumb, one fingertip just within each point of the pentagram. The star should be almost your hand-spread in size.

Once this is completed, then place an appropriate link or talisman upon the center of the pentagram. This can be anything associated with the target object or desire, such as a lock of hair, a ring, a key, etc. The size of this talisman should be no larger than the center

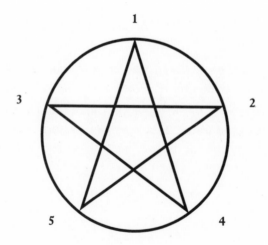

Figure 28
The Witches' Pentagram

section of the star. If necessary, you may simply concentrate upon the center and visualize the desired goal, without the use of a talisman.

The Spell: Place your palm out over the pentagram and state your desire. Then perform the following:

1. Place the tip of your middle finger upon the first point and say:

   I call upon the Source of All Things, to send me power!

2. Place the tip of your right-hand ring finger or left-hand index finger upon the second point and say:

   I call upon the God to give strength to my spell.

3. Place the tip of your right-hand index finger or left-hand ring finger upon the third point and say:

   I call upon the Goddess to give life to my spell.

4. Place the tip of your right-hand little finger or left-hand thumb upon the fourth point and say:

   I call upon the Astral forces to receive the image of my spell.

5. Place the tip of your right-hand thumb or left-hand little finger upon the fifth point and say:

   I call upon the Elemental forces to draw the desire of my spell (concentrate upon the elemental properties, mentally visualizing them in action).

6. At this point you draw upon all your powers of concentration, visualization, and expectation, saying:

   By the Power of the God and Goddess, and by the Forces of the Planes, and by my desire (state desire), I declare my purpose manifest!

7. Now quickly draw all your fingers forcefully together into the center of the pentagram, and press down firmly upon the talisman (or center space, if no talisman was used).

8. The spell is completed. Do not allow your thoughts to dwell upon your desire, as this will only serve to deplete its energy. If a charm or talisman was charged by this spell, then carry it upon your person for seven days (especially if coming into contact with the target of the spell).

INCANTATION TO BEFANA

This is performed to remove evil of any kind, or to invoke good fortune. Items required:

An ounce of high quality frankincense

An ounce of low quality frankincense

A pinch of cumin seed

1 incense burner dedicated solely to Befana

2 pieces of coal for burning the incense

1. Preparations: Place a burning coal into the incense burner (*scaldino*), then take 3 pinches of both high- and low-quality frankincense and line them up in a row across the threshold of your front door. Take the cumin seed and mix it into the remaining separate portions of incense. Then drop three pinches of the high-quality frankincense upon the burning coal in your burner, followed by three pinches of the low-quality frankincense (cumin seeds should be mixed in both).

2. Carry the incense burner throughout your house, from back to front, ending at the threshold (wave the smoke over every bed and in every corner).

3. Speak the incantation as you go from room to room:

   In nome del cielo!
   Delle stelle e della Luna!
   Mi levo questo mal d'occhio
   per mia maggior' fortuna!
   Befana! Befana! Befana!

   Chiunque mi ha dato mal d'occhio;
   Befana! Befana! Befana!
   Me lo porta via
   e maggior fortuna
   Mi venga in casa mia !

   (In the name of the sky,
   and of the stars and Moon,
   may this trouble change
   to good fortune soon!
   Befana! Befana! Befana!)

(Whoever gave me this misfortune;
Befana ! Befana ! Befana!
Take it away and bring good fortune I pray
into this house of mine!)

4. When the incense has been used up, light the piles of incense at the threshold and say three times (spit over your left shoulder each time you complete the incantation):

Befana! Befana! Befana!
Chiunque mi ha dato il mal d'occhio!
Me lo porta via!

(Befana, Befana, Befana
whoever gave me this bad luck,
carry it away!)

5. Complete by passing three times backward and forward before the burning incense, spitting over the left shoulder, and repeating the same incantation. It is completed.

SPELL OF ST. ANTHONY

When a girl wishes to win or reclaim a lover, or, indeed, if anybody wants anything at all, he—or generally she—puts two flowerpots, containing lilies of Saint Anthony, one on either side of an open window at midnight, with a pot of rue in the center. These must be bound with a red-scarlet ribbon, made in three knots, and pierced or dotted with pins, as a tassel. Then, turning to the window, he or she should say:

My benign Saint Anthony! I am not worthy to pray to thee. This grace I modestly require; please light for me three flames of fire and of these the first in turn on my head may storm and burn, one I pray within my heart, that all pain from me depart and the third beside my door that it may never leave me more. If this grace be granted me, let three sounds be heard by me: a knock at a door, a whistle, before, or the bark of a dog.

When this prayer shall have been uttered, wait attentively at the window, and if a knock at a door be heard, or a man whistling, or a dog barking, then the request will be granted. If a dark horse or mule passes by, or a hearse is seen, then the prayer is refused. If a white horse is seen then the favor will be granted, but at a later time than you desired.

Faun and Female Lasa

16

Moon Magick

In Moon Magick, the ritual altar is the focal point for the lunar forces which are drawn upon. Women are the vessels for lunar energy, receiving and directing the magickal force.

from the text

The accumulation and direction of the subtle forces of the Moon is one of the arts of La Vecchia Religione. Moon Magick is a personal art, even though there are basic guidelines. In ancient times, the Strega held the position of the Moon Priestess. In coastal regions and upon islands, Strega were also Sea Priestesses. The use of water from the sea was an important aspect in Moon Magick. The "charging" of water and the release of the "charge" through evaporation was an important aspect. So too was the soaking of woods and herbs in seawater. These items were later dried and burned as incenses and offerings. Two excellent books on this subject are *Moon Magick* and *The Sea Priestess*, both by Dion Fortune. The use of portals to gain access to the Lunar Realms, and the building of magickal images there, is a very important aspect of Moon Magick. This will be covered as the chapter continues.

The actual essence of the power used in Moon Magick originates out among the stars. The Sun transmits it into our solar system giving it a concentrated energy. The planets within our system absorb this energy which then merges with their own vibrations or energies. The planets, in turn, then emanate a composite energy within our solar system. Each planet's energy or vibratory pattern is unique, and influences other planetary bodies and forces within each planet's sphere of influence. This is the basis of astrology, and planetary correspondences, in magick.

The Moon is the focal point of power upon the Earth. The Moon absorbs, condenses, and channels all forces, which are then received by our planet. Agrippa, the fifteenth-century magician, understood these principles when he wrote:

> . . . *but the receptacle of all the heavenly influences, by the swiftness of her course, is joined to the Sun, and the other planets and stars, as a conception, bringing them forth to the inferior world, as being next to itself, for all the stars have influence on it, being the last receiver, which afterwards communicates the influence of all the superiors to these inferiors, and pours them forth upon the Earth . . .*

Aradia (the Holy Strega) told her followers to seek the Moon above all others for the purposes of magick. In this, she was instructing them to employ the Moon for magickal purposes (and the Moon Goddess). In the closing prayer of the Full Moon Ritual, we find these words, which Aradia's followers later wrote:

> *O Goddess of the Moon . . . teach us your ancient mysteries . . . that the Holy Strega spoke of, for I believe the Strega's story, when she told us to entreat Thee, told us when we seek for Knowledge, to seek and find Thee above all others.*

Agrippa understood this also when he wrote:

> *Therefore her (the Moon) motion is to be observed before the others, as the parent of all conception . . . [And again he wrote] . . . hence it is, that without the Moon intermediating, we cannot at any time attract the power of the superiors . . .*

What Agrippa spoke of is what Strega have known for ages: the Moon is the focal point of power upon the Earth. Without the Moon we cannot make use of the Universal Forces. Although solar magicians are sure to disagree, the Moon is essential to the art of magick. Without the Moon we can accomplish nothing. Some magicians claim that planetary bodies are secondary considerations, and that the Universal Force can be tapped directly, regardless of traditional magickal "timing."

The Universal Force is indeed a greater force than the planetary forces, yet we need to understand how it is that we "tap" that force. The force (or whatever you prefer to call it) originates out among the stellar bodies. As I stated, our Sun condenses this energy and channels it into our solar system. Each planet within our solar system absorbs a portion of the force and then emanates it outward. These individual emanations contain aspects of the planet's energy mixed with those of the original Force.

The Mistress of Magick

The important thing to remember is that the Moon draws these energies in, and then projects them out upon the Earth.

The electromagnetic field of the Earth receives and "collects" these energies. The Earth's field is greatly influenced by the Moon. Because of the swift orbit of the Moon, it can absorb and direct all the stellar and planetary forces within twenty-eight days (a lunar cycle).

Many magicians emphasize the forces of the Earth in magick, and they certainly can't be ignored, but again, we must look at the Moon's influence. The Moon influences plant growth (and the chemical/magickal potency of plants), biological functions (and fluids), emotions, bodies of water (tides), psychic energy, vibratory rates, and much, much more.

It is clear that the Moon is the mediator for the Universal Force in human experience and magickal practice. The role of the Sun is that of an amplifier. It generates raw power and enhances those energies already present in the electromagnetic sphere of the Earth. This is the primary difference between the Sun and Moon in the art of magick.

205

In Moon Magick, the phases of the Moon are observed and magickal rites are timed accordingly. Rituals or spells that involve a new beginning are performed during the new moon. Spells designed to influence something already in progress are performed at the "Half Moon." The Full Moon is for workings that require great force. It is the time in which the other "planes of existence" can be influenced and when the subconscious spheres of influence are most active (and receptive). Rituals or spells dealing with death and decline are performed when the Moon is waning.

The energy of the four quarters of the Moon begins and ends in a cycle running seven days. Rituals or spells should be designed to coincide with these energies and are best divided into seven stages that culminate on the last day of the lunar phase.

The use of silver in the ritual setting will greatly aid the accumulation of lunar energy for magickal purposes. This is because the silver (bell, chalice, bowls, etc.) sets up a subtle, harmonious, vibration of the Moon's energy. Colored glass or plastic can also be employed to enhance the lunar power. Liquids can be "charged" by placing them in a closed, colored bottle beneath the Full Moon. Colored filters can be made under which amulets, talismans, ritual tools, or even herbs can be placed, and through which the Moon's light may pass for the purpose of "charging."

What this means is that you can alter the vibrational rates of these materials and attune them to the vibration rates of those energies which will exert the sphere of influence desired. Green is best used to act upon the emotions, to balance, and to cleanse and heal. Red is used to stimulate, activate, and motivate. Purple is used to influence the subconscious and other astral levels, and to contact the planes. Dark blue will depress, and light blue will aid with spiritual connections. Brown will tend to ground, and amber will help to stabilize. Yellow will irritate, and thus stimulate, the mental sphere.

When using the Moon's light for "charging," it will help to ring a silver bell nine times near the object being charged. This will help to increase the vibratory rate and will aid in the absorption of the magnetic properties of lunar energy. Don't forget to retrieve the object before sunrise and wrap it securely, because direct sunlight will negate the magickal lunar charge. This is especially important in the case of charging crystals.

The general influence of the Moon changes with the zodiac sign which the Moon "occupies." It is also influenced by the twenty-eight lunar "Mansions" of the Moon (daily placements) and by the Moon's Nodes. These too will be covered in this chapter.

In Moon Magick, the ritual altar (Figure 29) is the focal point for the lunar forces that are drawn upon. Women are the vessels for lunar energy, receiving and directing the magickal force. Men can also become lunar vessels, but women are much better suited. The method used by both women and men is given following the Moon altar setup.

The Moon altar is placed facing the west quarter. The altar itself should be round, but a rectangular table will do. In the center of the altar, place a bowl of salt water. Set a white seashell in the center of the bowl. As this is done, whisper the name of the goddess who rules the current phase of the Moon. The New (and Waxing) Moon is Diana, the Full Moon is Jana, the Waning Moon is Mania. Around the bowl are set nine white stones, pearls, or shells, forming a crescent shape.

If the work of magick is for the gain of something, place the shells (stones or pearls) right to left. If the work of magick is for the loss of something, then place the objects from left to right.

As each shell is put in place, chant the name of the goddess who presides over the goal of the magickal influence. Matters concerning beginnings are under the influence of Diana. Matters involving forces, energies, or powers are under the influence of Jana. Matters of death, decline, and stagnation are ruled by Mania.

Censers of Moon incense are placed around the bowl upon the altar, forming a triangle (Figure 30) with a censer placed at each corner. A reversed triangle (base facing upward) is formed for manifestation desired in the Physical Plane. Upright triangles are formed for manifestation upon the Astral Plane. To complete the altar setup, place a black

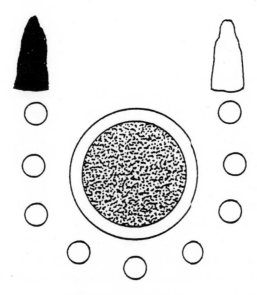

Figure 29
The Moon Altar

207

standing stone (or a candle) to the left of the bowl and a white standing stone (or a candle) to the right of the bowl.

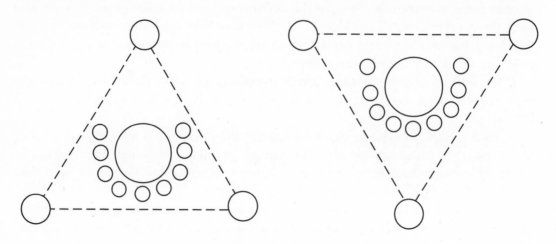

Figure 30
The Moon Altar Triangle

CHARGING THE ALTAR BOWL

During magickal work, the energy is focused into the altar bowl (or Moon bowl, as it is often called). This can be done by several different means. In group rituals, members may point their ritual blades at the High Priestess, who stands before the altar. The members visualize their energy flowing from their blades and into the aura (not the body) of the High Priestess. The High Priestess then visualizes the energy surrounding her, flowing out her own ritual blade, and into the bowl of water; or she may simply place her palms over the bowl and focus the energy through her hands. During this method she may recite an incantation stating the purpose of the charge, or the group may chant the spell.

Another method is to "enchant" the water. Begin by passing your right hand, palm down, over the bowl in a clockwise manner. Perform nine passes and then do the same with your left hand. Next sprinkle some ground herbs that are appropriate to the desired magickal influence, into the water. Then place your palms out over the bowl, index fingers and thumbs together, forming a triangle called the Gesture of Manifestation (Figure 24) and recite your incantation. As you chant, blow gently upon the water, slightly disturbing the surface. Formulate the incantation to be as descriptive of your intent as possible.

Releasing the Charge:

There are several different ways in which the magickal charge may be released into the ether.

One of the best techniques is to boil the water, observing the evaporation in steam, and chanting the formulated spell. Boil the water until it is completely evaporated. A similar method is to pour out small portions of water upon burning charcoals or hot rocks, until it is used up. The use of the steam is the same as the above.

A very old method is to pour the contents of the Moon bowl into a stream or river, saying something similar to:

> *Water to water*
> *a Witch's spell*
> *I give this stream*
> *to speed it well.*

RECEIVING THE MOON'S LIGHT

For Women

The Priestess receiving the Full Moon will need an assistant. The assistant will require a silver disk, smooth and highly polished. If absolutely necessary, a hand mirror may be used in place of the silver.

The Priestess will stand or kneel at the altar, with her head bowed down. The assistant will part her hair at the base of the skull, using water or oil to help part it if the hair is short.

While the Priestess visualizes the form of the Goddess merging from behind, with her own form, the assistant will reflect the Moon's light upon the base of the skull, using the silver disk.

You will find that the light pollution of the city will make this quite difficult. If possible perform this in a very isolated country setting (deserts work quite well also).

Once the Priestess receives the Moon, she can channel it into the Moon bowl, or she can "store" it within her being for seven days.

For Men

The Priest receiving the Full Moon does not need an assistant, but may choose to use one. Men cannot receive the Moon in the same manner as women, nor should they visualize the Goddess merging with them.

The Priest will stand, or kneel, before the altar with his head slightly bowed. Using a polished brass disk, the Moon's light is reflected upon the forehead of the Priest. At this point the Priest will visualize himself as the Full Moon itself.

Once the light is received, the Priest can channel it into the bowl. Men do not "hold" Moon light very well, and it is best to channel it off before the seven days that the Priestess can enjoy.

MOON PORTALS

Moon Portal symbolism is an aid for Astral Projection and a doorway to the lunar realms. Through the use of portals, "Inner Planes" awareness and magickal images may be established. Using a poster board, draw or paint a symbolic setting like the Moon altar's standing stone arrangement (Figure 31). The background can be colored to enhance the desired energy (see Correspondences).

To include water in the portal symbolism is to gain access to the magnetic properties of the Moon, and is a link to the subconscious mind (and therefore the Astral Realms). This imagery appears in the Major Arcana card of The Moon (Rider-Waite deck). The white and black "standing stones" imagery also appears in this tarot card, along with other significant images.

The portal is a focal point for meditation, as well as a doorway to other dimensions. When constructing the portal, the Moon's image should be placed directly center upon the poster board. Symbols of the polarity of the lunar force should be placed to represent a threshold. This can be the black and white standing stones, or temple pillars, etc. Water should be represented in the symbolism in one form or another. Ideally, water should cover the bottom of the card. A path should lead from the water to the Moon. This can be a path of light or a land "trail."

When using the Moon portal, the phase and "sign" of the Moon must be considered. Sit comfortably in front of the portal with only candles for lighting. If you desire, you can fix the poster to the ceiling above your bed, and mentally/astrally project as you drift off to sleep. Whatever you decide, simply gaze upon the portal, using the Moon as a focal point. Imagine yourself drifting off into the Moon (over the water, through the threshold, and so on). Allow your imagination to animate your experience. This

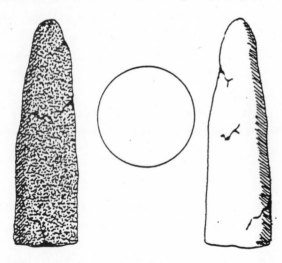

Figure 31
Moon Portal

is especially effective when drifting off to sleep, as the portal will influence your Dream World Reality.

MIRROR WORKING

In this technique a mirror is used as a doorway to the Astral Realm. Once established it can be used to establish an Astral temple, or to explore past lives, and so on.

Method One: Past Life Recall

To begin, obtain a full-length mirror. Next set a bowl of water out under the Full Moon (which should be in the sign of Pisces, Cancer, or Scorpio). If possible, use a green or blue filter through which the Moonlight can be focused (a colored glass jar will do). Leave this under the Moon for at least three hours, but in any case, remove it before sunrise.

Using the water, wash the surface of the mirror completely. Next, dry the mirror, leaving no streaks whatsoever. This must be done within three days following the Full Moon. If you do not complete this, then you must wait until the next New Moon.

When you are ready to begin using the mirror, set it upright on the floor in a quiet setting. Place a candle in front of the mirror. Sit before the candle and mirror so that the candlelight falling upon your face slightly changes your appearance. Study this face until you begin to feel that this "person" is not you (your reflection). Then allow yourself to "sense" this person, seeking an impression. Try to visualize the surroundings of this person's time. Repeat this exercise until you have "seen" at least one or two people. Feel free to use your intuition as you explore this technique. With patience, you will be able to link with some of your past-life personalities.

Method Two: The Astral Doorway

Prepare the mirror as you did before. The mirror is now used to reflect a painting or drawing of the desired realm you wish to enter. This can be a temple, sanctuary, or whatever you wish to encounter. Ideally, a wall mural is best so that the entire mirror is filled with the reflected image.

Sit off to the left of the mirror, so that your body is not reflected in it. The only lighting should be from candles near the painting. The mirror itself must be placed in the west quarter of the room being used.

When you are ready to begin, mentally walk into the mirror doorway, and explore the setting using your imagination/ visualization. You will need to perform this many times, so that your mind can fix (or bind) the reflected image within the structure of the mirror. Once you become adept at this, you can visualize a setting within the mirror (when the mirror reflects only a blank wall) and enter it. With practice, you will find that you can enter almost any setting you desire (in the Physical or Astral Realms).

MOONBEAM MAGICK

This is a very old and very simple technique for spell casting. It can be used for the initial charge of an amulet or talisman, or to enhance a charge which is already set. I have modernized it a bit in order to make it usable by non-initiates.

Using the Full Moon, you must consider the zodiac sign it occupies:

Aries, Leo, Sagittarius: for works of love or friendship

Taurus, Virgo, Capricorn: for works of an astral nature or spirit dealings

Gemini, Libra, Aquarius: for works of consciousness and mental processes

Cancer, Scorpio, Pisces: for works of the subconscious and psychic matters

Go out beneath the Full Moon between 9 P.M. and midnight. Take a small round mirror (such as a compact mirror) and place it on the palm of your left hand. Set the object to be charged upon the mirror, and hold it out at about eye level, as you face the Moon.

Looking toward the Moon, squint your eyes until it appears that you can see three sets of three beams, emanating from the Moon (Figure 32).

Do not squint to the degree that your eyes perceive another set of beams on top of the Moon. With your right hand, throw three kisses (***) to each aspect of the Goddess, saying:

*Three for the Maiden ***, three for the Crone ***, three for the Mother ***, for the light they have shown.*

Now, simply and briefly state your purpose or desire. You may create a rhyme for this purpose if you wish. After this, concentrate upon the bottom beams and squint slightly more so that these beams expand downward. Do this so that the descending middle beam appears to touch the charm upon the mirror, as you say:

Oh Great Goddess Moon, send me your light,
Fire of Ether burn clear and bright.
Let Spirits fly swiftly,
Your Magick bind fast,
until my Spell is done at last!
Oh Queen of the Heavens,
Consort of the Sun,
In the name of Thy Goddess,
so now be it done!

As you finish the last verse, saying "done," quickly close your eyes and cover the charm with your right hand. Give thanks to the Moon and go into a dark room so that you can wrap the charm in a dark cloth until you will need it. Avoid letting direct sunlight fall upon it. When you carry the charm, carry it hidden upon your person.

Should you encounter the person, or situation, etc., for which the spell was cast, then touch the charm and say (quietly):

> *Three for the Maiden—Three for the*
> *Crone—Three for the*
> *Mother—whose target is shown.*

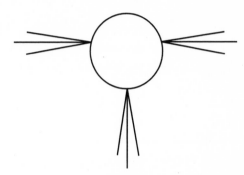

Do this as you look upon the "target." If you don't encounter the target, don't worry about it.

When the next Full Moon appears you must go out beneath the light again with your charm and the mirror. Stand with your back to the Moon and hold the charm against the mirror with your thumbs.

Figure 32
Moon Beam Magick

Manipulate the mirror so that the Moon appears in it. When you see it, say:

> *Three for the Maiden—Three for the Crone—Three for the Mother—return*
> *again home!*

With this, fling your arms up and back, so that the charm is flung up toward the Moon. Leave the area without looking back. If you want the physical object back again, then look for it after the sun has risen.

Be careful; this spell works quite well. Remember the Law of the Threefold Return: that which you do, shall return to you threefold! Don't misuse it, because it will come back: *three from the Maiden—three from the Crone—three from the Mother—if evil's been shown.*

MOONSTONES

The use of various gems for magickal purposes has long been an aspect of occult lore. Here we shall consider the use of moonstones.

Moonstones are a variety of feldspar, and have a milky opalescence. They are very valuable to Witches and magicians because of their spiritual qualities. Moonstones are highly magnetic on the Astral level, and when worn on the body, will draw together the higher and lower "natures" of the individual. This action results in a balancing of the inner being. Moonstones also have a soothing influence and can help to control emotional energies.

The magnetic properties of this gem upon the Inner Planes are very useful in the art of magick. This is because moonstones can draw and condense the subtle energies of the Astral substances. They are also useful when worn during Astral projection or dream working (conscious dream control), as they have a stimulating effect upon the pineal gland. This gland is the "Third Eye," and deals with extrasensory perception. The benefit here is that the stone strengthens the influence of the pineal, allowing more psychic control and stronger Astral/dream images.

Moonstones, when worn or carried, seem to reflect the inner person. It is for this reason that they are very useful in the art of psychometry. Many covens give prospective members a moonstone to carry for one month, at which time the coven members retrieve the stone and pyschometrize it. Thus do they gain a truer image of the prospective member.

Moonstones are sacred to the Moon Goddess and can be used as ritual offerings. They can also be incorporated into jewelry as symbols of Priesthood or Priesthood. Meditation upon a moonstone may lead you to other uses of this gem.

THE LUNAR MANSIONS

The influence of the Moon can be seen in the star sign it occupies during its travels, and in the twenty-eight Mansions of the Moon. The north and south Nodes of the Moon, which are linked to the Dragon of the Moon, are also of noted importance. An interesting study of the Moon Mansion in magick can be found in Francis Barrett's *The Magus*. In Book One, Part 2, Chapters 33, 42, 43, and 44, you will find a record of old magickal images and spells, along with some ancient Moon lore.

The old order of Moon Mansions begins with the star called Alcyone, which is the Pleiades. The current order now begins in Aries. The problem with using the Moon Mansion System is that it differs, with regard to stellar correspondence, from cultural system to cultural system. The Arabs, Hindus, and Chinese all place the Lunar Mansions within constellations which are outside of the Moon's current orbital path. Janarric Witches place the Mansions along the ecliptical path, incorporating those constellations which lie across it. The Janarric System begins in the Pleiades and ends in Perseus. The following is the current formation of the Mansions in the Janarric System.

The Janarric Mansions

1. Pleiades
2. Taurus
3. Auriga
4. Orion
5. Gemini
6. Cancer
7. Hydra
8. Leo
9. Leo (tail)
10. Crow
11. Virgo
12. Virgo
13. Bootes
14. Libra
15. Centaur (small section)
16. Scorpio
17. Ophiuchus
18. Sagittarius
19. Capricorn
20. Eagle
21. Aquarius
22. Pisces S
23. Pisces W
24. Pisces N
25. Cetus
26. Aries
27. Aries
28. Perseus

The most commonly used system today is the Chaldean. It was also very popular during the Middle Ages. I include it here so that you will be familiar with it for future reference. It must be remembered that the Chaldean System differs from the Janarric, but the associated "powers" of each Mansion are compatible.

The Chaldean Mansions

1. Al Thurayya	(Taurus)	15. Iklil Al Jabhah	(Scorpio)
2. Al Dabaran	(Taurus)	16. Al Kalb	(Scorpio)
3. Al Hak' ah	(Orion)	17. Al Shaulah	(Scorpio)
4. Al Han' ah	(Gemini)	18. Al Na' am	(Sagittarius)
5. Al Dhira	(Gemini)	19. Al Baldah	(Sagittarius)
6. Al Nathrah	(Cancer)	20. Al Sa'd Al Dhabih	(Capricorn)
7. Al Tarf	(Leo)	21. Al Sa'd Al Bula	(Aquarius)
8. Al Jabhah	(Leo)	22. Al Sa'd Al Su'ud	(Aquarius)
9. Al Zubrah	(Leo)	23. Al Sa'd Al Ahbiyah	(Aquarius)
10. Al Sarfah	(Leo)	24. Al Farch Al Mukdim	(Pegasus)
11. Al Awwa	(Virgo)	25. Al Fargh Al Thani	(Pegasus & Andromeda)
12. Al Simak	(Virgo)	26. Al Batn Al Hut	(Andromeda)
13. Al Ghafr	(Virgo)	27. Al Sharatain	(Aries)
14. Al Jubana	(Libra)	28. Al Butain	(Aries)

Lunar Influence of the Mansions

1. Good fortune
2. Ill will, separation, revenge
3. Favor with authority
4. Secures love
5. Secures material desires
6. Aids in battle
7. Causes illness
8. Aids in childbirth and healing
9. Causes fear or reverence
10. Causes disharmony between lovers
11. Creates harmony between lovers
12. Influences divorce and separation
13. Influences friendship and good will
14. Material increase
15. Inhibits thieves
16. Aids against poisons
17. Aids childbirth
18. Aids the hunter
19. Causes misfortune for enemies
20. Aids the fugitive
21. Influences destruction and decline
22. Aids fertility in animals
23. Aids the harvest, and plants in general
24. Influences love and favor
25. Fouls liquids
26. Aids the fisher
27. Aids in the destruction of enemies
28. Aids in reconciliation

The 28 Spirits of the Moon Mansions

These are the Tuscan (phonetic) Pagan names of the Lunar Spirits who rule over the Moon Mansion:

1. Arisham
2. Estanacohn
3. Evonacus
4. Miracohn
5. Sendomahr
6. Therassus
7. Viracus
8. Lucinus
9. Selahna
10. Mensus
11. Kirahm
12. Morgronus
13. Thera
14. Atava
15. Trutus
16. Tiniah
17. Satur
18. Venu
19. Totorum
20. Arogus
21. Diona
22. Pahnus
23. Niah
24. Silvus
25. Aquosus
26. Undia
27. Cosus
28. Poscinia

MAGICK MANSIONS IMAGES

Agrippa, in the year 1531, recorded a collection of magickal images related to the twenty-eight Mansions of the Moon in his work on Occult philosophy. These images were to be designed during the influence of the desired Mansion, in order to bind the flow of energy within a magickal seal. These seals were either carried upon the person intended, or placed in the appropriate setting, etc.

The following is a list, common during the Middle Ages, of the twenty-eight images for sealing the power of the Mansion of the Moon.

1. The figure of a well-dressed woman, sitting in a chair with her right hand lifted up on her head. This is to be fumed with an incense of musk, camphor, and calamus. The seal is to be set upon a silver square, set upon a silver ring.

2. The figure of a soldier sitting upon a horse, with a serpent in his right hand. This is to be fumed with an incense of red myrrh and storax. The image is set upon red wax.

3. The figure of the head of a man, set upon silver. This is fumed with an incense of red sanders.

4. Upon white wax, the figures of two people embracing. This is fumed with an incense of aloes and amber.

5. Upon silver, the image of a well-dressed man, whose hands are raised in prayer. This is fumed with an incense of frankincense and myrrh.

6. Upon tin, the image of an eagle, with the face of a man. This is fumed with an incense of sulfur.

7. Upon lead, the image of a man holding his genitals in one hand, and covering his eyes with the other. This is fumed with an incense of pine.

8. Upon gold, the head of a lion, fumed with amber.

9. Upon gold, the image of a man riding a lion. In his left hand he holds the lion's ear, and in his right he extends a gold bracelet. This is fumed with an incense of myrrh, frankincense, and saffron.

10. Upon blackened lead, the image of a dragon and a man in combat. This was fumed with the hairs of a great cat mixed in an incense of assafoetida.

11. Upon a white wax seal, the image of a woman, and upon red wax, the image of a man. These images are then pressed against each other, so that the couple embraces. The seal is then fumed with an incense of aloes and amber.

12. Upon copper, the image of a dog biting his tail. This is then fumed with the smoke from burning the hair of a black dog and cat.

13. The figure of a man who is seated, writing letters. This is fumed with frankincense and nutmeg.

14. Upon silver, the image of a man sitting upon a chair with a balance scale in his hands. This is fumed with cinnamon.

15. Upon iron, the image of an ape. This is fumed with the hair of an ape.

16. Upon copper, the image of a snake with its tail raised above its head. This is fumed with hartshorn.

17. Upon copper, the image of a woman holding her face with both hands. This is perfumed with liquid storax.

18. Upon tin, the image of a male centaur. This is fumed with the burnt head of a wolf.

19. The figure of a man, with his own image behind, and in front of him. This is fumed with sulfur and jet, then placed in a brass box along with your enemies' link (hair, nails, etc.) and some sulfur and jet.

20. Upon iron, the image of a man with winged feet, and a helmet upon his head. This is fumed with argent vine.

21. Upon iron, the image of a cat with a dog's head. This is fumed with hair from a dog's head, and buried where the destruction, or decline, is intended.

22. Upon iron, the image of a woman suckling her son. This iron seal is then heated to brand with. In herd animals the "leader" is branded, usually upon the horn.

23. Upon a piece of fig wood, the image of a man planting. This is fumed with the flowers of a fig tree, and then hung in the area to preserve.

24. Upon white wax, the image of a woman brushing her hair. This is fumed with orris and coriander.

25. Upon red clay, the image of a winged man holding an empty vial. The seal is then mixed in with asafoetida and liquid storax, and burned. The burned remains are then dropped into the body of water to be influenced.

26. Upon copper, the image of a fish. This is then fumed with the skin of a sea fish, and the seal is tossed into the water in which you desire to fish.

27. Upon an iron ring, the image of a black man covered with hair and girdled the same, tossing a lance with his right hand. This is then sealed with black wax, and perfumed with liquid storax while stating the desired effect.

28. Upon white wax (with mastic), the image of a crowned king. This is fumed with aloes.

Alpena, Goddess of Flowers

17

Herbs and Witchcraft

Plants, like all natural objects, possess a Numen, or spirit consciousness. They are not singularly as "powerful" as stones, but they are more versatile, and can be used in more varied ways.

from the text

In the long and rich tradition of herbs associated with the Old Religion, two herbs may be singled out for special mention: rue and fennel. In this chapter we will examine each herb, its properties, and its associations with the ancient Craft, and we will explore the symbolic and magickal aspects of various plants.

RUE (*RUTA GRAVEOLENS*)

Rue is an herb native to Italy and southern Europe. It is a hardy evergreen perennial, growing to a height of approximately three feet. Rue contains a powerful stimulant known as rutin. Herbalists have long employed rue as a stimulant and antispasmodic. Ancient writings attribute the curing of many illnesses to rue, as well as restoring good eyesight. Piperno, a physician in Naples (1625), recommended rue as a

Rue

treatment against epilepsy and vertigo. Hippocrates considered it an essential ingredient in antidotes to poison.

Along with its many physical attributes, this herb also has a rich magickal and religious history. An Italian Witch charm called the Cimaruta (sprig of rue) depicts a rue branch hung with symbols (see Figure 1). During the Middles Ages, it was a symbol of recognition for witches. Each branch divides into three offshoots, symbolizing the Dianic Triad: maiden, mother, crone. Ironically, the Catholic Church used a branch of rue to sprinkle holy water on its followers, and referred to rue as "the herb of grace."

Rue is used in several rituals where it represents the God (as well as the power of the God). The Mythos of the God, as reflected in planting, growing, and harvesting, is played out using the herb in a series of seasonal rites. Various parts of the plant are employed as they relate to the symbology of the God. The following are a few of the traditional associations connected to rue:

Ruler: Sun

God Form: Faunus

Goddess Form: Fana

Medicinal: Healing

Magickal: Protection

Ritual: A God-form plant

FENNEL (*FOENICULUM VULGARE*)

An herb indigenous to the shores of the Mediterranean, fennel was well known among the ancients, and was cultivated by the Romans for its aromatic fruits and succulent edible shoots. It also had a reputation for strengthening eyesight. In medieval times, fennel was hung over doors on Midsummer's Eve to ward off evil spirits. In the Cult of Dionysus the fennel stalk was capped with a pine cone, symbolizing fertility, and was used as a wand by ancient priests and priestesses.

Fennel has a thick root stock, growing to five feet or more in height. Roman fennel is distinguished by its greater length, and stronger, anise-like fragrance. Florentine fennel is a

Fennel

smaller variety, growing only a few feet in height, and being more "bushy" in appearance. In the midsummer festivals of Adonis, fennel was among those seeds planted in pots for the rituals, depicting his death and resurrection. The seeds sprouted quickly, and then the sprouts were allowed to wither from sun and drought.

During the sixteenth and seventeenth centuries, Italian witch trials revealed a curious tradition associated with fennel. Certain Witches, calling themselves Benandanti, gave accounts of ritual battles (performed in "dream states") which occurred four times a year. These battles were waged against an evil cult, the Malandanti, over the harvest yields. The Benandanti fought with long stalks of fennel, and the Malandanti with sorghum stalks. In these battles, the Benandanti carried a standard bearing a banner of white silk with a gilded lion embroidered upon it. During medieval times the fennel stalk was a symbol of St. Lucy, a patroness of the blind, and the Benandanti employed the stalk to evoke St. Lucy and seek her aid in granting night vision as the Benandanti battled in the darkness.

The Malandanti carried a banner of red silk emblazoned with four black devils. A very detailed account of this appears in *The Night Battles: Witchcraft & Agrarian Cults in the 16th & 17th Centuries,* by Carlo Ginzburg. In Roman mythology, fire was stolen from the gods on a staff of fennel, and fennel was associated with Lucina, a Roman goddess of light. In Italian Craft rituals today, fennel is used as a symbol of victory and is presented at each of the elemental quarters during the Spring and Summer rites. At these times, it represents a successful harvest empowered by the magick of the coven. The following are traditional associations of fennel:

Ruler: Mars

God Form: Dianus

Goddess Form: Diana

Medicinal: Stomach problems

Magickal: Protection

Ritual: Victory, success, dominion

TREE LORE

In ancient times trees were worshipped as gods and goddesses. This is also reflected in Greek and Roman mythology where we find many tales of individuals being transformed into various trees. In the oldest tales of European folklore we find legends where evil spirits can be imprisoned in trees. This may be the foundation in the folkore of later periods where wooden stakes are used to destroy vampires.

In this section we will consider several trees that appear frequently in material related to the Old Religion. Italian Witchcraft employs many types of trees, some of which were imported to Italy during ancient Rome's occupation of other European regions. The following trees have special ritual and magickal associations connected to the Old Religion.

Ash:

The flowering ash (*fraxinus ornus*) is native to Italy. Each leaf has seven leaflets, a symbol of the seven worlds in occult cosmology. Some witches prefer to make their wands from the ash tree because of its association with the creation of the occult worlds. In Greek and Roman mythology, Nemesis carried an ash branch as a symbol of divine justice. Therefore the ash wand is also a symbol of the higher self.

Beech:

The beech tree was one of the sacred trees at Lake Nemi in Italy. In part, its magickal nature is linked to the fact that each husk contains three triangular shaped nuts. Both the triangle and the number three in Italian Paganism represent manifestation. In the seventeenth century Italian work titled *Compendium Maleficarum*, Francesco Guazzo writes that Witches use beech twigs to trace ritual circles on the ground.

In Greek and Roman mythology this tree was a symbol of ancient wisdom and knowledge. Connected to this theme is some evidence to indicate that thin slices of beech wood were once used to make book pages.

Elder:

Elder was used by the ancient Greeks to make a wind instrument known as the sambuke. Because of this the elder is sacred to the woodland god known as Pan. In ancient lore the elder was favored by Nature spirits as a dwelling place. In some traditions the elder is preferred as the material for making wands because of this association.

Oak:

Before the ancient Romans cleared much of the forests that once covered Italy, oak stood mixed with other trees in the Sacred Grove of Diana at Nemi. The oak was worshipped as a god among Italic peoples just as it was in other parts of Europe. At Nemi the oak tree was the God and the lake was the Goddess, a divine marriage. Acorns were dropped into a stream that flowed into Lake Nemi as a magickal act to invoke fertility. This stream was sacred to Egeria, a nymph serving in the Sacred Grove.

Mountain Ash (Rowan):

Mountain ash is found now mainly in northern Italy and is an old tree associated with Witchcraft. It is mentioned in Greek and Roman mythology where legend says it sprung from drops of blood shed by a wounded eagle sacred to Zeus/Jupiter.

Ancestral guardian spirits were said to live in ash trees, and the red berries of the tree were signs of the ancient blood link.

Olive:

Olive is one of the sacred trees mentioned in Greek and Roman mythology. Athena created it in a contest against Neptune to rule over the city of Athens. The gods of Olympus were pleased with the tree because Athena told them that olive oil could be burned by humankind in offertory lamps for acts of worship. Therefore, the olive tree is a special link to the gods, bearing the fruit that unites divinity with humankind.

Walnut:

The walnut tree has long been associated with Italian Witchcraft. In the ancient Aegean/Mediterranean cultures the walnut tree was believed to possess and impart the gift of prophecy. It was also believed to grant fertility, and traditionally a walnut tree was planted when a female was born into a family. When the daughter married, the tree was cut down and her marriage bed was made from the wood. In the ancient city of Benevento, a great legendary walnut tree once stood. According to legend, Witches from all over Italy would come to gather beneath the tree for seasonal festivals. In Roman mythology the walnut is sacred to Proserpina, Diana, and Hecate.

HERBAL MAGICK

Generally, when considering any plant for Magickal use you must break it down into symbolic aspects. Its coloring, habitat, fragrance, taste, peculiarities, and chemical properties are all important to correspondences. It is necessary to understand the Elemental associations, as well. The root is earth, the stem is water, the leaves are air, and the flower is fire. Fragrance is considered to be the fifth element of spirit. Determining any correspondence for a plant to a zodiac sign, planet or whatever, will relate to the part of the plant used.

The moonflower plant is a good example of the mixed symbolism of plants. Its leaves are heart-shaped, which, together with their green color, links the plant to Venus. Its flower is white and opens only after sunset, linking it to the Moon. If it bore thorns, then this would show a Mars influence. The seeds of the moonflower are hallucinogenic, making it a truly shamanistic plant. Most of the powerful magickal plants have either trance-inducing, or hallucinogenic properties.

Plants, like all natural objects, possess a Numen, or spirit consciousness. Singularly, they are not as "powerful" as stones, but they are more versatile, and can be used in more varied ways. In magick, the plant (or, more properly, its Numen) is employed to add power to spells or rituals. The plant can be used as an incense, an ingredient in an oil, or to empower a potion. The plant can also be used as a Familiar, which is an older and less-known aspect of plant magick.

THE PLANT FAMILIAR AND MAGICKAL PLANTS

The purpose of the following technique is to "raise," or grow a plant, as a Familiar (serving spirit) or as a magickal plant. In ancient times, a circle of small stones was set around the chosen plant, to "bind" the Numen there. Then a hole was dug toward the roots (being careful not to damage them), and a chosen power stone was set in place, to "charge" the plant.

Today's method is somewhat different, but equally effective. You can begin with a seed, or young sprout or plant. Choose a secluded area that is suitable for the needs of the plant (sunlight, drainage, etc.), and prepare the soil for planting. Bury the stone or crystal of your choice about three inches—or more—deep in the soil. Quartz crystals are best. Next, fill in the soil over the crystal and plant the seed (or plant) as is appropriate. Lay a circle of eight stones around the plant site. At each of the four quarters (of the circle) place a crystal of the same type as the one you buried. The other four stones may be of the same type, or may be assorted, as long as they complement each other. The spacing of the stones is determined by the physical needs of the plant.

Method One

If you planted a seed, wait seven days after a sprout appears to proceed with the following steps. If you started with a young plant, wait seven days after planting. Remove the stones between the quarter stones and plant a seed at each point. These seeds may be of the same type as the plant within the circle or may be an assortment. Next bury the quarter stones where they lay, at least an inch deep.

Each day place both palms upon the ground within the circle, forming a triangle with your fingertips (index fingers and thumbs touching). The stem of the plant will be in the open center of the triangle. Using your imagination and visualization, sense your power flowing out through your arms and into the soil. The "source" of the power can begin from one (or more) of your personal power centers, or you may employ techniques for drawing or raising power.

You must also talk to the plant and send it visuals, communicating your needs and desires through mental pictures. You must take good care of the plant, watering, fertilizing, and protecting it from damage. To create a strong bond with your plant Familiar, add three drops of your own blood to a quart of water, using this to water your plant as needed.

Magickally, you have first increased the level of the Numen through the crystal. Second, you have extended its power and influence to the other plants, because these plants became alive under the influence of the center crystal and plant. They were also bathed in a cross-quarter current of energy, controlled from the center entities, through the quarter crystals.

If you need to use the physical properties of the plant for spells, potions, or whatever, use only the circle plants (never the center). The center plant is the Familiar, the other plants are simply extensions.

The final step in creating this plant Familiar is to establish your "linking" and rapport. To do this you must sit comfortably before the plant, at the north quarter facing south. Stare at the plant and allow your vision to slightly blur. In this state, observe the general shape of the plant, trying to leave your mind blank. The plant will send you a mental image as you gaze. You will receive this "formed thought" as a distortion of the plant; in other words, its "shape" will resemble something else. This could be an animal, insect, or some other creature. Whatever shape is revealed to you will be the "Familiar" spirit.

The Familiar will give you extra power in any magickal work whenever you summon it. House plants can become protective entities for your home through this technique. Plants given as gifts can be very useful for magickal purposes as well.

To summon your Familiar, you simply imagine your plant in its setting, and visualize it becoming the image of the spirit Familiar. Mentally draw it to yourself and allow it to merge within your thoughts. Experience the entity form, imagining that you are that creature. See yourself as the entity form, be the form, act like the form. This is how it becomes a "Familiar" spirit. Once you can perform this successfully, then you truly possess the Familiar.

Method Two

On the New Moon, plant a seed over the buried crystal. Each day, after sunset, focus your power through your hands (as in Method One). Your "source" of power must be "drawn" before you begin, as follows: Sit comfortably before the plant, at the west quarter, facing east. Close your eyes and visualize the Full Moon above you. Mentally draw the Moon down until it sits just above your head. Next, visualize its light glowing brightly, then draw the Moon down to your stomach area. Finally, visualize the Moon expanding until it encloses you totally. The image would be similar to you sitting inside a glowing white balloon. At this point, you will begin to pour the light out through your hands. You may drain the light out completely if you wish, or just a portion of it, releasing the rest back into the air. In any case, you must rid your body of the gathered power.

At this point, send your visual communications to the plant, establishing what is desired of the Familiar. This method works extremely well for the formation of magickal plants. Create an "image play" for the plant, running through how you will use the plant (or Familiar) and showing it the successful outcome of the spell, potion, or whatever. In other words, focus a "day dream" upon the plant. Include the summoning of the Familiar, and the work of the Familiar, in your visual communication. As in Method One, you must take good care of the plant. You also may add other plants to the stone circle if you desire. Talking to the plant is important, as it will aid in the bonding.

On the night before the Moon is full, perform the following: Beneath the Moon, set out an open jar of the water you are using for the plant. If possible, use a green glass jar or a green filter over the jar. Leave this out for the night, but be sure to remove it before sunrise. On the night of the Full Moon, pour this water out upon the plant. Then take some white flour and mark the symbol of the Power of the Moon (see Symbols & Sigils, Figure 13) upon the soil. The plant will occupy the center of the "X" mark, with the stones of the circle surrounding the sigil. If you desire, you can set a crystal at each end of the "X," to enhance the power focused upon the plant.

Method Two will make the chemical properties of the plant more potent and increase its magickal potential. Being attuned to lunar energy, Method Two allows the plant to be more active within the astral and subconscious spheres of influence. It is a method well suited for the Craft of Witches.

Working with the Plant Familiar

In Method One, you were shown the technique for summoning the Familiar. Now we will look at some techniques for using the Familiar.

Potions — In the case of herbal potions (or other liquids), you can charge them with the aid of your Familiar. Set the potion before you and summon the spirit Familiar; then mentally project the Familiar out into the potion. See it enter the potion, swimming and diving within the liquid. As it performs these acts, see the liquid begin to glow with a color that corresponds to the desired magickal effect.

Incense — For powdered or herbal bulk incense, summon the Familiar and send it to rest upon the material. Mentally see it walk upon the surface, occasionally digging down into the material and reappearing through the surface. See the material begin to glow with the symbolic color of the desired magickal effect, until it seems fully charged. Then recall the Familiar and return it to the plant.

Healings — Summon the plant Familiar and project it into the body of the person (or animal, etc.) concerned. First visualize it being the size of the patient, and see it merge with him or her. Mentally see the patient glowing with the symbolic color of the desired effect. If a specific area of the body is concerned, then focus the Familiar there. See it move in and out, removing and discarding the illness. This can be visualized as bits of dark material, or whatever may seem appropriate. Intensify the magickal color in this area for the healing. Finally, recall the Familiar and return it to the plant.

Amulets and Talismans — Plant Familiars can be used to add power to an amulet or talisman, but they usually are not powerful enough to "break" someone else's. Summon the Familiar and project it onto the object. Visualize it grasping onto the edges, and see it glowing with the symbolic color of the desired effect. Carry the amulet or talisman with the Familiar attached to it. However, be sure to return the Familiar to the plant within two days.

Minds — Familiars can be used to influence the thoughts and emotions of other people. Through your Familiar you can lend someone else some "creativity," "inspiration," "motivation," or whatever. Normally, this is most effective when the person is asleep or under the influence of a drug, as in the case of major surgery. Even when the person is fully conscious this method can still be effective.

Summon your Familiar and project it into the mind of the person you want to influence. See it "perched" upon the crown of the head, then mentally have it enter through the "Third Eye" power center. Leave your Familiar within the person's mind while they sleep (or for several hours if the person is conscious) and then recall it, returning it to the plant. As always, you must instruct the Familiar mentally (or verbally) as to what you want it to accomplish, and you must direct it during the work.

HERBS AND RITUAL TOOLS

Herbs can be used to enhance the power of ritual tools. This can be in the form of incense, potions, charms, etc. The following are some techniques that can be used to accomplish this.

Loading

This technique involves the placing of certain herbs within a ritual tool. Most commonly this is done with candles and with the ritual wand. For candles, hollow out the bottom of the candle, about an inch or so deep. It is best to do this with a hot metal shaft, pushing and twisting it gently into the candle. Place the herbs in the hole, and seal them over with wax.

For wands, hollow out the shaft, or you can hollow the head of the wand out and later glue it back to the shaft. Herbs are then placed inside (traditionally with a power stone) and sealed. In ancient times, tree sap was used to glue wands together, and to seal them.

The following herbs are only a few of the possibilities:

For Matters of Love: Balm of Gilead, coriander, lovage, laurel

For Protection: Angelica, bloodroot, cinquefoil, fennel, rosemary, rue, wormwood

For Extra Power: Periwinkle, pennyroyal, Solomon's seal, Dittany of Crete, mandrake

Potions

This aspect concerns the brewing of an herbal potion into which a ritual tool may be placed. To prepare the potions, bring water to a boil in a suitable pan, and steep the appropriate herbs in the water. After a few minutes, the ritual tool may be dipped into the potion. Depending upon your needs, you may wish to use several different potions for each tool.

To Purify

Use equal parts of vervain, basil, woodruff, hyssop, and myrrh. Add a pinch of salt to the water and herbs. Allow them to steep for five minutes, then bathe the tool in the mixture (the water will still be hot, so be careful!). Rinse the tool with fresh water when you are finished.

For Added Potency

Use equal parts of periwinkle, Solomon's Seal, and mandrake. Place the herbs in the pan, and drop a loadstone in with them. Let the herbs steep for five minutes, then plunge the tool into the mixture.

If you are using a knife or metal amulet you will find it effective to heat the object before plunging it into the herbal potion. The reaction of the water and the hot metal will add an extra charge. Rinse with fresh water afterwards.

To Bless — A General Blessing

Use equal parts of pennyroyal, rosemary, hyssop, and acacia. Steep for five minutes, then strain the liquid through cheesecloth. Add the herbal liquid to another bowl, half-filled with pure spring water. Add a few freshly picked roses to the water, letting them float. Wait a few minutes, then bathe the ritual tool. Rinse with fresh water afterward.

To Bless — Lunar/Goddess Blessing

Use the same mixture of herbs as above, and strain in the same manner. To the new bowl of herbal liquid, add nine drops of almond extract. Next drop in three moonflowers (or white jasmine or lotus flowers). Then bathe the ritual tool, and rinse it off when finished.

Incenses

This involves the grinding or powdering of herbs, which are burned upon charcoal blocks as incense. The ritual tools are passed through the smoke to purify, bless, or empower.

Purification: Dragon's blood, myrrh, mint, vervain

Extra Potency: Dittany of Crete, periwinkle, pennyroyal, mandrake

Blessing: Acacia, rosemary, orris root, hyssop, moonflower

MAGICKAL FAIRY DUST RECIPE

This mixture can be used to charge ritual tools for Nature or fairy magick. It is also used to sprinkle over fairy stones, and according to legend helps one to see fairies through the hole in the stone.

1. The contents of three ripe foxglove seed pods
2. A pinch of scrapings from the stone rhyolite (A fine grain of volcanic granite)
3. A pinch of pollen (from selenetrope or evening glory)
4. Seven vervain blossoms
5. A pinch of lavender blossoms
6. A pinch of sand (west shore)

The Horned God

18

Starlore and Magick

The association of human destiny with the stars was directly due to the belief that the stars were powerful Beings and to the belief that the Stellar Realm was the final dwelling place of the soul.

from the text

Presented in this chapter are some of the Tanarric teachings dealing with the stars and their influences, and lore in Witchcraft and the Occult. Star Magick is one of the most ancient forms of Magickal practice. Remnants of Star Magick can still be found in published grimoires such as *The Key of Solomon*, *The Magus* (by Francis Barrett), and *The Book of the Sacred Magick of Abra-Melin the Mage*.

THE STARS OF MAGICK

Aldebaran

Aldebaran is the pale red star that forms the left eye in the constellation of Taurus the Bull. Throughout the early history of astrology, it was considered to emanate a powerful and fortunate influence, up until the dawn of Christianity.

In ancient times, Aldebaran was one of the Four Guardian Stars, known as the Watcher of the East. This was the station it commanded when the star marked the Vernal Equinox. Aldebaran was also called the "Eye of God" and the "Leading Star of Stars." This comes from the time when Taurus was the first of the Star Signs (before Aries replaced it).

Aldebaran lies slightly south of the ecliptic, in the path of the Moon's orbit. Here it marks one of the twenty-eight Mansions of the Moon. Mystics and occultists associated many powers and influences with Aldebaran. Ptolemy linked it to the nature of Mars, as did Agrippa. Francis Barrett, in his book *The Magus*, placed Aldebaran in the 4th Moon Mansion, and associated it with destructive forces (Christianity strikes again).

In La Vecchia, Aldebaran occupies the 2nd Moon Mansion and is a star of both positive and negative qualities. It is magickally linked to the ruby because of its color, and to the milky thistle because of its mixed nature. The mystic symbol of Aldebaran is shown in Figure 34.

In medieval times, talismans bearing a ruby, and the inscription of Aldebaran's seal, were anointed with the juice of the milky thistle and blessed in the name of Azariel, under the constellation of Taurus. It was used for protection against black magick and to bind other magicians. Aldebaran's influence was also said to hinder anything associated with mines, wells, or fountains.

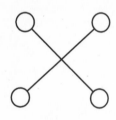

Figure 34
Aldebaran

One medieval spell involves drawing the image of a soldier upon parchment. He should be shown on a horse, holding a snake in his right hand. The seal of Aldebaran was then set in red wax upon the parchment, and perfumed with red myrrh and storax. The parchment was then buried in the place where the curse was desired.

The desired influence of this spell was upon mines, wells, fountains, and the construction of buildings.

CAPUT ALGOL

This star marks the head of "Medusa" in the constellation of Perseus. In medieval times, Algol was called the Demon Star. Under Christian influence, this star was greatly maligned, and was considered to cause violence and misfortune. Francis Barrett, in his book *The Magus*, stated that Algol was of the nature of Saturn and Jupiter, and was the most evil star in the heavens.

In astrology, this star is considered to exert a negative influence. I suppose that its ill reputation is gained by its link with the head of "Medusa." Ancient Hebrews called this star "Satan's Head." Prior to this association, they called the star "Lilith." In Hebrew mythology, Lilith was the first wife of Adam, in Eden.

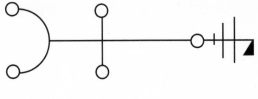

Figure 35
Caput Algol

Lilith was aggressive, and considered herself equal to Adam. Adam rejected her and she became an evil demon.

Actually, Algol is an ally to magicians. Tanarric Witches teach that this star can protect against another Witch's spells, and cause the "sender" to receive them instead. It is also said to strengthen the body.

In magick, the diamond is associated with Algol, along with the herb mugwort, and the metal lead. In spells, a sharp blade was prepared as a charm under Algol. These objects were prepared when the Moon and Algol were in conjunction. The talisman, or amulet, was made of lead and fumed with an incense of mugwort. The sigil of Algol (Figure 35) was inscribed upon the charm and blessed.

HIRCUS

Hircus is also known as the "Goat Star," and by the Arabs as the "Shepherd's Star." In astrology, Hircus was said to be fortunate in civic and military honors. This star is located in the constellation of Auriga, and is set upon the body of the Goat of Auriga's arms.

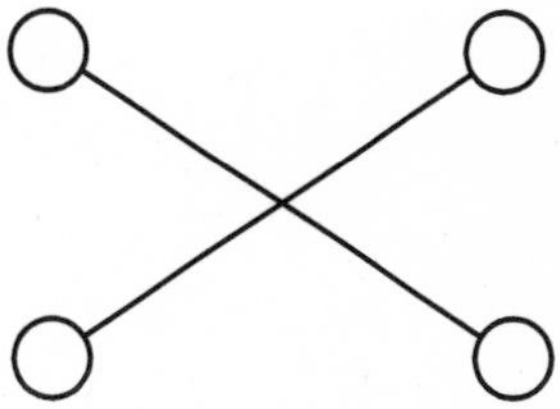

Figure 36
Hircus

Ptolemy ascribed the nature of Mercury and Mars to Hircus, but Tanarric Witches teach that this star is of the nature of Jupiter and Saturn. In magick, Hircus is used to gain the favor of authority, and to heal disorders of the teeth and bones.

A talisman of tin should be prepared, with a sapphire set upon it. The sigil of Hircus shown here (Figure 36) must then be placed upon the face of the talisman.

On the reverse side, place the image of a wandering minstrel. Next, an incense of equal parts of horehound, mugwort, and mandrake is used to fume the talisman.

The talisman is then held in the left hand, and a fig in the right. The Moon must be in a harmonious aspect, or conjunction, with Hircus during the Magickal work. All that remains is to call upon the name of the star three times, and to then state the desired effect.

A TRADITIONAL STAR SPELL

In medieval magick, the most common method of using a stellar force was to magickally bind it within a ring of power. The traditional manner of constructing these rings is as follows:

1. When the desired star shall fortunately ascend the horoscope, with the fortunate aspect or conjunction of the Moon, take a stone and herb of that star and make a ring of the metal that corresponds to the star. In the ring, under the stone, put a piece of the required herb or root. Upon the bottom of the stone place the symbol, name, and image of the star. If the stone is too small, then place these items upon a piece of parchment and seal them in with the herb.

   Next, set out the required stones of the star, forming the design of the constellation in which it is found. In the center of this, place a censer of incense containing the required herbs. Light the incense and call out the name of the star three times, saying:

   Hear me _____ I summon you, I evoke you!

2. As you do this, suspend the ring over the smoking censer. Next you must state clearly the exact effect that you desire. If you wish, you can formulate an incarnation to help focus your mind. Once the ring is charged, it is worn only when its magick is desired. To activate the ring, you must tap the stone setting with another stone of its type and speak the name of the star.

STARS AND THE AFTERLIFE

During the fourteenth century, Aradia taught that departed souls moved through a cycle of other worlds, eventually reaching the Realm of the Stars. From the Earth, the soul passed into the Lunar Realm, where it abided for a time. This was the Realm of Luna, known in some Craft Traditions as the Summerland. In Luna, the soul was renewed and purified.

If the soul had evolved beyond the need for physical existence, it then passed on to the Solar Realm. There a new "body of light" was "forged" in Divine Fire, and the soul became a totally spiritual being, who then dwelled in the Solar Kingdom of its deities. If the soul had not evolved beyond the Physical Plane, then it passed from Luna and was returned to the Earth. Ultimately the soul would reach the Stellar Plane.

In ancient times, the constellation of Cancer was believed to be the "portal" through which the soul returned to Earth. According to ancient legend, it was in this constellation that the Moon was located at the time of Earth's creation. Here it was guarded by the god Mercury.

The Moon itself was the portal through which the soul crossed over from the Physical Plane. According to the ancients, the Moon grew (waxed) as it received departed souls, and declined (waned) as the souls were released. Departed souls were drawn to the Sun god, as the Sun rose, and were carried off to the Underworld at sunset. Here they dwelled until their attachment to the physical life was dissolved. Then they rose with the Moon into the sky, and to the Realm of Luna.

At various times during the reign of the Stellar Mysteries, the stars were either viewed as the divine bodies of transformed souls, or as the souls of deities (or sometimes both). The planet Venus, then thought to be a star, was known as the Star Goddess, who oversaw the cycles of the soul. The Pole Star was considered to be her consort, the Star God.

The Watchers, themselves associated with stars, were believed to assist and guide departed souls to their proper Realms. In this same mythos, the Milky Way was believed to be the path which led to the Divine Abode, and was called "The River of Tana" by Tanarric Witches. Here were the nine heavenly crystal circles from which issued the "Harmony of the Spheres," universally believed in until the time of Copernicus.

The remnants of these stellar beliefs can be seen in the writings of many well-known people. Aristotle wrote, "Heaven is full of gods to who we give the name of stars," and Milton, in his *Paradise Lost*, says "Those argent fields more likely habitants, translated saints, or middle spirits hold, betwixt the angelical and Humankind . . . " The Christian Father Origen, using the books of Job and Matthew, stated that the stars were actually living beings.

In the Book of Job, 38:7, there appear to be two classes of stellar beings. These are called the "Morning Stars" and the "Sons of God." It is interesting also to note the mention of several constellations in Chapter 38:31–32.

The association of human destiny with the stars was directly due to the belief that the stars were powerful beings and to the belief that the Stellar Realm was the final dwelling place of the soul. I think that even the modern practice of calling celebrities "stars" may be rooted in the ancient belief that "stellar beings" were greater than Earth-bound ones. Perhaps especially so in the case where someone is said to have been destined to become a star. In essence, according to ancient belief, we're all destined for stardom, and someday the stars will call us home.

THE STARS' INFLUENCE IN OUR LIVES

Anyone even slightly aware of the Occult knows of the ancient belief that the stars influence our lives. In the Aridian Mythos, the Realm of the Gods is known as Aster. It is the plane upon which the gods dwell, properly known as the Divine Plane. The ancients, perceiving the vastness of the night sky, believed this to be the place where the gods first dwelled.

The Greek word for star was *aster*. This word is defined in today's dictionary[1] as:

aster: (Gk. aster, star) A combining form denoting relationship to a star.

It is interesting to note that the word "disaster," of which we all know the meaning, has its roots in Star Lore. The dictionary gives the following definition:

disaster: (Ofr. desastre. Gk. astron, a star: from astrological notions: ill-starred.) Any happening that causes great harm or damage; serious or sudden misfortune; calamity.

If we look up the prefix "dis," we find that it means "away, apart, deprived of, expelled from, cause to be the opposite of." If we take these meanings and connect them, we see that anyone who was experiencing severe misfortune (another interesting word) was believed to have been deprived of the influence of the stars.

Looking at the notion that a person could be expelled from the influence of the stars, we come into the realm of divine intervention. Apparently, to live in a way which would be the opposite of the stars was also a state of disaster. This leads us back to the Realm of Asteris. As surely as the ancients believed that living opposed to the stars brought misfortune, we know that living opposed to the gods (whatever we conceive them to be) will bring disharmony into our lives.

The structure of the Old Religion is such that it brings us into the harmony of those forces that influence our plane of existence. This is accomplished through seasonal rituals, and through the mental and spiritual training which is the essence of the Old Religion.

When we are experiencing strife, it is because we are moving against the forces which are unharmonious with ourselves. We are, in a sense, swimming against the current. We must either move within the flow, redirect the flow, or deflect it.

But to live in harmony with the influences emanating from Asteris is to become part of the natural way of things. It is by this means that we avoid disaster in our lives. In the stellar mythos, the influencing realms consist of seven spheres. Earth is last, although it is first from our perspective. Immediately surrounding the Earth Sphere is the vaporous, or Elemental Sphere. Next comes the sphere of Lunar influence, followed by the Planets. Then the sphere of the Sun begins, joined on the outer ridge by the Stellar Sphere. The last, but actually the first sphere is the Ultimate Realm, known as Aster.

Each plane in descending order was believed to influence the next sphere. This format became the formula for magickal workings, concepts, and symbolism. It also came to represent the realms through which the soul journeyed, after the physical body it had dwelled in perished.

All power originated out among the stars, having come from the gods of Aster. These powers were then attracted by the Sun, and directed into our sphere. The planets absorbed some of these diverse energies, and emanated them back outward, slightly altered by the vibrations of the planets themselves. This was the foundation of planetary influences in astrology. The Moon then attracted these emanations, and absorbed them, likewise emanating an altered vibrational energy of its own, down upon the Earth.

Through knowledge and worship of the Moon, Sun, and stars, it was believed that a ripple of energy could be sent back up through the spheres, to influence the gods themselves. Chants became the Music of the Spheres, and magick became the Harmony of the Spheres, just as it is today.

ENDNOTES

1. *Webster's New World Dictionary*. 1970.

A Traditional Witch Image

19

Shadow Magick

This was the earliest form of spell casting, and perhaps that is where the term "casting a spell" originated (as in "casting a shadow"). Perhaps even the Wiccan "Book of Shadows" may have originally been a record of these shadow forms.

from the text

Here we will examine a very ancient form of magick known as Shadow Magick. There is a metaphysical connection between the shadow and the body (or object) that casts the shadow. Charles Leland, in his book *Legends of Florence*, addresses this concept as follows:

> *. . . It is born of light, yet is in itself a portion of the mystery of darkness; it is the facsimile of man in every outline, but in outline alone; filled in with uniform sombre tint, it imitates our every action as if in mockery, which of itself suggests a goblin or sprite, while in it all there is something of self, darkling and dreamlike, yet never leaving us . . .[1]*

In ancient Egypt, the shadow was believed to be a portion of the soul itself. There were eight bodies which comprised a human entity in the theology of Egyptian religion. These were the *Khat*, a body; *Ba*, the spirit;

Khon, the intellect; *Khaibit*, the shadow; *Ren*, the name; *Ka*, the eternal vitality; *Ab*, the heart; and *Sahu*, the mask.

It is interesting to note that the ancient Etruscans believed that a portion of each human survived in a shadow-like form. They used the word *Hinthial* as the term for this surviving form (which they believed lived in, or around, the tomb or burial site). Leland makes reference in his book to the Hinthial, of which he says:

> *I had the belief, derived from several writers, that Hinthial in Etruscan meant simply a ghost or revenant; the apparition of someone dead. But on mentioning my discovery of this legend (the Legend of Intialo) to Professor Milani, the Director of the Archaeological Museum in Florence, and the first of Etruscan Scholars, he astonished me by declaring that he believed the word signified a shadow, and that its real meaning in its full significance had apparently been marvelously preserved in the Italian witch Tradition.[2]*

The legend of Intialo, which Leland recounted to Professor Milani, deals with an entity who takes on the form of a shadow. In this form, Intialo terrorizes anyone whom he selects as a target. The legend originates from the old region of Tuscany, which is in the north of Italy (the early site of the Etruscan civilization). In Leland's particular tale of Intialo, an evil sorcerer is attacked by the shadow form of Intialo, and tries to fend him off. In this story, of interest to Witches is the fact that the sorcerer banishes Intialo by declaring that he (the sorcerer) is protected by a "lovely witch." Italian witches will be delighted to know that mention of the walnut tree (a famous site of witch gatherings in Benevento, mentioned in the writings of Saint Barbato as early as A.D. 662) is also made in the legend, confirming the antiquity of the Strega Tradition. Leland gives this account of the words spoken to Intialo by the sorcerer:

> *Intialo! now, confess*
> *that with all thy craftiness*
> *thou didst not know what now I tell,*
> *that I am protected well*
> *by a lovely witch, and she*
> *is mightier far, O fiend than thee.*
>
> *Intialo! ere we go,*
> *if thou more of me wouldst know,*
> *come at midnight — I shall be*
> *'neath the witches' walnut tree,*
> *and what I shall make thee see*
> *I trow will be enough for thee.*

Intialo! in that hour
thou shalt truly feel my power
and when thou at last shalt ween
that on the witches' tree I lean,
then to thee it shall be known
that my shadow is thine own.

Intialo! everywhere
with me magick charms I bear,
ivy, bread, and salt and rue,
and with them fortune too.

Intialo! hence away,
unto thee no more I'll say;
now I fain would go to sleep,
see that thou this warning keep.
I am not in power thine,
but thou truly art in mine.[3]

Leland had obtained this legend, along with other treasures, from the good Witches of Tuscany. He spent many years there studying Witch lore, and made many significant discoveries.

Having labored the point here of the lore of the shadow, let us look now at the use of the shadow in Italian Witchcraft. Traditionally, shadows symbolizing a power animal were cast upon an object, or person, in order to transfer the nature of the animal into the target. This was the earliest form of spell casting, and perhaps that is where the term "casting a spell" originated (as in "casting a shadow"). Perhaps even the Wiccan "Book of Shadows" may have originally been a record of these shadow forms.

To perform this type of spell, you must first select the target object, and then determine which animal would most likely be associated with the desired "charge" for which the spell was designed. For example, you might choose a wolf shadow for hunting skill, or even for protection of a home, or a personal object. You might choose a panther shadow for tracking skills, swiftness, or war magick. A rabbit shadow symbolizes fertility, while a snake represents craftiness and virility. These are only a few good examples. A children's book on casting hand shadows will demonstrate the necessary hand positions needed to create a shadow.

Once you know how to cast the desired shadow image, and you have chosen the target, you are now ready to begin. Make sure that the light is strong enough behind you so that the shadow is quite clearly visible, when projected. Join your hands together, so that a "shapeless" image is cast on the target. Then begin to think about the animal form whose image you are about to cast. Imagine how the animal moves and sounds. Picture it clearly in your mind. Imagine how it might "feel" to be that animal. As you do this, look upon the target. Then slowly begin to arrange your hands into the necessary positions, so that the animal image begins to appear on the target.

Once the image is clearly cast upon the target, then you must instruct the shadow-form about the intent of the spell. You may either create a rhyme, or simply state the intended purpose. For example, a woman could charge a key chain with the wolf shadow, and then instruct the shadow that it will protect her from anyone who tries to physically assault her. When going out to her car at night, she would hold the key chain, and think of the wolf as though it were "escorting" her. The energy of the charge would tend to make her appear less of a victim, and an attacker would most likely not select her as his victim. Depending upon the personal power of the person casting the spell, it is even possible that a thought-form of the wolf might appear visible to the attacker, and he would move off, thinking that she had a dog with her.

Once the intent is firmly established in the spell, close your eyes and drop your hands to your sides. Say out loud that the spell is cast, then turn away from the target, and open your eyes. This is a very old form of magick, preserved in the Hereditary Tradition. This is the first time that I am aware of that this method has ever been made public.

Other methods of casting shadows may also be employed. A carving can be the source of the shadow; even an image cast from a piece of stained glass can be used quite effectively. I have a stained glass with a pentagram image on it; by placing a candle behind it, a beautiful image is cast. I have used this to charge a person with protection by letting the image fall upon them in the area of the head, heart, and genitals, and saying:

> *Strict charge and watch I give thee,*
> *that to this person,*
> *no evil thing approach, or enter in.*

I did not make up these words, but I like to use them, and they are effective (actually, they are based upon a verse in Milton's *Paradise Lost*). Concepts can also be placed in your target—such as the blessing of a goddess—with a crescent Moon image, or of a god, with a stag horn image, for example. Whatever symbols are meaningful to you will be the ones which are most effective.

In closing, it is unwise to place within the target other images that are not harmonious to one another in Nature. For example, a bird and a cat shadow would not be proper. Several compatible images may be safely placed together. Should you wish to remove a shadow charge, then simply reverse the process. Place the shadow image on the target once again, and then begin to picture the animal moving away from you. Tell it to return to its own realm, and then slowly move you hands together, allowing the shadow image to collapse. Close your eyes at this point (after you have seen the image collapse) and drop your hands to your side. Then open your eyes, and look at the target. Everything is now as it was before the spell was cast.

ENDNOTES

1. Leland, Charles. *Legends of Florence*, Macmillan and Co., 1895, page 237.

2. *Legends of Florence*, 1895, page 244–245.

3. *Legends of Florence*, 1895, page 244.

The Book of Strega

Part 3
Aradia and the
Teachings

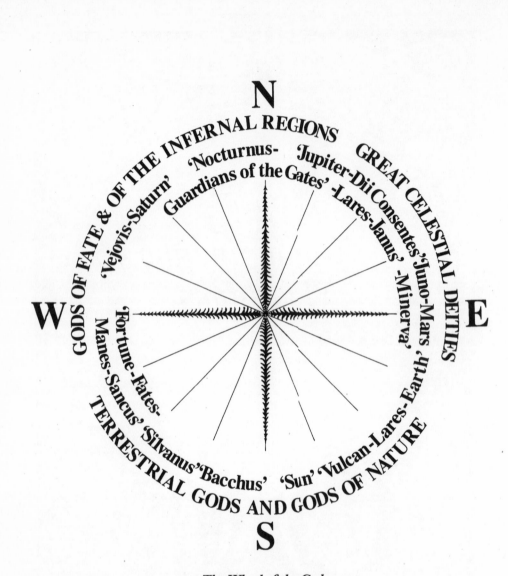

N

GODS OF FATE & OF THE INFERNAL REGIONS

GREAT CELESTIAL DEITIES

'Nocturnus- Guardians of the Gates' 'Jupiter-Dii Consentes'Juno-Mars

'Vejovis-Saturn'

'Lares-Janus' -Minerva'

W

E

'Fortune-Fates-

'Lares- Earth-

Manes-Sancus' 'Silvanus''Bacchus' 'Sun' 'Vulcan-Lares- 4th'

TERRESTRIAL GODS AND GODS OF NATURE

S

The Wheel of the Gods

20

The Strega's Story

Then having obtained a pilgrim's dress, she traveled far and wide, teaching and preaching the religion of old times, the religion of Diana, the Queen of the Fairies and of the Moon, the goddess of the poor and the oppressed. And the fame of her wisdom and beauty went forth over all the land, and people worshipped her, calling her La Bella Pellegrina (the beautiful pilgrim).

Charles Leland
Aradia; Gospel of the Witches

Long ago, in the Alban hills of Italy, a disheveled group of outcasts gathered by the fireside one Summer's eve to hear the tales of a forgotten age. In their midst sat a woman whom they called La Bella Pellegrina: the beautiful pilgrim. Her name was Aradia de Toscano, and in time she came to be known as the Holy Strega. Here in these ancient hills, she brought about the revival of the Old Religion of Italy (La Vecchia Religione), after centuries of Christianity and feudal lords had robbed the people of their heritage and their hope.

The Old Gods of Nature lay silent, carved in the mute stones that supported the ceilings of Christian temples. The cult of saint worship arose, and arrogated the offerings once sanctified by Pagan deities. It was a time of enslavement and abuse of power. Aradia came to deliver these peasants from slavery and to return their ancient Pagan heritage.

Many people are already familiar with the Legend of Aradia, as told by Charles Leland in his book, *Aradia; Gospel of the Witches*. Unlike his other works, Leland sought out what he thought was a pre-existing "gospel," instead of researching it on his own (as was his custom). He paid a local fortuneteller to obtain the text for him once she claimed to have knowledge of its existence.

The legend that was eventually given to Leland is a distortion of the original Italian legend. It was unlike anything that Leland had previously published, and contradicted his general theme of the "good witches" of Italy. Some people say that Leland created the text himself, and others say that he was deceived by the fortuneteller, whose only motive was a quick profit. If Leland had indeed created it himself, then it would certainly have supported his basic stand on Italian Witchcraft, but clearly it does not.

In this chapter, we will look at both portrayals of Aradia, through the eyes of Leland, and through the eyes of the Tradition that actually evolved out of her original teachings. To begin, we turn to the gospel of Aradia that was presented to Leland.

Leland's *Aradia; Gospel of the Witches* has been read and quoted by many Witches over the years. Yet how many have understood the potential danger hiding within its words? A close look at the published "*Gospel*" itself quickly reveals many of the flaws in its alleged "validity." These we will examine as the chapter continues, along with several fragments of actual Strega material woven into the deceptive fabric of the text.

Telling the Strega's Story

The Strega's Story

Charles Leland began his search for material pertaining to Italian Witchcraft in the late 1800s. In Italy he met a woman named Maddalena, who claimed to be a Witch. It was through her that Leland obtained the material that resulted in his book (published in 1899). I'm sure that anyone who has had to seek out the Craft in America is aware of all the obstacles and pitfalls, even with the many excellent Pagan organizations available today. You can imagine what it must have been like for Leland in Italy during the latter part of the nineteenth century. Despite his good intentions, Leland ended up with a mixture of folklore and fabrication (with a dash of authentic witch lore thrown in).

In chapter one, the text describes medieval Italy, and then quotes the Goddess Diana as saying (to Aradia):

> *Thou must go to Earth below to be a teacher unto women and men who fain would study Witchcraft in Thy school . . .*

> *and Thou shalt be the first of Witches known; and Thou shalt be the first in all the World . . .*[1]

What this is trying to tell us is that Aradia was the first Witch in the world, and that she appeared in medieval Italy. This would mean that there was no Old Religion of the Craft predating Christianity. This would then support the Christian claim that Witchcraft is a perversion of Christian belief. No true Witch of the Old Religion would ever write such nonsense, nor ever desire to see it be published as representative of the Old Religion. If Maddalena were actually a Witch, then why would she pass on such nonsense? Chapter one also links Diana to Lucifer, a theme that plays right into the hands of Christian propaganda. The matter is somewhat resolved by the fact that Leland's Gospel of Aradia does not reflect the Witchcraft tradition actually practiced by Maddelena. It is likely that Maddelena was simply passing on to Leland the material he requested, and she may not have known he was going to publish it as a book. By Leland's own account he never again had any contact with her after receiving the Witches' Gospel from Maddelena.

In chapter two, we find a very disturbing invocation to Diana for the charging of ceremonial cakes:

> *I bake the body and blood, and the Soul of great Diana, that She shall know neither rest nor peace, and ever be in cruel suffering till She will grant what I request . . .*[2]

This is another thing that no true Witch would advocate, and therefore it was not a practitioner of the Old Religion who incorporated these words. I know of nothing like this in the Old Religion of Italy, but aspects of such practices by Catholic peasants in Italy do exist relating to saint worship. In a practice originating in the Middle Ages, statues of saints are sometimes bound with cords and placed in darkness. This is a punishment designed to extract favors from the saint in some type of sympathetic magick.

Leland's Aradia text is clearly a Christianized mutation of the actual writings of Aradia's followers. Again, in chapter one, we find another disturbing verse:

> *And when the Priests of the Nobility shall say to you that you should put your faith*
> *in the Father, Son, and Mary. then reply: "Your God, the Father and Maria are*
> *three devils!*[3]

This would certainly bring disaster to anyone who spoke these words in medieval Italy. So, why would a Witch advocate such a stand? Unfortunately, Leland fell victim to what some Italian Witches call the *Malandanti*. The Malandanti are people who practice black magick and disregard the true path of Stregheria, but claim to be Witches, just as many Satanists call themselves Witches, even though they are not. Is there anything positive to say about Leland's book? Yes, there are actually a few fragments of genuine Strega material.

In chapter one, we find part of the now well-known "Charge of the Goddess":

> *Whenever ye have need of anything,*
> *once in the month, and when the Moon is Full . . .*

This is part of what Aradia told her followers before she departed. The actual Strega text, as it appears today, can be found in the Full Moon ritual appearing in this book. In chapter two of Leland's *Aradia*, we find a writing that reflects one of the ancient symbolical mystery teachings. Here Leland associates the grain for the cakes of celebration with the seed that was planted in the ground "where all deep secrets hide," and the firefly (whose shape is like a wheat grain) with the forces which aid plant growth (pollination and sunlight). They also represent the Sun God, who is the harvest grain.

In chapter eleven, we find the term *La bella pellegrina* (the beautiful pilgrim) connected to a story about a woman born in Volterra. This was a phrase actually used by followers of Aradia, and it is curious to find it here in Leland's book. Finally, in chapter thirteen, Leland gives an excellent description of the offering to, and invocation of, Diana.

Even though there are a few almost redeemable segments in Leland's book, the material itself cannot be taken seriously by anyone knowledgeable in the Old Religion as an indication of Italian Witchcraft beliefs and practices. It is certainly a far cry from his excellent book, *Etruscan Roman Remains*, which also addresses Italian Witchcraft. Why he chose to publish the Aradia material, clearly contradicting his life's work, remains an unsolved mystery.

Despite the many errors in Leland's book, the portrait of Aradia as a rebellious leader is quite accurate. To better understand this, we shall now turn our attention to the original legend of Aradia.

According to the teachings, Aradia was born in Volterra, Italy during the early part of the fourteenth century. Legend states that she was born on August 13, 1313. Many people dismiss this date as a fabrication, feeling that it is a bit too "witchy." Others see it as symbolism, for August 13 was the sacred Festival day of the Goddess Diana, and thirteen was the mystical number of the Moon (Aradia and Diana being thirteen twice). This may not be so far off, however, when we consider that there is some evidence that Aradia did exist, and was alive during the fourteenth century.

According to the original legend, Aradia brought about a revival of the Witch Cult in Italy during the mid-fourteenth century. She was taught the Old Ways by her aunt, and she later returned this ancient Pagan heritage to the oppressed peasants of Italy.

The Italian Inquisitor, Bernardo Rategno, documented in his *Tractatus de Strigibus* (written in A.D. 1508) that a "rapid expansion" of the "witches sect" had begun 150 years prior to his time. Rategno had studied many transcripts concerning Witchcraft from the trials of the Inquisition. Tracing back, he discovered the time at which the trials had first begun, and noted how they have increased over the years.

After a thorough study of these records (kept in the Archives of the Inquisition at Como, Italy), Rategno fixed the time the persecution began at somewhere in the mid to late 1300s. If Aradia had been born in 1313, she would certainly have been old enough to teach and influence others, and for groups to form to carry on her teachings.

There are no public records concerning Aradia by name, and no references to her in any published literature (that I can find) until Leland's account of her in 1890. In 1962, T. C. Lethbridge (former Director for Cambridge University Museum of Archaeology and Ethnology) published a book called *Witches*, which does refer to Aradia in several chapters. In chapter two, he writes:

> *We can then, I think, assume that Leland's Vangelo and Dr. Murray's trial evidence are more or less contemporary and that it is reasonable to use the two together to form a picture of the witch cult at about A.D. 1400 . . . Aradia was sent to earth to teach this art to Mankind. That is, she was, in the opinion of her devotees, a personage, known in Hindu Religion as an Avatar, who taught them how to harness Magick power. Aradia, at some far-off time, may have been as much an historical person as Christ, Krishna or Buddha . . .*[4]

This is one of the few references to Aradia having possibly been a real person in history, written by someone not personally connected with Witchcraft. It is also interesting to note that *Ecstascies: Deciphering the Witches' Sabbath*, by Carlo Ginzburg, contains a passage that may also be a historical reference to Aradia. On page 189, he speaks of a medieval pagan sect known as the Calusari, who (as late as the sixteenth and seventeenth centuries) worshipped a mythical Empress. The Calusari called her "Arada" or "Irodeasa," and also used the term "mistress of the fairies" for her. Could this sect have still been practicing a form of worship initiated by Aradia over 100 years earlier?

According to the original legend of Aradia, she left Italy at some point in her quest, and traveled out of the country. Serbia, the home of the Calusari, lies a short distance across the Adriatic from central Italy, and travel by ship was not uncommon in that era. Aradia would not have traveled west to France because the Papacy was still established in France, and the Church was still hunting her. It would have been too dangerous to go to northern Europe, because Witches were being burned or hanged in that region (Italy did not begin the burning of Witches until after the time of Aradia). So, in fact, an eastern exodus would have been the only logical action that Aradia could have taken. At the very least, there is a striking coincidence between Aradia's Witches and the Calusari of Arada.

Many people will refute this circumstantial evidence and demand some solid historical documentation. Unfortunately, such evidence is not available to the public, so the truth of her existence may never be made known. However, there are no historical records of there ever having been a Jesus Christ either, except for references to the persecution of his followers, and the existence of his gospel. The same can be said for Aradia. As we know, all myths have their basis in fact (and the most effective lies are based upon the truth).

Leland's public account of Aradia includes a legend about the "Beautiful Pilgrim," and we believe this to be a remembrance of Aradia, preserved for generations by Tuscan peasants. In part, this legend says:

> *Then having obtained a pilgrim's dress, she traveled far and wide, teaching and preaching the religion of old times, the religion of Diana, the Queen of the Fairies and of the Moon, the goddess of the poor and the oppressed. And the fame of her wisdom and beauty went forth over all the land, and people worshipped her, calling her La Bella Pellegrina (the beautiful pilgrim).*[5]

An interesting connection can be found in classical Roman mythology. The Roman deities Faunus and Fauna had offspring known as Fatui, who were considered to be prophetic deities of the fields. These resemble the later beings known in Celtic folklore as *Fays*, or fairies.

In Italian Witchcraft, the name Fauna (or Fana) is another name for Diana, just as Faunus is another name for Dianus. Leland names Diana as the Queen of all Fairies (Fays) and Roman mythology names Fatua/Fauna as the mother of Fays. Leland's Aradia contains several stories connecting fairies to Diana, Aradia, and to Witchcraft in general. He also mentions that La Bella Pellegrina was converted to Moon Worship and taught others the Old Religion of Diana.

In the original story of Aradia, we find a woman who was rebelling against her parents and their religion. In the fourteenth century, this was not met with much understanding (not that it is today, by any stretch of the imagination). According to the legend, Aradia would often go for long walks through the Alban Hill region near Lake Nemi. It was here that she one day experienced a vision that shaped the course of her life. In a manner not uncommon among mystics, Aradia encountered a moment of spiritual enlightenment.

It is said that she heard a "voice" that told her that she was chosen to fulfill a quest, and that she must challenge the established order of things, and provide hope to those who were enslaved by the wealthy nobility. Whether this was an inner voice, or some other phenomenon, we do know that it was significant enough for her to set out on a course of which few women of that era would ever dare dream.

Aradia came to be known as the Holy Strega, a spiritual teacher and wise woman. Her natural healing abilities and her knowledge of herbal potions was legendary during her time. She collected a small band of followers from the outlaw camps in the Alban Hills, and traveled the countryside, teaching the Old Religion of pre-Christian Europe. During her brief time as a holy woman among the peasant people, Aradia came to be regarded as the daughter of the Goddess Diana, and after her disappearance many people worshipped her as a goddess herself. But Aradia had come as the avatar of a forgotten age, and not as a goddess. It was never her intention to be worshipped.

In the final instruction to her followers, she asked them to remember her through a sacred meal of wine and cakes, and to always keep to the Old Ways. She told them to gather together when the Moon was full, and to worship the Great Goddess. She told them that they must be free when they came together, and that as a sign of their freedom they were to be naked in their rites, to celebrate in joy, and to make love with one another.

The freedom of which she spoke was the freedom of the mind, body, and spirit. She urged her followers to reject the Judaic-Christian "morality" that served to control them, and to practice the Old Ways. Today, many people have personal issues with these old Pagan ways, and cling to the moral values of Judaic-Christian culture.

Many involved in the Craft today come from this kind of background, and it is difficult for them to shed the beliefs of their parents and teachers. They do not strive to embrace the Old Ways which lead to liberation, but allow their own inhibitions and fears to stunt their Pagan spiritual growth. Sadly, this attitude, which is better suited to Christianity than to Paganism, quite often causes the initiate to remain in the Outerworld, outside of the abilities of the Old Ways to bring them the peace and harmony which so many seek, but cannot sustain.

Throughout the original legend of Aradia, we find a woman who was capable of both great spiritual peace and great social anger. In one particular event, she is confronted by Christian priests being escorted by a group of soldiers. When she is told that they have come to arrest her, Aradia unleashes her anger upon them, saying:

> *I rebuke you and I cast you out because you teach punishment and shame to those who would free themselves from the slavery of the Church. These symbols and apparel of authority that you bear serve only to hide the nakedness which we are all equal. You say that you serve your God, but you serve only your own fears and restriction.*

This is quite a contrast to some of the gentle spiritual teachings that she so eloquently delivered in other parts of the original text.

Above all things, Aradia stressed the seeking and obtaining of an inner and outer balance. She spoke of the equality of the masculine and feminine in an age where this was most unwelcome. Aradia challenged the authority of the Church and the "right" of the wealthy nobility to oppress the peasants. This behavior brought her many enemies and eventually resulted in her arrest for heresy and treason.

She suffered humiliation and torture at the hands of her captors, but never lost sight of her spiritual quest. In prison, she used her sexual power over men to secure her escape. She did not allow herself to become a victim of their power over her, but instead used hers against them.

Today, many people have bought into the Judaic-Christian myth concerning a woman's sexuality. Even many modern Pagans hold to the myth that a woman who is free with her sexuality, according to her own needs and desires, is somehow cheap or used, and is a "slut." Somehow men do not seem to fall into this same category, and at worst are considered "animalistic," which to a Pagan does not necessarily carry the same demeaning connotations (even to non-Pagans, it's still not quite the same meaning).

Aradia used her entire being as a tool for self-empowerment. She employed her intellect and spiritual nature when she spoke with friends and enemies alike. She used her feminine instincts and sexuality as a resource upon which to establish power over those who sought to control her. Aradia employed magick as a tool for self-empowerment, to reach beyond to her full potential.

To her, the totality of a person, both experientially and potentially, had to be nurtured and brought into fullness. This was what the Church feared most, and was the real reason for the persecution of Witches. Men basically fear a woman's sexual power over them and seek to control it, harnessing it for their own use. *If she denies it to him, she is called a bitch. If she shares it with anyone but him, she is called a slut.*

Aradia is the image of the powerful female Witch. She is bold, independent, sexual, confident, and self-empowered. Even in the distorted version provided by Charles Leland, Aradia appears as a woman who draws people together into the Society of Diana, displaying leadership abilities and personal charisma. Overlooked for far too long by modern Witches, Aradia should be a symbol of women in the Craft today, for in Aradia is the Amazon Warrior, the Enchantress, the Healer, and the Matriarch.

In fourteenth-century Italy, Aradia taught hope and personal empowerment to an oppressed peasant population. She taught them freedom and openness in a time when the Church taught them shame and guilt. She gave peasants hope and self-worth, in an age that offered them only slavery and servitude. She taught them how to discover their roots, and to remember who they were, so they could start to live the lives of the people they truly were. She returned their heritage and pride to them, teaching them that they did not simply labor for the fancy of the wealthy.

The message of Aradia is much the same today, and her teachings offer the same path to freedom and personal empowerment. Every woman who has ever stood her ground, faced her fears, or met her death defending her beliefs, knew the spirit of Aradia. She still lives on today inside of all women. Sometimes she whispers her message, sometimes she sets it on fire, but it is always there for those who have the courage to listen. All women are Daughters of Aradia, and she asks only these few things of those who will follow her ways.

THE COVENANT OF ARADIA

Observe the times of the Treguenda, for therein is the foundation of the powers of Stregheria.

When good is done to you, then do good to another. If someone wishes to repay you for a kindness, then bind them to go out of their way to help three others; then this shall clear the debt.

Do not use the arts of Stregheria to appear powerful among others. Do not lower the standards of the Art and thereby bring contempt upon the Old Ways.

Do not take the life of anything unless it is to preserve life, yours or another's.

Do not give your word of honor lightly, for you are bound by your words and by your oaths.

Do not bow before any authority over you unless it is of the gods. Instead, cooperate with others but do not be a slave and always preserve your honor. Give respect to others and expect respect in return.

Teach all who appear worthy and aid the continuance of the Old Religion.

Do not belittle another's religious beliefs, but simply state your own truths. Strive to be at peace with those who differ.

Do not purposely cause harm to another, unless it is to prevent true harm to yourself or another.

Strive to be compassionate to others, and to be aware of the hearts and minds of those around you.

Be true to your own understanding and turn away from those things which oppose the good in you, or are harmful to you.

Hold reverence to all within Nature. Destroy nothing, scar nothing, and waste nothing; live in harmony with Nature, for the ways of Nature are our own ways.

Remain open in your heart and in your mind to the Great Ones who created all that is, and to your brothers and sisters alike.

ENDNOTES

1. Leland, Charles. *Aradia; Gospel of the Witches* (1890). Phoenix Publishing, Inc. (1990 reprint), page 4.

2. Leland, Charles. *Aradia; Gospel of the Witches*, pages 13–14.

3. Leland, Charles. *Aradia; Gospel of the Witches*, page 5.

4. Lethbridge, T. C., *Witches*. The Citadel Press (1962), pages 13–14.

5. Leland, Charles. *Aradia; Gospel of the Witches*, page 69.

21

The Teachings of
the Holy Strega

Not shall this time pass quickly, for the Church shall grow in power. But their time
of power shall not last, for the Age of the Son will pass away, and the Age of the
Daughter shall come upon the world in all its glory. Now when the Age of the
Daughter shall come, then shall reason be restored and the world shall be complete.

from the text

The Strega's gospel of Aradia, as it appears here, is a modern compilation of written and oral tradition blended together to present the story of Aradia, and her teachings, during the Middle Ages in Italy. The stories and legends of Aradia have been passed down through family lines since the fourteenth century. It would be nice to believe that the teachings have come to us unchanged through the centuries, but there is no way to be sure of such things.

In the final analysis, it is really unimportant whether the teachings are ancient or modern, for the Strega find them today to be sound and practical. They are as much a part of the Strega's spirituality as the Wiccan Rede is to modern Wiccans. Such debates of authenticity are best left to those who are so unsure of their own spirituality that they feel the need to dismantle another's.

The material that follows in this chapter is divided into the Gospel and the Teachings. It is the purpose of this chapter to present the reader with a clear image of Aradia and her teachings, and therefore of the Strega's mentality as a whole. If you stay in the company of an Italian Witch for any time at all, you will hear the Strega's story. Let us begin now with the legend of Aradia.

PART ONE: THE GOSPEL OF ARADIA

Aradia was born in Volterra, Italy in the early part of the fourteenth century. Even as a child there was a sense of spirit about her, and her parents believed that she might someday become a Catholic nun, themselves being of the Catholic faith. Her aunt had other ideas, for she was of the Old Religion.

In the course of time the aunt was hired to care for Aradia, and she began to tutor the young child in the Old Ways. Aradia listened with great interest to the tales of forgotten gods and ancient spirits. Her spirit grew and she understood the inner truths of these stories. Then, on her thirteenth birthday, Aradia was initiated into the Old Religion. Something inside of her then awoke, and she began to remember other realities.

Up in the hills of Nemi, near the lake upon whose shores the ancient temple of Diana had stood, Aradia sat and listened to the inner voices. A voice spoke to her, telling her to open her eyes and look upon the sky. It was then that she noticed that the sky had begun to darken, but the afternoon had not yet passed. The voice spoke again and whispered the word "Moonshadow."

Looking about her, she saw the beauty of all things, and the equality of all things. She understood, and with the enlightenment that had come upon her, Aradia opened her heart and mind to the vastness of all she perceived.

She decided not to return to her home, and was taken in among the outlaw camps that were hidden in the woods. Here she learned of the sorrows of those who lived in slavery, and listened to tales of cruelty and evil task masters. She learned also of the hypocrisy of the Church, which aided the nobles in controlling the peasants.

Aradia began to contemplate the plight of the peasants who labored for the wealthy lords. She embraced their sorrow and was moved with compassion for them. In the months that followed, she began to go among the villages to heal and counsel the people, giving them comfort and hope.

The people came to love her, and they called her "the Beautiful Pilgrim." Her fame spread throughout the towns and villages, and she began to teach the Old Religion. It was not long before the Church became aware of her, and the priests who were accompanied by a group of soldiers confronted her. Aradia rebuked them for the hypocrisy of the Church, and she was arrested for heresy. When it was learned that she wanted to free the peasants from servitude, she was also charged with treason against the kingdom.

While awaiting execution in prison, an earthquake toppled the structure and the word spread that Aradia had died. Later she appeared in the outlaw camp and chose a small group of followers to accompany her on a journey. In the months that followed, Aradia initiated them and taught them all the secrets of the Old Ways.

One day she announced that she must leave them, and she presented them with a set of nine scrolls. Aradia departed to the east and was never seen again. Her followers began to form groves throughout the Kingdom of Naples, and the Church was greatly concerned over the revival of the Old Religion. In time the followers of Aradia were hunted down by the soldiers and the scrolls of Aradia were captured and given over to the Church.

The last few remaining survivors of Aradia's original followers took refuge in the town of Benevento, and began to teach the Old Ways there once more. Benevento had once been the main gathering place for the Strega, and the town was a sanctuary for followers of the Old Religion. One of Aradia's disciples wrote down all that she could remember of Aradia's teachings. She had once lived in the home of a noble family and was taught to read and write. What she preserved has come to be called "The Words of Aradia."

PART TWO: THE WORDS OF ARADIA

Concerning Nature

Nature is the Great Teacher. In Her are all things revealed. Nature reflects the Higher Ways of Spirit. The Creators established the Laws of Nature so that through them we might come to know the laws of the Great Ones. Therefore, observe the ways of Nature around you, both great and small. Everything has purpose and reason. Be not confused by its seeming cruelty, for there is a duality in all things.

Respect Nature in all ways. Take only that which you must from Her, and remember nothing can be taken except that something be given. This is law for all Strega.

Know that the wind speaks of the knowledge of the Earth, and the spirit of the kindredness of all living things emanates from everywhere.

Nature teaches all living things all that must be known. She teaches birds to make their nests, animals to hunt and survive, children to crawl and walk. She teaches life. Once She taught all people of Her ways, but they chose to go their own way. They chose to oppose Her and to control Her. But for Strega there can be no other way than Nature. A Strega must live in harmony with the Forces of Nature.

Concerning the Earth

The Earth is the nurturing power of the Mother. She nourishes us and from the soil She returns that which we sow. She gives us healing herbs and herbs by which we work our magick. The very Earth gives us life, without which we would perish.

There is a healing power in the Earth, and a vital force. We know that a wounded animal will lay against the Earth to heal its wounds. They understand, and we are one with them through our religion.

I have taught you the secrets of the circle, for therein is the secret of the power of the Earth. Everything that the world does, it does with a circle. The Earth teaches us the doctrine of Cycles. The Sun, the Moon, and the seasons come and go, and return again and again. Even so is it with the cycles of our own lives. The Earth teaches us just as Nature does, for they are one. Earth is the body, and Nature is the Spirit.

We must live in harmony with the Earth and with Nature. To do otherwise is to court disaster. The forces of the Earth are greater than any power we can safely master. To strive against these forces is foolish.

Do nothing to the Earth that shall take away from the purpose it serves in Nature, for this is the natural balance. And the Earth shall always move against us to restore itself.

Is the tiller greater than the soil he tills? Is the family greater than the crops they help grow? Is not the life within the soil, and within the crops, our own? How shall we be without them? What you do to the Earth you do to yourself.

Do not think that we are greater than the Earth, or than Nature. For surely they shall both crumble and dissolve all that we shall erect. And there shall be floods and earthquakes, and hostile weather to show us our errors and teach us perspective.

Concerning Life

We live upon the Earth because we are not prepared to live in the ways of the spirit. We are not physical beings, and this is why physical life is often difficult.

It is not our way to disregard the physical, for we dwell within it. So it is best to live in harmony with the world. But for us to become involved in the physical so as to disregard the spirit is likewise harmful. This binds us to rebirth, and to unhappiness.

A Strega respects life, and all living things. Life must not be taken without necessity. The purpose of physical life is to learn the higher ways of spirit through knowledge of the lower, and to prepare our spirit for the existence for which it was created.

Concerning Death

Every beginning is also the ending of that which came before it. Every ending is likewise a beginning of that which is to follow. Coming and going are simply the two sides of the one journey.

Death is merely a change of awareness and of form. It is unfeared by the spirit, but often feared by the personality of the dying one. Yet the realm of death is like the dream worlds to which we journey in our sleep, and just as brief. Know that the spirit always moves to a higher state, and always toward the Light. The shadows of death cannot keep us.

Upon dying we are purified by the elements as we rise into the ether. From life we go to dwell upon the Moon (within the Lunar and Astral Realms) and there await our return. In Luna we are given vitality and made strong again.

If the Great Ones, who created all things, have seen within us the purity of Light, then shall we go forth to be forged by the Sun and taken to dwell among the stars, in our new divine form. If this is not to be, then shall we be given unto rebirth (according to our deeds) within the world of physical matter.

Concerning Love

Love is the gift of the spirit's blessings. It is the emanation of spirit within. Love is the Great Attainment.

Receive love when it is offered, and offer love regardless. Yet do not allow the duality of love to cause you despair. For love can lift up your heart and it can likewise drag it down.

Accept love in the manner in which it comes to you. Do not possess it, or attempt to control it or shape it. For love is free, and shall come or go in its manner.

Concerning Sexuality

The sexual power of a man or woman is the strongest power that may be raised from the body. The Christians teach that sexuality must be repressed, and thereby rob people of their personal power.

Do not be confused by the duality of sex, for it can be physical alone or it can be spiritual alone. It can also be both together.

Share your sexuality with whomever you may, in whatever manner you may. For all acts of love and pleasure are rituals to the Goddess and to the God.

It has been written that you shall be free, and so shall you be free in body, mind, and spirit.

Be not like the Christians who teach shame and modesty, and false morality. Blessed are the free.

You have heard it said that homosexuality is unnatural, yet I say to you that heterosexuality is likewise unbalanced. Everything is masculine and feminine in essence, and all bear the divine spark of the God and Goddess within them. Realize this, and do not exalt the one above the other. A Strega must live with inner and outer harmony.

You have heard the Christians condemn adultery, and say that the spouse is the property of the other. Yet no one may rightly dictate the will of another. Do not confuse love with sex nor sex with love.

Remember that pleasure belongs to everyone, and rightly so. Therefore harm no one through your own will, nor place your will above another's.

Concerning Marriage

When a man and a woman join their lives together through ritual, and the love which they share, then are they linked to each other in another life to come.

Yet being together, know that each of you must be alone. Understand that even though you are bound together, let this not be as captives.

There shall always be others with who each of you may desire to share a closeness, either physical or spiritual. This is as it should be. Let your love desire fullness of life for each other and also pleasure for each other. Honor each other with openness and honesty.

Because you have joined your lives together, you are sanctuary and comfort for each other. Together shall you stand in all things, for you are true friends.

You are together because of your love, and you remain for this reason. Yet if this reason for coming together is forgotten, or fades, then it is well to part if needs be such. You do not honor the joining by remaining without love. Neither do you honor each other.

Concerning the Gods

Know that the gods need our worship, even as we need food and drink. Do not think that they serve us, for we are the servants. Therefore do not bargain or demand through prayer or ritual. The gods shall provide that which is needed.

Do not blame the sorrows of life upon the gods. For it is humankind which creates the despair on Earth.

Do not doubt the reality of the gods, for they do exist and are many. They have been since long before the people walked upon the Earth. Yet as we are capable of understanding them, they are no older than we. For they are not the personifications, nor the images which we establish. But the gods do respond to us through these things. We are linked to them by virtue of our yearning toward a higher nature.

The gods are attracted to our rituals because of the sacred signs that we use, and because of our worship (which is vitality). They are attracted by the ritual fires and incense, and by the purity of our naked bodies. They give and take the vital essences that we both need, through the power that we raise.

Each god is like us for our ways are but reflections of theirs. Each god has likes and dislikes and must be approached in accordance. Each god is linked to the culture of the people who give worship to it, and must be called by the appropriate ties.

Yet beyond all of this are the God and Goddess who together are the One; herein does the true worship belong.

Concerning the Goddess

The Goddess is the life force inasmuch as she is the fertility in all things. It is through Her activity that we are born, and that seeds push up through the Earth and grow into plants. She moves the God to create through His desire for Her.

The Goddess is the joy of life. She is the passion to live. Compassion, love, gentleness, and kindness are the essence of Her spirit. All women carry the Goddess within in various aspects and degrees.

Yet there is a duality in all things, and the Goddess can manifest as sterility, vengeance, and destruction. She is the Soul of Nature.

The Goddess rules the night and the Moon is Her symbol. All women are linked to Her through the Moon, which influences the flow of blood. The night is the essence of the mystery which all women possess. This is the elusive quality which all women bear, but which can never be known or touched upon.

The desire of men for women is the desire of God for Goddess. It is the attraction of the life force.

The Goddess is known as the Queen of Heaven. She is clothed in stars and wears a silver crown adorned with a crescent moon. She is the Earth Mother, clothed in green and endowed with large breasts that rise as rounded hills rise beyond the lush green meadows. She is pregnant with the Child of Life, which She bears each year. She is the Virgin Maiden, naked and beautiful. She is youth and lust for life. She is the Enchantress and Temptress. She is all women.

The Goddess does not accept live sacrifices as were given in ancient times. She is the Goddess of life and all living things. She demands respect for life. If you give offerings in Her honor, then better it be of fruits or grains, or things of beauty.

The Goddess is Queen of all the Strega, which She calls Her Hidden Children. We are Her servants; She is not ours. She gives us life and receives us in the Afterworld. She teaches us the ways of Nature and Spirit. She gives us power and magick. She reveals all mysteries and gives light to the night. And to the wise, She imparts Her sacred name.

Concerning the God

The God is known as the stern and demanding aspect of divinity. He is perceived as the death force that transforms. He is Lord of the Afterworld who restores and rests the Soul, which is prepared for a new life. This is performed through the union of the God and Goddess.

Yet there is a duality in all things, and the God is also the vitality and strength. He is the Sun, the Lord of Light. He can give life or death through His activity. He ascends and vitalizes all living things, but in His journey He descends and brings darkness and cold. This is His Realm of Shadows, to which He carries all departed beings.

The God is the desire to create, dwelling in the state prior to creation. Through the attraction of the Goddess He is moved to create.

He is the Lord of the Heavens, clothed in the Sun and bearing a golden rod. He is Lord of the Earth, horned and hooved. He is Lord of the Afterworld, dark, lonely, stern, and just. (Thus are the two faces of Janus.)

Through Him is order established and discipline mastered. He is the inner strength of the individual. He is the essence of inner strength and defense.

Yet He is also the warrior and the destroyer. He is power and strength. All men bear His essence. He is all men.

There is a side of the God that can be seen by those who desire to love Him. It is a gentleness, a compassion, and an understanding. His gentleness comes from His awareness of His strength and power. His compassion is born of His understanding of justice.

The God is sexual desire and virility within the male. He is attraction, sensuality, and sexuality. He is physical nature, just as the Goddess is spiritual nature.

In death, He is the comforter and the renewer. He is the great initiator and teacher. He rules the Afterworld and dispels the darkness with His presence. He is the illuminator and reveals all that is hidden. He scatters all falsehoods and establishes truth.

Concerning Tana and Tanus

Tana is the sacred name of the Great Goddess, She who is All Goddesses. Upon the Earth She is known as Fana, in the heavens She is Diana (the Moon), and in the Universe She is Tana (containing them all).

Lakes, hills, streams, and beaches are sacred places to Tana. The animals that are sacred to Her are dogs, owls, and cats. Her sacred plants are moonflowers and willows. Lemons and apples are also sacred to Tana.

Tana is all that is feminine. She is total beauty and love. She is the Divine Lover, Enchantress, Temptress, and Mother. At times She is the Eternal Virgin; at times the

266

Mother; but truly, She is free, loving, sexual, independent and powerful. Tana loves Her followers with unequaled passion. She never forgets nor neglects Her own. She is generous and protective to all who love Her.

Tanus is the Great God, who is All Gods. On Earth He is Faunus, in the heavens He is Janus (the Sun), and in the Universe He is Tanus.

All mountains are sacred to Tanus. His sacred animals are horses, wolves, woodpeckers, and ravens. His sacred plants are the fig tree, oak, dogwood, laurel, and the bean plant.

Tanus is all that is masculine. He is strength and will. He is the power of fertility (which is shared with Tana) and the desire behind all of creation. Tana is the source for all creation.

At times He is the hunter and provider, and at times He is the destroyer. But truly, He is wise and powerful. He is the freedom of things that are wild. He is loving and sexual, independent and powerful. Tanus loves His followers with a demanding love. He protects and provides, but He is stern and judgmental. He expects strict adherence to His ways and His laws. But He is always fair and just.

Faunus is the Eternal Child, for we see in Him the frolicsome Pan. Yet the noble side of Faunus can be seen in the grace of a beautiful stag in the forest. We can see His spiritual nature in the circling of a hawk, and in the playful bunting of young goats can we see the lighthearted Faunus. All of these are lesser reflections of Janus and Tanus in their own natures.

Tana is the balance to Tanus, and He is the balance to Her. Without Tana, the God would be a judge without compassion, He would be stern without understanding, He would control without loving.

Without Tanus, the Goddess would have compassion without direction, understanding without foundation, love without form.

The God and Goddess complete each other, and together they are the One True Creator and Maintainer of the Universe.

Concerning Worship

Remember to keep—and observe—all the sacred gatherings. For therein does the power flow, and emanate forth into our Being. Observe the time of the Full Moon, and all the Holy Days of the Goddess.

Honor the Sun and Moon, for they are the sacred symbols of the God and Goddess (which they placed in the heavens as a token of their covenant with us). But do not worship them, for they are but images of the Great Ones.

And you who are priests and priestesses, remember the times of union (and the rite thereof).

All acts of reverence toward Nature, and towards life, are acts of worship. So is it too with love and pleasure. Therefore, let each day be your rituals of adoration to the Great Ones.

The Times of Gathering: Shadowfest: October 31st

Winter Solstice

Lupercus: February 2nd

Spring Equinox

Tana's Day: May Eve/May 1st

Summer Solstice

Cornucopia: August Eve

Autumn Equinox

The Holy Days: Festival of Diana: August 13th

Festival of Fana: December 19th

Festival of Tana: May 1st

Festival of Jana: January 1st

Concerning Freedom

We have been enslaved. We are persecuted, hunted, and murdered by the Christian Church. We are outlaws.

Because of our plight we have come to know the meaning of Freedom. To be free is the essence of life.

Freedom allows the mind, body, and spirit to be rid of shame, guilt, and restriction (which the Christians teach).

The freedom to act as you desire, harming no one by your deeds, is the gift of Freedom. The Old Ways free us from the restrictions of society and the expectations of other people.

Therefore, you shall be free. And as a sign that you are truly free, you shall be naked in your rites. And you shall sing, dance, and make love.

Concerning the Law of Return

Every act that you perform will draw to itself three times the nature of the act (affecting us on three levels: the soul, mind, and body). Such is the Law. This effects not only the acts of each day, but reaches into the future as well. Here the Law establishes those debts that must be paid.

Therefore, consider well your actions. Nothing escapes the Law, nor is anything hidden from it. The Law does not punish nor reward. It only returns the intent of each action to its origin.

If you step off from a high place you will fall, and this is consistent. There is no intent; there is nothing good nor evil. It may be good to leap upon your enemy from a high place and surprise him, or it may be bad to fall and be injured. But the nature of the descent itself is only a law. So too is the nature of the Law of Return.

Concerning the Prophecies

Now it shall come to pass that our ways will no longer be mere heresy in the eyes of the Church. But they shall make of our practices an evil thing, and they shall seek to destroy us. So shall they steal independence from the people, and make them dependent upon the Church and its priests.

When the Pope shall come again into Rome and establish his power anew, then shall you know the first of all the sorrows. With this shall the eyes and ears of all the Churches be upon our ways. And they shall make strict laws against us. Then shall come the great sorrows, for they will openly hunt us down and slay us. In their prisons shall they torture us and create all manners of lies, forcing us to bear witness to all that they say.

Not shall this time pass quickly, for the Church shall grow in power. But their time of power shall not last, for the Age of the Son will pass away, and the Age of the Daughter shall come upon the world in all its glory.

Now when the Age of the Daughter shall come, then shall reason be restored and the world shall be complete.

To herald the coming of the Daughter, and to keep it remembered upon the Earth, there shall arise a prophet. And a prophet shall come among the people every two hundred years, that our ways shall not be forgotten.

Then when the Age is near my prophet shall arise, and prepare the way for She who will establish reason. When the Age is near there shall be an awakening in the awareness of women, and their wills shall be asserted. Laws will then change and women shall walk in the ways of men. And the followers of the Old Religion shall receive a sign, for the last of the laws which persecute us shall vanish. In that year my prophet will be born, and will prepare the way for She who will come. This prophet shall be a teacher of the Old Ways, whom many will call the Silent Prophet.

When the Age of the Daughter replaces that of the Son, then shall the Daughter appear and establish her power. And she shall be thirty-six at this time. Such changes will occur in the Earth, which the people of that time have never seen before. And there shall be upheaval and renewal. Out of the ashes shall arise the new world of reason.

People shall no longer be ruled by governments. Nor shall one people oppress another. There shall be no rulers, but only teachers and counselors. No one shall possess power over another, nor shall anyone restrict or control any other person.

The Earth shall be of one people, and they shall all live under the emanating rays of love, peace, and reason.

Concerning Magick

There is a force that dwells in all things, which is called the Numen. The power of an object is the power of its Numen. This essence has, of its own accord, a definite consciousness. If you are in harmony with the Ways, then you may call upon any Numen that you desire, and it will assist you. This is but one aspect of magickal rapport.

Know that all things of the same nature (or essence) are as links in a chain. Through one you may influence the other. By this law do we make use of clay puppets. Yet even the mind is linked by thoughts and has power to reach out on its own.

The substance of magick is best controlled and directed through the use of ritual. Ritual attracts power, and through repetition it is then accumulated.

Certain channels of power are formed through ritual, which becomes a link to the desired response or contact. Thus do we make use of the secret signs, symbols, and gestures (which are thus empowered). Repetition is necessary, as well as is consistency.

As Strega, we draw power down from the Moon, and also do we draw power from Nature. The God and Goddess oversee our works, as do the Grigori. When our magick does not produce the desired effects, it is because a greater power resists its power. This is often a sign that the nature of the magick was improper. Yet it can be that another Strega works against you. If this becomes the matter, then seek this person out and resolve your differences.

Understand that you must always work in harmony with the phases of the Moon, and under the blessings of the God and Goddess, and in accordance with the laws and ways.

The Moon symbolizes the hidden things revealed in the darkness. The night is the side of life that is unknown. The light of the Moon is subtle and active on hidden levels. So too is our magick.

The powers which are obtained through the knowledge of the Old Ways are neither good nor evil; it is only the way in which you use them that is good or evil. The mind is most receptive to the influence of power when the person is intoxicated or asleep (within two hours of awakening). This is true also of trance, which is induced through chant and dance.

The mind that dreams (the subconscious) is directly linked to the Moon Worlds (the Astral Realms), just as the mind that knows the daylight (the conscious mind) is directly linked to the Physical World. It is through the dream mind that the Moon Worlds are contacted. It is through the Moon Worlds that magickal influences, and magickal forms, are created. These, in turn, influence the Physical World.

It is the purpose of symbols to speak to the dream mind, and plant the magickal seeds that will manifest. It is the purpose of rituals (and spells) to establish the patterns of power. These patterns are established to either draw upon power or to raise power (or both).

Magickal and ritual correspondences are incorporated to take advantage of the Numen qualities in objects, times of power, links to Deities, and states of consciousness (awareness).

The art of magick is a blending of inner or personal power with that of natural powers and divine powers.

Concerning the Elements

There is a vaporous, subtle, and invisible quality to each of these things that are called the physical elements. The ancients have told us that all of creation was brought into being when the spirit drew the four elements unto itself. These elements are called earth, air, fire and water. And they are controlled by spirit.

Each of these elements possess an etheric double. It is this essence which gives vitality, or fertility, to the physical object.

Just as the physical realms of matter contain their own forms of life, so too do the etheric realms. These entities have been personified as the many spirits and creatures of myth and legend. It is their activity that creates and maintains the vital essence within all matter.

The etheric powers of the elements also give potency to spells and works of magick. It is within their realms that magickal powers ebb and flow. Thus are the spirits of the elements summoned to assist us.

Concerning the Grigori

Before the people walked upon the world, there dwelt those beings which we call the Grigori. Some have called them spirits and gods. Some have spoken of them as powers and forces.

The old legends tell us that the Grigori once were physical beings, but that they are no longer. It is said they dwell among the stars.

They are the Watchers of the Worlds, and of the entrances and exits to the Worlds. Once it was said that the stars were the campfires of their armies, ever watching over us.

The Grigori have set their towers at the four quarters of the world, and they stand vigil over the portals which lay between the worlds.

Once they were called the powers of the air, and so did they come to be linked to the winds. Then were they known by the Latin names of Boreas, Eurus, Notus, and Zephyrus. Yet these were but their titles. Know now their ancient names: Tago, Alpena, Settrano, Meana.

The Old Ones come to our rituals to witness our rites, for we have a covenant with them. So do they watch over our works and help us. Our covenant with them was established at the end of the Second Age, and from this time do we mark the years of our ways.

The Grigori observe our rites, protect us, and escort us to the Moon Worlds when we pass from the Physical World.

Concerning Rebirth

The human body will eventually fade away after the death experience. Yet the soul cannot be destroyed, nor is it subject to physical actions or restrictions. After the death of the body, the soul is still connected to its form for three days. For a period of seven days the soul is earthbound. After this it will be escorted by the Old Ones to the Moon Worlds.

For the Strega the desire is to enter the world of Luna and be prepared for rebirth. The Strega also desires to be born among the loved ones that he or she knew in lives that have passed.

The ancient teachings tell us that the soul enters a cycle of seven lives through which it strives to be complete. Each cycle is followed by another until the soul is complete and physical life is no longer necessary.

The memory of a past life is often hidden from the present consciousness so that each life is unique. Yet the memory can be recalled if truly desired. The memory of each life is contained within the soul. The soul is the True Self. Each physical body (and personality) is only a garment worn by the soul. It is not important whether you are a man or a woman, for each is but a small lesson, and you shall be both many times.

The Law of Return governs the life experience and condition in each new life. But beyond all of this is the realm of Tartaru, which is the abyss. Here are the Souls that are inclined toward evil. Here are they kept in restriction until the Great Ones decree their fate.

Concerning the Act of Rebirth

After the death experience has been completed, then the soul is made ready to be born again.

When a couple is engaged in sexual union, a whirlpool of energy (a vortex) is created above them. This energy attracts souls who are awaiting rebirth, from the plane which is harmonious to the energy of the Union (the vortex is a composite aura of the couple).

Once attracted, the soul will be drawn into the female womb and will enter into a new physical life (all conditions being procreant).

Before being born again, the soul will obtain knowledge of the life to come. Then is the plan realized.

Concerning Luna

Luna is the purest of all the Moon Worlds. It is where the soul is taken to rest and be renewed. It is the place of eternal youth. Here there is union with the Gods and with those Strega who have gone before.

The portal to Luna is in the West, beyond the sunset and beyond the Ocean. Luna is a place of beautiful forests and meadows. It is a place of clear streams, rivers and lakes. Nature spirits inhabit these places as do all the beautiful creatures of ancient myth and legend. In Luna it is always Summer.

Each soul experiences Luna in the manner that is most suited to its life experience. This is as it should be.

In ancient times, it was said that the shape of the Moon grew as it received the souls from the Physical World, and that it depleted as they were reborn. But we must realize that the Moon is not truly the World of Luna, but only a symbol. Yet if you could see between the Worlds, you would see that the Moon is Luna.

From the Physical World, and by the physical senses, you can never see or know the World of Luna.

Concerning the Astral Plane

The Astral World, through the Plane of Forces, receives the thoughts and vibrations of actions from the Physical World. Just as solid materials are used to create objects in our world, thoughts and vibrations create etheric objects on the Astral Plane.

Therefore, what people strongly believe in enough can be created astrally. This is one method by which ritual magick is performed. Energy is first raised with a specific purpose in mind, then this is given up to the Plane of Forces, where it is drawn and channeled to the Astral World, and so obtains a thought form.

The true purpose of the Astral Plane is to prepare us for future lives and existences by burning out (purifying), or exhausting, all of our fears, desires and false concepts. These bind us to the lower worlds. So it is with our Afterlife experiences in the lower astral worlds which transforms us.

The Astral World is under the Divine Law of Cause and Effect, action and reaction. It is the essence of the Three-fold Law.

The Astral Planes contain all the heavens and hells which the followers of all religions believe in. They will experience that which they believe awaits them. On the Astral Plane, thoughts are things. And as you believe, so shall it be.

Concerning Christianity

You have heard the Christians say that only through Jesus Christ can you enter into the Great Realm. So I tell you that Jesus was the spirit of love, and only by love may you enter in.

You have heard the Christians say much concerning the teachings of Jesus, but how many have you seen follow them? So I say to you that Christianity, as Jesus taught it, died with him on the cross. Even his own disciples were more concerned with their self-images, and self-importance.

The Christians say that we are evil and dangerous, but who is the more so? They believe the world will end, and teach others concerning this, speaking of the destruction which their god will bring. The mind has great power, and many minds of one belief have much power (even to accomplish a great destruction). So I say to you that there shall indeed be this time of sorrow. But out of the ashes shall arise the new World of Reason. For the Great Ones shall use this to fulfill the plan, through the teachings of the Daughter.

There shall never be peace between our religions, for they ever strive against us. It is useless to attempt to reason with them, for they have never been known for their ability to reason. They choose to have faith in place of understanding.

Therefore, it is best to avoid them so as not to anger them. For anger always follows lack of understanding. Remember also the time of persecution to come, and reveal nothing to them that shall harm our people or our ways.

It is sad that our ways of spirit cannot be extended to, nor be shared with, the Christians.

Here end the Words of Aradia

22

Conclusion

Many people feel that the Old Religion is long gone, fragmented and faded, perhaps a bit like a jigsaw puzzle with most of the pieces missing. Others maintain that it never existed in the first place, and that it is a modern invention based upon bits of lore and legend. Still others do not even speculate, but simply enjoy it as it is today, no questions asked. Hereditary Witches simply grin or walk by the skeptics, whistling, maintaining the legacy of secrecy that has preserved the Old Religion for centuries.

In this book we have looked at the historical documentation of the Witch Cult and its association with the goddess Diana down through the centuries. We have seen that, as early as 30 B.C., writers in Italy were commonly addressing Witches as followers of Diana. The trail of this Society of Diana has been preserved through the records of the Inquisition at Como, Italy, and clearly attests to this ancient tradition, as is evident in the chronology appearing in chapter 2. Supporting evidence of this antiquity is also noted in the appearance of ancient Etruscan elements discovered in Tuscan Witchcraft as late the nineteenth century.

We have seen that the trial transcripts of the Italian Inquisition (as late as the seventeenth century) note that the Benandanti and Malandanti Witches held rites associated with the fertility of crops and animals. They also performed marriages and other customs that clearly address the structure of a func-tioning Witch community. Such a structure is also noted in the *Compendium Maleficarum* concerning Italian Witchcraft. The image of Witches worshipping a Queen of the Sabbat, seated with a Horned Deity (as depicted in Jan Ziarnko's seventeenth-century print) also adds credence to the concept of a Witches' God and Goddess pantheon. Despite the views of those whose writings negate the existence of the Old Religion, clearly enough historical evidence exists to give one pause for thought.

We know from the writings of the Italian Inquisitor Bernardo Rategno that something apparently took place in the mid-fourteenth century that caused the Church to focus upon those who were believed to be involved in the practice of Witchcraft. Bernardo Rategno refers to it as a "rapid expansion of the witches sect." What was the catalyst to this resurgence? In Italian folklore, we have seen that native Witches believed that Aradia brought about the revival of the Old Religion at that same period in Italian history that Rategno refers to. Skeptics may be interested to know that I first wrote about Aradia as an historical Witch of the fourteenth century, who brought about the revival of the Old Reli-gion, in *The Book of the Holy Strega* (published in 1982). The first time I came across the reference to Rategno's comments concerning the fourteenth-century expansion of Witch-craft was when they were reported in *Ecstasies: Deciphering the Witches' Sabbath*, by Carlo Ginzburg (published in 1991).

Some scholars may feel that the works of Frazer and Leland, upon which I have drawn in this book, are no longer given the importance they once enjoyed in those authors' day. While it is true that academia may no longer consider their books to represent main-stream thought, this in no way detracts from individual points raised within their works as a whole. Like most persecuted people, Witches know how incorrect public thought can be anyway, even at its best.

In the final analysis, it is not the historical evidence, or claims to ancient traditions by those who profess a membership therein, that attest to the survival of the Old Religion. It is what everyone who practices the Old Ways knows in their hearts, and in their spirits, that confirms the living legacy of the Craft. When we look upward upon the same Moon as did the ancients, and we gather in the celebration of Nature beneath her, we all know then that it never passed away. When we join in kindred celebration at festivals or ritual gatherings, we know the ancient joys, and we all feel the love that cannot die. Perhaps it is simply that here, at the close of the twentieth century, Pagans and Witches still call upon the ancient deities, still recall their names and times of celebrations, truly proclaiming the survival of the Old Religion. As Italian Witches say, "As it was in the time of our begin-ning, so it is now, so shall it be."

Charles Leland wrote, in the closing of *Aradia; Gospel of the Witches*, "It would be a great gratification to me if any among those into whose hands this book may fall, who possess information confirming what is here set forth, would kindly either communicate it or publish it in some form, so that it may not be lost." I hope that this book has accomplished what he wished for in his final days.

Part 4
Appendices

A
Comparison of Wiccan Aspects with Leland's Italian Witchcraft

USE OF THE TERM: THE OLD RELIGION

From *Etruscan Roman Remains*, the introduction:

> *Among these people, stregeria, or witchcraft—or, as I have heard it called, " la vecchia religione" (or "the old religion")—exists to a degree which would even astonish many Italians.*

From *Aradia; Gospel of the Witches*, appendix:

> *The result of it all was a vast development of rebels, outcasts, and all the discontented, who adopted witchcraft or sorcery for a religion, and wizards as their priests. They had secret meetings in desert places, among old ruins accursed by priests as the haunt of evil spirits or ancient heathen gods, or in the mountains. To this day the dweller in Italy may often find secluded spots environed by ancient chestnut forests, rocks, and walls, which suggest fit places for the Sabbat, and are sometimes still believed by tradition to be such.*

FULL MOON RITUAL

From *Aradia; Gospel of the Witches*:

> *When I shall have departed from this world,*
> *Whenever ye have need of anything,*
> *Once in the month, and when the moon is full,*
> *Ye shall assemble in some desert place,*
> *Or in a forest all together join*
> *To adore the potent spirit of your queen,*
> *My mother, great Diana. She who fain*
> *Would learn all sorcery yet has not won*
> *Its deepest secrets, then my mother will*
> *Teach her, in truth all things as yet unknown.*

RITUAL CAKES AND WINE

From *Aradia; Gospel of the Witches*:

> *You shall make cakes of meal, wine, salt, and honey in the shape of a (crescent or horned) moon, and then put them to bake. . . .*

> *O Diana!*
> *In honor of thee I will hold this feast,*
> *Feast and drain the goblet deep,*
> *We will dance and wildly leap . . .*

> *And thus shall it be done: all shall sit down to the supper all naked, men and women, and the feast over, they shall dance, sing, make music. . . .*

From *Aradia; Gospel of the Witches*, appendix:

> *The supper of the Witches, the cakes of meal, salt, and honey, in the form of crescent moons, are known to every classical scholar. The moon or horn shaped cakes are still common. I have eaten of them this very day, and though they are known all over the world, I believe they owe their fashion to tradition.*

From *Aradia; Gospel of the Witches*, chapter one:

> *Thus do I seek Aradia! Aradia! Aradia! At midnight, at midnight I go into a field, and with me I bear water, wine, and salt, I bear water, wine, and salt, and my talisman— my talisman, my talisman, and a red small bag which I ever hold in my hand. . . .*

Appendix A

SKYCLAD PRACTICE (NUDITY)

From *Aradia; Gospel of the Witches*:

> And so ye shall be free in everything;
> And as the sign that ye are truly free,
> Ye shall be naked in your rites, both men
> And women also. . . .

> And thus shall it be done: all shall sit down to the supper all naked, men and women, and the feast over, they shall dance, sing, make music. . . .

A GOD AND GODDESS MYTHOS

From *Aradia; Gospel of the Witches*:

> Diana was the first created before all creation; in her were all things; our of herself, the first darkness, she divided herself; into darkness and light she was divided. Lucifer, her brother and son, herself and her other half, was the light.

> Lucifer was extremely angry; but Diana with her wiles of witchcraft so charmed him that he yielded to her love. This was the first fascination; she hummed the song, it was as the buzzing of bees (or a top spinning round), a spinning-wheel spinning life. She spun the lives of all men; all things were spun from the wheel of Diana. Lucifer turned the wheel.

> (Chapter nine) The ancient myth is, to begin with, one of darkness and light, or day and night, from which are born the fifty-one (now fifty-two) weeks of the year. This is Diana, the night, and Apollo, the sun, or light in another form. . . .

From *Aradia; Gospel of the Witches*, appendix:

> Now be it observed, that every leading point which forms the plot or center of this Vangelo, such as that Diana is Queen of the Witches; an associate of Herodius (Aradia) in her relations to sorcery; that she bore a child to her brother the Sun (here Lucifer); that as a moon-goddess she is. . . .

GODDESS WORSHIP

From *Aradia; Gospel of the Witches*, chapter four:

Diana, beautiful Diana!
Who art indeed as good as beautiful,
By all the worship I have given thee,
And all the joy of love which thou hast known,
I do implore thee. . . .

(Chapter ten) Why worship a deity whom you cannot see, when there is the Moon in
all her splendor visible? Worship her. Invoke Diana, the goddess of the Moon, and
she will grant your prayers. This shalt thou do, obeying the Gospel of (the Witches
and of) Diana, who is Queen of the Fairies and of the Moon.

THE WATCHERS

From *Aradia; Gospel of the Witches*, appendix:

All things were made by Diana, the great spirits of the stars, men in their time and
place, the giants which were of old, and the dwarfs who dwell in the rocks, and once
a month worship her with cakes.

From *Aradia; Gospel of the Witches*, chapter three :

. . . Then Diana went to the Fathers of the Beginning, to the Mothers, the Spirits
who were before the first spirit, and lamented unto them that she could not prevail
with Dianus. And they praised her for her courage; they told her that to rise she
must fall; to become the chief of goddesses she must become a mortal.

INITIATION

From *Etruscan Roman Remains*, chapter ten:

As for families in which stregheria, or a knowledge of charms, old traditions and
songs is preserved . . . as the children grow older, if any aptitude is observed in them
for sorcery, some old grandmother or aunt takes them in hand, and initiates them
into the ancient faith.

REINCARNATION

From *Etruscan Roman Remains*, the introduction:

Also that sorcerers and witches are sometimes born again in their descendants.

From *Etruscan Roman Remains*, chapter ten:

> *It is also believed in the Romagna that those who are specially of the strega faith die, but reappear again in human forms. This is a rather obscure esoteric doctrine, known in the witch families but not much talked about. A child is born, when, after due family consultation, some very old and wise strega detects in it a long-departed grandfather by his smile, features, or expression.*

From *Etruscan Roman Remains*, chapter ten:

> *Dr. O. W. Holmes has shrewdly observed that when a child is born, some person old enough to have triangulated the descent, can recognise very often the grandparent or great-uncle in the descendant. In the witch families, who cling together and inter-marry, these triangulations lead to more frequent discoveries of palingenesis than in others. In one of the strange stories in this book relating to Benevento, a father is born again as his own child, and then marries his second mother. But the spirit of the departed wizard has at times certainly some choice in the matter, and he occasionally elects to be born again as a nobleman or prince.*

From *Etruscan Roman Remains*, chapter ten:

> *Sometimes in his life a man may say, "After my death I may be born again a wizard, (for) I would like to live again!" But it is not necessary even to declare this, because if he has said such a thing, even unthinkingly to witches—senza neppure pensarvi ai stregoni—they hear and observe it. So it will come to pass that he may be born again even from the children of the children of his children, and so be his own great-great grandson, or great-grandson, or grandson.*

From *Etruscan Roman Remains*, chapter ten:

> *In this we may trace the process by which the witch or sorcerer, by being re-born, becomes more powerful, and passes to the higher stage of a spirit.*

ELEMENTALS

From *Etruscan Roman Remains*, the introduction:

> *Closely allied to the belief in these old deities, is a vast mass of curious tradition, such as that there is a spirit of every element.*

B

Charles Godfrey Leland

Many people today think of Gerald Gardner as the founder of modern Wicca/Witchcraft. Gardner's books on Witchcraft published in the mid-twentieth century brought about a growing interest in the Old Religion of pre-Christian Europe. However, over half a century earlier a man named Charles Godfrey Leland wrote on many of the same topics later popularized by Gerald Gardner. For example, the theme of witches meeting at the time of the Full Moon in the nude, calling their ways The Old Religion, celebrating with ritual cakes and wine, and worshipping a God and Goddess all appear in Leland's writings on Italian Witchcraft circa 1896.

In chapter four of his book, *Gypsy Sorcery & Fortune Telling*, published in 1891, Leland makes the earliest connection between Wicca and modern Witchcraft:

> *as for the English word witch, Anglo-Saxon Wicca, comes from a root implying wisdom* . . . (Leland's footnote here reads:)
> *Witch. Mediaeval English wicche, both masculine and feminine, a wizard, a witch. Anglo-Saxon wicca, masculine, wicce feminine. Wicca is a corruption of witga, commonly used as a short form of witega, a prophet, seer, magician, or sorcerer. Anglo-Saxon witan, to see, allied to witan, to know* . . .

What I find interesting is Leland's "pre-Gardnerian" reference to Wicca and Witchcraft. Of further interest is the fact that there is no single element of the basic structure of Gardnerian Wicca that cannot be found in Leland's earlier writings. The only exception would be the clear mention of a ritual circle. However, in the Italian witchhunter's manual (*Compendium Maleficarum*, 1608) we do find a woodcut of Italian Witches gathered in a circle traced upon the ground along with a reference to ritual circles being traced in the ground using a beech twig. Therefore, the historical support for this aspect of Italian Witchcraft may have been obvious enough for Leland to feel no need to address it specifically.

But who was this Leland character, and why should we take particular notice of his writings in the first place? Charles Godfrey Leland was a famous folklorist who wrote several classic texts on English Gypsies and Italian Witches. He was born in Philadelphia on August 15, 1824 and died in Florence, Italy, on March 20, 1903. Leland was fascinated by folklore and folk magick even as a child, and went on to author such important works as *Etruscan Roman Remains*, *Legends of Florence*, *The Gypsies*, *Gypsy Sorcery*, and *Aradia; Gospel of the Witches*.

In 1906 a two-volume biography of Charles Godfrey Leland was written by his niece, Elizabeth Robins Pennell. In chapter one, recounting his personal memoirs, Pennell writes of his infancy:

> *In both the 'Memoirs' and the 'Memoranda' he tells how he was carried up to the garret by his old Dutch nurse, who was said to be a sorceress, and left there with a Bible, a key, and a knife on his breast, lighted candles, money, and a plate of salt at his head: rites that were to make luck doubly certain by helping him to rise in life, and become a scholar and a wizard.*

Pennell goes on to tell us that Leland's mother claimed an ancestress who married into "sorcery." Leland writes in his memoirs:

> *My mother's opinion was that this was a very strong case of atavism, and that the mysterious ancestor had through the ages cropped out in me.*

The biography of Charles Leland is filled with accounts of his early interest in the supernatural, an interest that turned to a life-long passion. Of this passion Pennell writes:

> *It is what might be expected . . . of the man who was called Master by the witches and Gypsies, whose pockets were always full of charms and amulets, who owned the Black Stone of the Voodoos, who could not see a bit of red string at his feet and not pick it up, or find a pebble with a hole in it and not add it to his store—who, in a word, not only studied witchcraft with the impersonal curiosity of the scholar, but practised it with the zest of the initiated.*

As a young boy Leland grew up in a household that employed servants. According to Pennell, Leland learned of fairies from the Irish immigrant women working in his home, and he learned about Voodoo from the black servant women in the kitchen. Leland writes of his boyhood:

> *I was always given to loneliness in gardens and woods when I could get into them,*
> *and to hearing words in bird's songs and running or falling water.*

Pennell notes that throughout Leland's life, he could never get away from the fascination of the supernatural, nor did he ever show any desire to.

Fluent in several foreign languages, at age eighteen Leland wrote an unpublished manuscript English translation of Pymander of Trismegistus, a Hermetic text now commonly known as *Hermes Trismegistus: His Divine Pymander*. The *Pymander*, as it was often called for short, was the foundation for much of the Hermetic writings that inspired many Western Occultists during the later part of the nineteenth century and early part of the twentieth century.

In 1870 Leland moved to England where he eventually studied Gypsy society and lore. Over the course of time he won the confidence of a man named Matty Cooper, king of the Gypsies in England. Cooper personally taught Leland to speak Romany, the language of the Gypsies. It took many years before Leland was totally accepted by the Gypsies as one of their own. In a letter dated November 16th, 1886 Leland wrote to Pennell: " . . . I have been by moonlight amid Gypsy ruins with a whole camp of Gypsies, who danced and sang. . . . " Having penetrated their mysteries to such a degree, Leland went on to author two classic texts on Gypsies, establishing himself as an authority on the subject among the scholars of his time.

In 1888 Leland found himself in Florence, Italy, where he lived out the remainder of his life. It was here that Leland met a woman whom he always referred to as Maddalena. Her real name was Maddalena Alenti, although some people have mistaken her for another woman Leland knew named Margherita Talanti. Maddalena worked as a "card reader," telling fortunes in the back streets of Florence, and later married a man named Lorenzo Bruciatelli, with whom she moved to America.

Leland soon discovered that Maddalena was a Witch, and employed her to help gather material for his research on Italian Witchcraft. Maddalena introduced Leland to another woman named Marietta, who assisted her in providing him with research materials. Pennell, who inherited the bulk of Leland's notes, letters, and unpublished materials, refers to Marietta as a sorceress, but Leland's own description of her in his published works is less clear. At one point Leland mused, in a letter to Pennell dated June 28th, 1889, that Maddalena and Marietta might be inventing various verses and passing them off as something of antiquity. However, Leland seems to have had a change of heart, as reflected in another letter to Pennell written in January of 1891. Here Leland writes:

> *It turns out that Maddalena was regularly trained as a witch. She said the other day, you can never get to the end of all this Stregheria—witchcraft. Her memory seems to be inexhaustible, and when anything is wanting she consults some other witch and always gets it. It is part of the education of a witch to learn endless incantations, and these I am sure were originally Etruscan. I can't prove it, but I believe I have more Etruscan poetry than is to be found in all the remains. Maddalena has written me herself about 200 pages of this folklore—incantations and stories.*

In another letter dated April 8, 1891 (written to Mr. Macritchie) Leland indicates still other Witches who assisted him in his research:

> *. . . But ten times more remarkable is my MS. on the Tuscan Traditions and Florentine Folk Lore. I have actually not only found all of the old Etruscan gods still known to the peasantry of the Tuscan Romagna, but what is more, have succeeded in proving thoroughly that they are still known. A clever young contadino and his father (of a witch family), having a list of all the Etruscan gods, went on market days to all the old people from different parts of the country, and not only took their testimony, but made them write certificates that the Etruscan Jupiter, Bacchus, etc. were known to them. With these I have a number of Roman minor rural deities, &c.*

In Florence, Leland spent all of his spare time collecting Witch Lore, and purchasing items of antiquity as he chanced upon them. In a letter written to Mary Owen, Leland says:

> *I have been living in an atmosphere of witchcraft and sorcery, engaged in collecting songs, spells, and stories of sorcery, so that I was amused to hear the other day that an eminent scholar said that I could do well at folk-lore, but that I had too many irons in the fire.*

Leland describes the Italian Witches he met as "living in a bygone age." It was an age that Leland apparently longed for himself.

Leland, apparently, did more than interview Italian Witches, or simply keep their company. A passage from his book *Etruscan Roman Remains* strongly suggests that Leland was himself initiated into Stregheria, as indicated in the last sentence of the following:

> *But, in fact, as I became familiar with the real, deeply seated belief in a religion of witchcraft in Tuscany, I found that there is no such great anomaly after all in a priest's being a wizard, for witchcraft is a business, like any other. Or it may come upon you like love, or a cold, or a profession, and you must bear it till you can give it*

or your practice to somebody else. What is pleasant to reflect on is that there is no devil in it. If you lose it you at once become good, and you cannot die till you get rid of it. It is not considered by any means a Christianly, pious possession, but in some strange way the strega works clear of Theology. True, there are witches good and bad, but all whom I ever met belonged entirely to the buone. It was their rivals and enemies who were maladette streghe, et cetera, but the latter I never met. We were all good.

There is another passage given in the same book. In the chapter titled "Witches and Witchcraft," Leland is interviewing a Strega, and asks her how a certain priest became a Stregone. In doing so he asks her how he (the priest) "came to practise our noble profession." Leland seems to be referring to the Strega and him as being part of something that the priest had also joined.

One of the most puzzling aspects of Leland's writings on Italian Witchcraft is the fact that he goes back and forth between speaking of Witchcraft in the common negative Christian stereotypes of the period portraying Witches as "good" and "noble" followers of the goddess Diana instead of the Devil. His book *Aradia; Gospel of the Witches* is certainly a shocking turn from his general theme of the good Witches of Benevento. Was he trying to please both sides? Or was he laying the foundation for a greater revelation to come? Perhaps we may never know, because Leland died without completing his work on Italian Witchcraft.

C

Befana

In Italy there still remains, from early times, a curious tradition involving a beneficent Witch named Befana. She is also one of the three goddesses of Fate in Tuscan Witchcraft: Rododesa, Marantega, and Befana. On the night of January 6th, Befana leaves presents in children's stockings hung upon the hearth, a tradition very much like the Santa Claus tradition associated with Christmas in America. The stockings hung for Befana on the hearth are derived from ancient offerings to the goddess of Fate and Time. For such goddesses have always been associated with weaving, the loom, the spindle, and distaff (of which the stockings are totems.) In Italian folklore, Befana arrives flying on a broom, or a goat. This is symbolic of her connection to the plant and animal worlds, making her a woodland goddess as well as a goddess of annual renewal (the cycles of death and rebirth within Nature.)

Befana is also connected to ancestral spirits as a mythical ancestress who returns yearly. Through her timeless visits to the family hearth, her function is that of reaffirming the bond between the family and the ancestors through an exchange of gifts. The children receive gifts from Befana—which in ancient times were representations of one's ancestors—to whom offerings of food were set near the hearth (very much like cookies and milk are set out for Santa Claus.) In Tuscany and elsewhere the Befana appears in street processions as a masked figure guiding a band of postulants who receive offers from families (and who, in turn, receive the gift of prosperity from Befana's blessings).

The hearth, in which fire is burned and the cooking cauldron is hung, symbolizes the elements of fire and water. The Epiphany holiday observed on January 6th includes purifying rites, and benedictions with water. The water prepared on the eve of Epiphany has a sacred and warding-off-evil-spirits value and is used in critical moments of family life. In the Abruzzo, it's called "Water of the Boffe." Fire, in particular, represents a recurring theme of cleansing and renewal.

In Italian folk tradition, an effigy of Befana is constructed of wood, depicting her holding a spindle and distaff. The effigy is stuffed with grapes, dried figs, chestnuts, pears, apples, carobs, sapa, and cotnognata. Later it is sawed open and the items are dispensed to the town folk, followed by the burning of Befana upon a pyre (thus returning the ancestral spirit to the kingdom beyond the tomb through the symbolism of the ascending fire.) The pyre is six to seven meters high and has to be conical. Chopped wood is placed on the bottom of the stack. Next is placed brambles, then horse chestnuts, and finally straw.

Pyromancy is performed by the sparks exploding from the chestnuts as the pyre burns. The burning of Befana is also designed to return the old life to the new life, the decay of Winter feeding the soil of Spring. For the figure of Befana as a crone is merely the reflection of her having been aged by Winter. From the Autumn Equinox, Befana is born again, life renewed, and she returns as Fana, the woodland goddess of Spring.

D

The Myth of Diana

Diana was the first created before all creation. In her were all things; out of herself, the first darkness, she divided herself into darkness and light. Dianus, her brother and son, herself and her other half, was the light.

And when Diana saw that the light was so beautiful, the light which was her other half, her brother Dianus, she yearned for it with exceedingly great desire. Wishing to receive the light again into her darkness, to swallow it up in rapture, in delight, she trembled with desire. This desire was the dawn.

But Dianus, the light, fled from her, and would not yield to her wishes. He was the light which flies into the most distant parts of heaven, the mouse which flies before the cat.

Then Diana went to the Fathers of the Beginning, to the Mothers, the Spirits who were before the first spirit, and lamented unto them that she could not prevail with Dianus. And they praised her for her courage; they told her that to rise she must fall; to become the chief of goddesses she must become a mortal.

And in the Ages, in the course of Time, when the World was made, Diana went on Earth, as did Dianus, who had descended, and Diana taught Magick and sorcery, whence came witches and Magickians, and all that is like man, yet not mortal.

And it came thus that Diana took the form of a cat. Her brother had a cat whom he loved beyond all creatures, and it slept every night on his bed. It was a cat beautiful beyond all other creatures: a fairy, but he did not know this.

Diana prevailed with the cat to change forms with her. So she lay with her brother, and in the darkness assumed her own form, and so by Dianus became the mother of Aradia. But when in the morning he found that he lay by his sister, and that light had been conquered by darkness, Dianus was extremely angry. But Diana sang to him a spell, a song of power, and he was silent. It was the song of the night which soothes to sleep, and he could say nothing.

So Diana with her wiles of Witchcraft so charmed him that he yielded to her love. This was the first fascination. She hummed the song which was as the buzzing of bees, and the spinning of a wheel: the spinning wheel spinning Life. She spun then the lives of Men, and all things were spun from the Wheel of Diana. And it was Dianus who turned the Wheel.

AN OFFERING TO DIANA

The following is one of the ancient ways in which offerings were made to the goddess of the Moon. If you would like to perform this timeless offering, then proceed as described.

First, an offering of any white woodland-type flower was placed before the statue of the goddess. The classic statue was the image of a beautiful woman, carrying a bow and quiver of arrows, with a dog at her feet. Upon her forehead, she wore a headband with a waxing crescent Moon upon it.

Next a wreath of these flowers was made and placed upon her head, like a crown.

Then the invocation was given (English translation of the original Italian):

> *Beautiful Goddess of the bow, beautiful Goddess of the arrows, and of all dogs and hunting. You who awakens in the Stars of Heaven, when the Sun sinks in slumber.*
>
> *You with the Moon upon your brow, who prefers the chase by Night, to hunting in the Day, with your Nymphs to the sound of the Horn. You are the Huntress, and the most Powerful. I pray that you will think of me, yet even for a moment, for I worship you!*

Following this, the worshiper remained in silent prayer and praise for a few moments. After this, nine white stones or shells were placed before the statue, forming a crescent moon. The points of the crescent were placed toward the feet of the statue. Under the middle stone or shell was placed a symbol representing any desire or aid which was requested. In later times, a written request was often used.

Three torches were placed around the statue, forming a triangle (two behind, off to each side, and the third one in front). Incense of the Moon was often placed within the semicircle made by the stone or shell pattern. A typical moon incense would have been either wormwood and camphor, or cedar, sandalwood, and juniper.

To complete the magickal influences, the worshiper left the area immediately, and never spoke to anyone concerning this or her actions.

ℰ

The Mythos

The Descent of the Goddess

Tana, our Lady and Goddess, would solve all mysteries, even the mystery of Death. And so she journeyed to the Underworld in her boat, upon the Sacred River of Descent. Then it came to pass that she entered before the first of the seven gates to the Underworld. And the Guardian challenged her, demanding one of her garments for passage, for nothing may be received except that something be given in return. And at each of the gates the goddess was required to pay the price of passage, for the guardians spoke to her: "Strip off your garments, and set aside your jewels, for nothing may you bring with you into this our realm."

So Tana surrendered her jewels and her clothing to the Guardians, and was bound as all living must be who seek to enter the realm of Death and the Mighty Ones. At the first gate she gave over her scepter, at the second her crown, at the third her necklace, at the fourth her ring, at the fifth her girdle, at the sixth her sandals, and at the seventh her gown. Tana stood naked and was presented before Dis, and such was her beauty that he himself knelt as she entered. He laid his crown and his sword at her feet, saying: "Blessed are your feet which have brought you down this path.

Then he arose and said to Tana: "Stay with me I pray, and receive my touch upon your heart."

And Tana replied to Dis: "But I love you not, for why do you cause all the things that I love, and take delight in, to fade and die?"

"My Lady" replied Dis, "it is age and fate against which you speak. I am helpless, for age causes all things to whither, but when men die at the end of their time, I give them rest, peace, and strength. For a time they dwell with the Moon, and the spirits of the moon; then may they return to the realm of the living. But you are so lovely, and I ask you to return not, but abide with me here."

But she answered: "No, for I do not love you." Then Dis said: "If you refuse to embrace me, then you must kneel to death's scourge." The goddess answered him: "If it is to be, then it is fate, and better so!" So Tana knelt in submission before the hand of death, and he scourged her with so tender a hand that she cried out "I know your pain, and the pain of love."

Dis raised her to her feet and said: "Blessed are you, my Queen and my Lady." Then he gave to her the five kisses of initiation, saying: "Only thus may you attain to knowledge and to joy."

And he taught her all of his mysteries, and he gave her the necklace which is the circle of rebirth. And she taught him her mysteries of the sacred cup which is the cauldron of rebirth.

They loved and joined in union with each other, and for a time Tana dwelled in the realm of Dis.

For there are three mysteries in the life of man, which are: birth, sex, and death (and love controls them all). To fulfill love, you must return again at the same time and place as those who loved before. And you must meet, recognize, remember, and love them anew. But to be reborn you must die and be made ready for a new body. And to die you must be born, but without love you may not be born among your own.

But our Goddess is inclined to favor love, and joy, and happiness. She guards and cherishes her hidden children in this life and the next. In death she reveals the way to her communion, and in life she teaches them the magick of the mystery of the Circle (which is set between the worlds of men and of the gods).

THE MYTH OF THE ASCENT

Now the time came in the Hidden Realm of Shadows that Tana would bear the Child of the Great Dark Lord. And the Lords of the Four Corners came and beheld the newborn god. Then they spoke to Tana of the misery of the people who lived upon the World, and how they suffered in cold and in darkness. So Tana bid the Lords to carry Her son to the World, and so the people rejoiced, for the Sun God had returned.

And it came to pass that Tana longed for the Light of the World, and for Her many Children. So She journeyed to the World and was welcomed in great celebration. Then Tana saw the splendor of the new God as He crossed the heavens, and she desired Him. But each night He returned to the Hidden Realm and could not see the beauty of the Goddess in the night sky.

So one morning the Goddess arose as the God came up from the Hidden Realm, and She bathed nude in the sacred lake of Nemi. Then the Lords of the Four Corners appeared to Him and said: "Behold the sweet beauty of the Goddess of the Earth." And He looked upon Her and was struck with Her beauty so that He descended upon the earth in the form of a great stag.

"I have come to play beside your bath," He said, but Tana gazed upon the stag and said "You are not a stag but a god!" Then He answered: "I am Kern, God of the Forest. Yet as I stand upon the World I touch also the sky and I am Lupercus the Sun, who banishes the Wolf Night. But beyond all of this I am Tanus, the first born of all the Gods!"

Tana smiled and stepped forth from the water in all Her beauty. "I am Fana, Goddess of the Forest, yet even as I stand before you I am Diana, Goddess of the Moon. But beyond all this I am Tana, first born of all Goddesses!"

And Tanus took Her by the hand and together they walked in the meadows and forests, telling their tales of ancient mysteries. They loved and were One and together they ruled over the World. Yet even in love, Tana knew that the God would soon cross over to the Hidden Realm and Death would come to the World. Then must She descend and embrace the Dark Lord, and bear the fruit of their Union.

F

The Gifts of Aradia and the Tenets of Belief

In the fourteenth century, Aradia taught that the traditional powers of a Witch would belong to any who followed in the ways of the Old Religion. Aradia called these powers gifts, because she stressed the point that these powers were the benefits of adhering to the Old Ways, and not the reason for becoming a Witch. These are the powers:

To bring success in love.

To bless and consecrate.

To speak with spirits.

To know of hidden things.

To call forth spirits.

To know the Voice of the Wind.

To possess the knowledge of transformation.

To possess the knowledge of divination.

To know and understand secret signs.

To cure disease.

To bring forth beauty.

To have influence over wild beasts.

To know the secrets of the hands.

BASIC TENETS OF BELIEF

We believe that the Source of All Things (The Great Spirit) is both masculine and feminine in nature.

We believe that humans bear the Divine Spark of their Creator within themselves (soul/spirit), and that we are actually spiritual beings who are temporarily encased in physical matter.

We believe in reincarnation and view it as a process for spiritual liberation from the physical dimension.

We believe in psychic abilities and the supernatural as normal conditions which have been suppressed by Judaic/Christian Culture, but can be restored through the practice of the Old Ways.

We believe in Magick as a manifestation of energy that is directed by the mind through various ancient techniques.

We believe in spiritual worlds and spirit beings.

We believe in the Law of Action and Reaction, and that what we do affects others, and what others do affects us. Therefore, we strive to live in peace with those around us.

We believe in karma, meaning that we believe in responsibility and consequences.

We believe in love, life, and harmony as the spiritual foundation of our ways.

We believe in the expression of religious beliefs through rituals and festivals.

We believe in Earth Energy, meaning that we acknowledge places of natural power existing upon our planet. We hold that the same is true for natural objects.

We believe in a positive Afterlife and a successful spiritual evolution.

We believe that everything in Nature is of equal importance. Everything is linked and entwined beyond separation.

GLOSSARY

Actaeon: Stag-horned God of the Forest.

Air: One of the four creative elements, associated with the east and with the ritual wand.

Alpeno: Guardian of the eastern Portal between the Worlds.

Aradia: A Holy Woman who lived in fourteenth-century Italy, taught Witchcraft, and is considered an avatar.

Aridian: One of several traditions of Italian Witchcraft. It separated from the Triad Clans in 1981 and became the first independent Italian tradition in America. It is a rejoining of the Triad traditions into one complete system.

Astral: Nonphysical etheric substance that forms around images and thoughts, creating duplicates within another dimension.

Avatar: A being who has evolved beyond the need for human existence, who returns and teaches the ways of liberation from this physical dimension.

Befana: The "Good Witch" who brings presents to children on Epiphany. Remnant of the goddess Fana.

Befano: Consort of Befana. Remnant of the god Faunus.

Benandanti: "Good Witches" who fought ritual battles over the fate of the harvest, against the Malandanti.

Boschetto: A grove (Italian word for a coven of witches).

Cavallino: An all-male Occult society linked to the Luperci.

Diana: Traditionally the goddess of all Witches in Italy.

Dianus: Horned God of the Woods, consort of Diana.

Earth: One of the four creative elements, associated with the north and with the ritual pentacle.

Elementals: Beings of the four elements of Creation: earth, air, fire, and water. They empower the natural forces within Nature, and help to maintain a balance.

Ether: The mystical property of atmosphere. The metaphysical counterpart of air.

Familiar: Any creature or spirit with which you establish a pyschic rapport, beneficial to both parties.

Family Tradition: A system in which the Old Ways have been preserved through superstitions, practices, or folkways among members of the same bloodline.

Fana: Goddess of the forests and wildlife.

Fata: Italian word for fairies.

Faunus: God of the forests and wildlife.

Fava: The first bean known to Europeans. Among the Greeks and Romans it was associated with funeral rites and the Underworld. Used as offerings.

Fire: One of the four elements of Creation, associated with the south and with the ritual spirit blade.

Folletti: Spirits of the air, similar to fairies.

Grigori: Guardians of the Portals between the Worlds.

Grimas: The director and guardian of a Tradition.

Holy Strega: A term of endearment for Aradia.

Hooded One: Also known as the Green Man. Lord of Vegetation, Lord of the Green-Wood. He who is hooded-in-the-green.

Horned One: Title of the Stag-horned Lord of the Forest and of all wildlife.

Jana: Italian Moon goddess.

Janus: Italian god of the Sun and of all Portals. God of all Beginnings and Ends.

Kern: Name for the Stag-horned God of the forest. Father of the Hooded One. Symbol of the waxing power of Nature.

Lare: Ancestral spirits who are evolving within the Spirit World. They assist and protect members of their former Clan. They are worshipped in home shrines.

Lasa: Spirits of the Old Ways. In Tuscan Witchlore they are the first spirits known in the world. They are protectors and helpers in the Spirit World, and can be evoked for assistance.

Lord of Misrule: The Lord of Misrule is a character who portrays the problems or regrets of the closing year. He represents chaos and disorder as well as licentiousness. He is another sacrificial king.

Luperci: Priests of the god Lupercus.

Lupercus: The Wolf God of Winter. Symbol of the waning power of Nature.

Magick: The ability to cause changes to occur in accordance with shifts in states of consciousness.

Malandanti: "Evil Witches" who fought ritual battles over the outcome of the harvest. Their war was against the rich feudal lords and the Church, but more often than not, this caused harm to the peasants.

Malocchio: Also known as "the evil eye" or the "overlook."

Mansions of the Moon: The daily placement of the Moon as it passes the constellations, in a cycle of twenty-eight days.

Meana: Guardian of the western Portal between the Worlds.

Mythos: The theology arising from all of the combined myths of Stregheria.

Nanta Bag: A magickal pouch intended to keep one linked with the forces of Nature.

Nemi, Lake: Site of the temple of Diana. Also known as "Diana's mirror" because the Full Moon reflected upon the water.

Old One: The human aspect of the God. The wise-bearded Elder God.

Old Religion: A pre-Christian religion in Europe. An ancient fertility cult worshipping the God and Goddess of Nature.

Old Ones: Another name for the Lasa.

Settrano: Guardian of the southern Portal between the Worlds.

Slain God: The Sacrificial King in pre-Christian religion. Lord of the Harvest, slain in the prime of his power as an offering to the Gods.

Spirit Flame: A blue flame burned upon the altar, believed to be the living essence of the gods and the Spirits of Old.

Strega: Italian word for a female Witch. In this book it is used to address all Witches regardless of gender, both singular and plural.

Stregheria: The religion of Witches.

Stregone: A male Witch.

Stregoneria: The magickal arts of Witchcraft.

Tagni: The most ancient name for the God of Witchcraft.

Taga: Guardian of the northern portal between the Worlds.

Tana: The star goddess, or Universal aspect.

Tanus: The star god, or Universal aspect, consort to Tana.

Thought-form: Literally a thought, image, or desire that has taken form within the Astral substance or Astral dimension.

Tregua: Slang term for Full Moon gatherings/celebrations.

Trequenda: Italian word for Sabbat. The eight seasonal rites.

Triad: After the departure of Aradia, three groups formed out of the original grove established by her, in order to preserve the ancient mystery traditions: the Earth Mysteries, Lunar Mysteries, and Stellar Mysteries. These groups are referred to as the Triad Traditions.

Uni: The most ancient name for the Goddess of Witchcraft.

Veglia: The oral family history and traditions.

Veglione: The Full Moon ceremony.

Watchers: (see Grigori).

Water: One of the four creative elements, associated with the west and with the ritual chalice.

Witch: A male or female practitioner of the Old Religion. In ancient times the village healer and shaman.

Witchcraft: The name used for the old pre-Christian religion of Europe, but also for the magickal arts practiced by Witches.

SELECTED BIBLIOGRAPHY

Agrippa, Cornelius. *Occult Philosophy or Magic*. New York: Samuel Weiser, 1971.

Allen, Richard H. *Star Names: Their Lore and Meaning*. New York: Dover Publications, 1963.

Ankarloo, Bengt, ed. *Early Modern European Witchcraft*. Oxford: Clarendon Press, 1993.

Baroja, Julio Caro. *The World of Witches*. Chicago: The University of Chicago Press, 1964.

_____. *Witchcraft and Catholic Theology* (from Early Modern European Witchcraft). Oxford: Clarendon Press, 1993.

Barrett, Francis. *The Magus*. New Hyde Park, NY: University Books, 1967.

Barstow, Anne Llewellyn. *Witchcraze: A New History of the European Witch Hunts*. San Francisco: Pandora, 1994.

Bonnefoy, Yves, ed. *Roman and European Mythologies*. Chicago: The University of Chicago Press, 1991.

Borgeaud, Phillippe. *The Cult of Pan*. Chicago: University of Chicago Press, 1988.

Cardini, Franco. *Il Giorno del Sacro, il Libra delle Feste*. Milano: Rusconi Libri, 1989.

Catabiani, Alfredo. *Calendario: Le Feste i Mitti le Leggende e i Ritti dell'Anno*. Milano: Rusconi Libri, 1988.

Crowley, Vivianne. *Wicca: The Old Religion in the New Age*. Wellingborough, England: The Aquarian Press, 1989.

Cumont, Franz. *After Life in Roman Paganism*. New York: Dover Publications, 1959.

_____. *Oriental Religions in Roman Paganism*. New Haven, CT: Yale University Press, 1920.

Davidson, Gustav. *A Dictionary of Angels, Including the Fallen*. New York: The Free Press, 1967.

Delaney, John. *Dictionary of Saints*. New York: Doubleday & Co., 1980.

De Martino, Ernesto. *Primitive Magic*. Bridgeport:, CT: Prism Press, 1972.

Dundes, Alan, ed. *The Evil Eye: A Folklore Casebook*. New York: Garland, 1981.

Eliade, Mircea. *Occultism, Witchcraft, and Cultural Fashions*. Chicago: University of Chicago Press, 1976.

Elsworthy, Frederick Thomas. *The Evil Eye*. New York: Julian Press, 1988.

Ericson, Eric. *The World, The Flesh, The Devil: A Biographical Dictionary of Witches*. New York: Mayflower Books, 1981.

Falassi, Alessandro. *Folklore by the Fireside: Text and Context of the Tuscan Veglia*. Austin: University of Texas Press, 1980.

Field, Carol. *Celebrating Italy*. New York: William Morrow & Co., 1990.

Fortune, Dion. *Moon Magic*. York Beach, ME: Samuel Weiser Inc., 1978.

_____. *The Sea Priestess*. York Beach, ME: Samuel Weiser Inc., 1978.

Frazer, Sir James George. *The Golden Bough*. New York: Macmillan Company, 1922.

Gardner, Gerald B. *Witchcraft Today*. Secaucus, NY: The Citadel Press, 1973.

_____. *The Meaning of Witchcraft*. New York: Samuel Weiser, 1959.

Gimbutas, Marija. *The Goddesses and Gods of Old Europe*. Berkeley: University of California Press, 1982.

Ginzburg, Carlo. *The Night Battles: Witchcraft & Agrarian Cults in the Sixteenth & Seventeenth Centuries*. London: Routledge & Kegan Paul, 1966.

_____. *Ecstasies: Deciphering the Witches' Sabbath*. New York: Pantheon Books, 1991.

Godwin, Joscelyn. *Mystery Religions in the Ancient World*. New York: Harper & Row, 1981.

Gray, William G. *Western Inner Workings*. York Beach: Samuel Weiser, 1983.

Green, Miranda. *Symbol & Image in Celtic Religious Art*. London: Routledge, 1989.

Harding, M. Esther. *Woman's Mysteries; Ancient and Modern*. New York: Harper Colophon Books, 1971.

Kelly, Aidan. *Crafting the Art of Magic: Book 1: A History of Modern Witchcraft, 1939–1964*. St. Paul: Llewellyn Publications, 1991.

Le Bohec, Yann. *The Imperial Roman Army*. New York: Hippocrene Books, 1994.

Leland, Charles. *Etruscan Magic & Occult Remedies*. New York: University Books, 1963.

_____. *Gypsy Sorcery and Fortune Telling*. New York: Dover Publications, 1971.

_____. *Legends of Florence*. New York: MacMillan and Co., 1895.

Lethbridge, T. C. *Witches*. New York: The Citadel Press, 1962.

Luck, Georg. *Arcana Mundi: Magic and the Occult in the Greek and Roman Worlds*. Baltimore: John Hopkins University Press, 1985.

Mallory, J. P. *In Search of the Indo-Europeans*. London: Thames & Hudson, 1989.

Malpezzi, Frances. *Italian American Folklore*. Little Rock: August House Publishers, 1992.

Murray, Alexander. *Who's Who in Mythology: A Classic Guide to the Ancient World*. New York: Crescent Books, 1988.

Neumann, Erich. *The Great Mother: An Analysis of the Archetype*. New Haven, CT: Princeton University Press, 1955.

Nuttall, P. A. *The Works of Horace*. Philadelphia: David McKay Publisher, 1884.

Perera, Sylvia. *Descent to the Goddess*. New York: Inner City Books, 1981.

Rose, Elliot. *A Razor for a Goat*. Toronto: University of Toronto Press, 1989.

Stewart, R. J. *The Underworld Initiation: A Journey Towards Psychic Transformation*. Wellingborough, England: The Aquarian Press, 1985.

Valiente, Doreen. *Witchcraft for Tomorrow*. New York: St. Martin's Press, 1978.

Vecoli, Rudolph J. "Cult and Occult in Italian-American Culture; The Persistence of a Religious Heritage." *Immigrants and Religion in Urban America*, edited by Randall M. Miller and Thomas D. Marzik, pp. 25–47. Philadelphia: Temple University Press, 1977.

Additional interior artwork was used from the following sources:

Doré Illustrations: Old-Fashioned Illustrations of Books, Reading & Writing; *Symbols, Signs & Signets*; and *Treasury of Book Ornament and Decoration*. Dover Publications.

Mortilogus, Reiter.

1,000 Quaint Cuts, Zucker Art Books.

Tableau de L' inconstance, Jan Ziarnko.

The Evil Eye, Frederick Thomas Elworthy.

INDEX

A

Actaeon, 77–78

Air, 6, 17, 37, 46, 58, 68, 71, 98, 102–107, 111, 122, 124, 155, 179–180, 187–188, 193, 198, 226, 228, 271–272

Alban hills, 249, 255

Alpena, 6, 220, 272

Altar, 20, 22, 30, 43, 53, 78, 99, 103, 110, 119, 121–125, 127–129, 133, 137–139, 141–144, 146, 152–157, 160, 162, 168, 179, 181, 203, 207–210

Aradia, xvi, 3, 8–9, 11, 16, 21–22, 25, 29, 36, 49, 65, 82, 88, 90, 92, 102, 107, 109–110, 120, 122, 130, 152, 157, 204, 236, 247, 249–261, 274, 276–277, 279–282, 285, 288, 292, 297

Aridian Tradition, xvi, 26, 73, 79, 81, 99–100, 165

Athame, 100, 122

Autumn Equinox, 26, 28–29, 68, 159–160, 268, 290

B

Befana, 22, 38, 41, 59–62, 64, 66, 79, 200–201, 289–290

Befano, 59–62

Benandanti, 14, 23, 73, 82–85, 223, 275

Benevento, xvii, 11, 15–16, 225, 242, 261, 283, 288

C

Calusari, 80, 253–254

Catholicism, 20, 57–59, 61

Cauldron, 105, 133–134, 138–139, 145, 148–149, 153, 155, 157–160, 163, 173, 289, 295

Cavallino, 80–81

Censer, 123–124, 208, 236

Chalice, 95–97, 99–100, 102, 122–123, 128, 130, 138, 142–144, 153, 157–160, 163, 206

Charge, 72, 90, 92, 101, 115, 124, 130, 137, 150, 152, 155–156, 187, 189, 197, 203, 206, 209, 212, 226, 229, 231, 243–244, 252

Christianity, 11, 13, 15, 18, 34, 45, 66, 71, 82, 100, 233–234, 249, 251, 255, 274

Circle, 54, 67–68, 71, 82, 104–105, 111, 119, 122–125, 127–130, 133–134, 136, 138–139, 141–146, 149–150, 152–156, 160, 166–168, 173–174, 179, 196, 199, 226–228, 262, 284, 295

Crone, 45, 212–214, 222, 290

Crowley, Aleister, xviii, 89

D

Diana, xiii, 4, 6, 11–12, 14–16, 18, 20, 36, 43–45, 47, 50, 52, 54, 62, 75, 77–78, 80, 88–90, 99, 120–121, 147, 154, 207–208, 223, 225, 249, 251–252, 254–256, 260, 266, 268, 275, 280–282, 288, 291–292, 296

H

Herbs, 4, 37–38, 51, 98, 100, 103, 178, 182, 185, 189–191, 203, 206, 209, 221, 223, 225, 227, 229–231, 236, 262

Holy Strega, xv, 23, 49, 55, 82, 120, 128, 132, 204, 249, 255, 259, 261, 263, 265, 267, 269, 271, 273, 276

Hooded One, 54, 74–75, 142, 161

Horace, 12, 15, 18, 22, 30, 43–45

Horned One, 74, 136, 139, 142

I

Italian, x, 4–23, 25–26, 28, 30, 32–36, 38–40, 42–47, 50–54, 58–62, 64, 66, 68, 70, 72, 74–76, 78–80, 82–84, 86, 88–92, 95–96, 98, 100, 102–104, 106–108, 110–112, 114, 116, 118, 120, 122, 124, 126, 128, 130, 132, 134, 136, 138, 140, 142, 144, 146, 148, 150, 152, 154, 156, 158, 160, 162, 165–166, 168, 170, 172, 174, 178, 180–182, 184, 186, 188, 190, 192, 194, 196, 198, 200, 202, 204, 206, 208, 210, 212, 214, 216, 218, 222–226, 228, 230, 232, 234, 236, 238, 242–244, 250–254, 256, 258, 260, 262, 264, 266, 268, 270, 272, 274–276, 279–280, 282, 284–290, 292, 295, 298

Italy, xv, 3–5, 7–12, 14–16, 18, 20–23, 25–26, 30–34, 36, 38–40, 42, 45–47, 54, 57–62, 64, 66, 73–74, 78–79, 82, 88–92, 99, 102, 105, 120, 165, 221, 224–225, 242, 249–254, 256, 259–260, 275, 279, 285–286, 289

J

Jana, 4, 149, 207–208, 268

Janarra, xvi–xvii, 50, 172

Janarric, xvi–xvii, 50, 52, 166, 215

Janus, 4, 6, 141–142, 149, 160, 266–267

K

Kern, 73, 147, 160, 296

L

La Vecchia, 4, 22, 39, 58, 203, 234, 249, 279

Lare, 7, 21–22, 27–28, 35, 38, 61, 77, 105

Lasa, 2, 4, 6–7, 21, 28, 34, 42, 105, 135

Lauru, 8

Leland, Charles, x, 9–11, 16, 22–23, 33, 36, 39, 42, 46, 57, 59, 87–88, 90, 92, 241, 245, 249–251, 256, 258, 277, 284–288

Linchetto, 6–7

Lord of Misrule, 30–31, 75, 79, 81, 144

Luperci, 80–81, 143

Lupercus, 28, 66, 73, 79, 81–82, 141–143, 145, 147, 268, 296

M

Magick, 3–6, 10, 13, 38–39, 43, 45–46, 55, 59, 61, 70–71, 81, 88, 91, 96, 98–99, 102–104, 110, 113, 115, 119, 133, 136, 138, 150, 168, 174, 177–185, 187, 189–191, 193, 203–207, 209, 211–215, 217, 219, 223, 225–226, 231, 233–237, 239, 241, 243–245, 251–253, 256, 262, 266, 270–271, 273, 285, 291, 295, 298

Maiden, 42, 44–45, 145–150, 153, 160, 162, 212–214, 222, 265

Malandanti, 14, 23, 82–84, 223, 252, 275

Malocchio, 4, 197

Meana, 6, 125, 272

T

Tagni, 4, 6

Tago, 125, 272

Tana, 4, 29, 101, 103, 106, 108, 110, 123–124, 128–132, 134, 136, 141, 146–153, 157–158, 166, 170, 172–173, 197, 237, 266–268, 294–296

Tanarric, xvi, 166, 233, 235, 237

Tanus, 4, 103, 107–108, 124, 130, 136, 138, 146–147, 149, 157–158, 166, 170, 197, 266–267, 296

Temptress, 265, 267

Treguenda, 25, 28–29, 104, 123, 133, 257

Triad, 89, 99, 166, 222

Tuscan, 3, 5–7, 18, 22, 33, 35, 37–43, 45–47, 57, 86, 105, 165, 217, 254, 275, 287, 289

U

Uni, 4, 6, 35, 169

V

Veglia, 18–21, 129

Vernal Equinox, 68, 234

Vervain, 47, 100, 191, 230–231

W

Watchers, 67–68, 70–72, 237, 271, 282

Werewolf, 78–79

Winter, 19–20, 26–28, 30, 62, 64, 66, 68, 73, 75, 79, 82, 84, 89, 133, 139, 147, 160–161, 268, 290

Winter Solstice, 20, 26, 28, 30, 68, 139, 160, 268

Witch, 4–6, 11–16, 18, 21–22, 36–37, 42–43, 46–47, 59–62, 64, 66, 68, 71–72, 75, 81, 83, 86–91, 95–96, 102, 154, 209, 222–223, 235, 240, 242–243, 251–253, 256, 260, 275–276, 282–284, 286–287, 289, 297

Witchcraft, 4–6, 8–23, 25–26, 28–30, 32–47, 49–55, 57–60, 62, 64, 66, 68, 70–72, 74–76, 78–80, 82–92, 94–96, 98–100, 102, 104, 106–108, 110–112, 114, 116, 118, 120, 122, 124, 126, 128, 130, 132, 134, 136, 138, 140, 142, 144, 146, 148, 150, 152, 154, 156, 158, 160, 162, 165–166, 168, 170, 172, 174, 178, 180, 182, 184, 186, 188, 190, 192, 194, 196, 198, 200, 202, 204, 206, 208, 210, 212, 214, 216, 218, 221–234, 236, 238, 242–244, 250–254, 256, 258, 260, 262, 264, 266, 268, 270, 272, 274–276, 279–282, 284–290, 292, 295, 298

Witches, 4–5, 7, 9–16, 18, 20–23, 25, 29, 32–33, 35–47, 50–52, 54, 57–59, 61–62, 66–67, 78, 80, 82–85, 87–92, 95–96, 103–105, 120–121, 130–132, 139, 152, 165, 190, 198, 214–215, 222–225, 228, 235, 237, 242–243, 249–254, 256, 258, 275–277, 279–285, 287–288, 291

Wolf, 34, 73, 75–82, 137, 142–147, 218, 243–244, 296

REACH FOR THE MOON

Llewellyn publishes hundreds of books on your favorite subjects!
To get these exciting books, including the ones on the following pages,
check your local bookstore or order them directly from Llewellyn.

Order by Phone
- Call toll-free within the U.S. and Canada, 1-800-THE MOON
- In Minnesota, call (651) 291-1970
- We accept VISA, MasterCard, and American Express

Order by Mail
- Send the full price of your order (MN residents add 7% sales tax) in U.S. funds, plus postage & handling to:

    Llewellyn Worldwide
    P.O. Box 64383, Dept. L259–3
    St. Paul, MN 55164–0383, U.S.A.

Postage & Handling
(For the U.S., Canada, and Mexico)
- $4.00 for orders $15.00 and under
- $5.00 for orders over $15.00
- No charge for orders over $100.00

We ship UPS in the continental United States. We ship standard mail to P. O. boxes. Orders shipped to Alaska, Hawaii, the Virgin Islands, and Puerto Rico are sent first-class mail. Orders shipped to Canada and Mexico are sent surface mail.

International orders: Airmail—add freight equal to price of each book to the total price of order, plus $5.00 for each non-book item (audio tapes, etc.).

Surface mail—Add $1.00 per item.

Allow 2 weeks for delivery on all orders.
Postage and handling rates subject to change.

Discounts
We offer a 20% discount to group leaders or agents. You must order a minimum of 5 copies of the same book to get our special quantity price.

Free Catalog
Get a free copy of our color catalog, *New Worlds of Mind and Spirit*. Subscribe for just $10.00 in the United States and Canada ($30.00 overseas, airmail). Many bookstores carry *New Worlds*—ask for it!

Visit our website at www.llewellyn.com for more information.

HEREDITARY WITCHCRAFT
Secrets of the Old Religion
Raven Grimassi

This book is about the Old Religion of Italy, and contains material that is at least 100 years old, much of which has never before been seen in print. This overview of the history and lore of the Hereditary Craft will show you how the Italian witches viewed nature, magick, and the occult forces. Nothing in this book is mixed with, or drawn from, any other Wiccan traditions.

The Italian witches would gather beneath the Full Moon to worship a goddess (Diana) and a god (Dianus). The roots of Italian Witchcraft extend back into the prehistory of Italy, in the indigenous Mediterranean/Aegean neolithic cult of the Great Goddess. Follow its development to the time of the Inquisition, when it had to go into hiding to survive, and to the present day. Uncover surprising discoveries of how expressions of Italian Witchcraft have been taught and used in this century.

1–56718–256–9, 288 pp., 7 1/2 x 9 1/8, 31 illus., softcover   **$14.95**

To order, call 1-800-THE MOON
Prices subject to change without notice

WICCAN MAGICK
Inner Teachings of the Craft
Raven Grimassi

Wiccan Magick is a serious and complete study for those who desire to understand the inner meanings, techniques and symbolism of magick as an occult art. Magick within modern Wicca is an eclectic blending of many occult traditions that evolved from the ancient beliefs and practices in both Europe, the Middle East and Asia. *Wiccan Magick* covers the full range of magickal and ritual practices as they pertain to both modern ceremonial and shamanic Wicca.

Come to understand the evolution of the Craft, the ancient magickal current that flows from the past to the present, and the various aspects included in ritual, spell casting, and general theology. When you understand *why* something exists within a ritual structure, you will know better how to build upon the underlying concepts to create ritual that is meaningful to you.

1–56718–255–0, 240 pp., 6 x 9, softcover   **$12.95**

THE WICCAN MYSTERIES
Ancient Origins & Teachings
Raven Grimassi

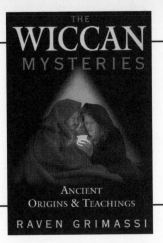

What you will encounter in *The Wiccan Mysteries* is material that was once taught only in the initiate levels of the old Wiccan Mystery Traditions, and to which many solitary practitioners have never had access. Learn the inner meanings of Wiccan rites, beliefs and practices, and discover the time-proven concepts that created, maintained and carried Wiccan beliefs up into this modern era. In reflecting back upon the wisdom of our ancestors, neo-Wiccans can draw even greater sustenance from the spiritual stores of Wicca—the Old Religion.

The Wiccan Mysteries will challenge you to expand your understanding and even re-examine your own perceptions. Wicca is essentially a Celtic-oriented religion, but its Mystery Tradition is derived from several outside cultures as well. You will come away with a sense of the rich heritage that was passed from one human community to another, and that now resides within this system for spiritual development.

1-56718-254-2, 312 pp., 6 x 9, softcover $14.95

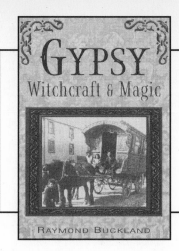

GYPSY WITCHCRAFT & MAGIC
Raymond Buckland

The Romany—or Gypsy—lifestyle has been a colorful one: living in brightly painted vardos and benders, cooking over campfires, moving about the countryside while scraping out an existence by one's wits. But the Gypsies, as an ethnic people, are disappearing. As a poshrat himself (a half-blood Romany), Raymond Buckland seeks to recapture the romance and charm of this culture's mystical past and present in *Gypsy Witchcraft & Magic*.

Learn of their origins and migration throughout the world, the truth about their religious beliefs, their daily life, and their magical practices. Try your hand at practicing authentic Gypsy magic, with spells and charms for love, healing, wealth, power, protection, and more. Learn to tell fortunes with beans, cards, coins, by scrying, and by reading the omens in nature.

1–56718–097–3, 192 pp., 7 x 10, illus., photos, softcover   **$17.95**

ANCIENT WAYS
Reclaiming the Pagan Tradition
Pauline Campanelli

Ancient Ways is filled with magick and ritual that you can perform every day to capture the spirit of the seasons. It focuses on the celebration of the Sabbats and of the wish for the magick to linger on. *Ancient Ways* can help you reclaim your own traditions and heighten the feeling of magick.

0–87542–090–7, 256 pp., 7 x 10, illus., softcover   **$14.95**